The Cannabis Business

As the largely illicit cannabis market transitions to a legal, regulated industry, the "canna-curious" and experienced industry participants alike are experiencing the harsh truth: Making a fortune in the legal cannabis industry is a challenge made even more difficult by a complex patchwork of state and federal laws.

The Cannabis Business clears the confusion around topics such as the distinction between hemp and cannabis and why it matters for consumers and regulators, why CBD isn't completely legal in the U.S., why and how states differ in their licensing processes, and how deal structuring is impacted by state regulations. Written by attorneys from the nation's leading cannabis law and policy firm, this comprehensive primer on all things cannabis law is a must-have for anyone seeking to understand the major practical legal issues facing the cannabis industry in the U.S.

Charles S. Alovisetti is a partner at Vicente Sederberg and chair of the firm's Corporate Practice Group, where he has focused his practice since 2015 on advising companies, investors, and other law firms on the nuances of executing financings, mergers, and acquisitions, and other corporate transactions involving licensed and ancillary cannabis companies. Charlie has been recognized by Chambers & Partners as one of the top cannabis lawyers in the United States.

Cassia Furman is a partner at Vicente Sederberg and managing attorney of the firm's California Practice Group based in Los Angeles. In addition to supporting the firm's policy and local government work in California and around the country, she counsels clients on a wide range of transactional, regulatory, and land-use issues related to the licensing and operation of California commercial cannabis ventures.

The Cannabis Business

Understanding Law, Finance, and Governance in America's Newest Industry

**Charles S. Alovisetti
and Cassia Furman**

Routledge
Taylor & Francis Group

NEW YORK AND LONDON

First published 2021
by Routledge
52 Vanderbilt Avenue, New York, NY 10017

and by Routledge
2 Park Square, Milton Park, Abingdon, Oxon, OX14 4RN

Routledge is an imprint of the Taylor & Francis Group, an informa business

Library of Congress Cataloging-in-Publication Data
Names: Alovisetti, Charles S., author. | Furman, Cassia, author.
Title: The cannabis business: understanding law, finance, and
governance in America's newest industry / Charles S. Alovisetti
and Cassia Furman.
Description: Milton Park, Abingdon, Oxon; New York,
NY: Routledge, 2021. | Includes bibliographical references and index.
Identifiers: LCCN 2020029491 (print) | LCCN 2020029492 (ebook) |
ISBN 9780367519964 (hardback) | ISBN 9780367519940 (paperback) |
ISBN 9781003055983 (ebook)
Subjects: LCSH: Marijuana industry—Law and
legislation—United States. | Marijuana industry—Government policy—
United States. | Marijuana industry—United States—Finance. |
Marijuana—Law and legislation—United States.
Classification: LCC KF3891.M2 A75 2021 (print) |
LCC KF3891.M2 (ebook) | DDC 343.7307/6353—dc23
LC record available at https://lccn.loc.gov/2020029491
LC ebook record available at https://lccn.loc.gov/2020029492

ISBN: 978-0-367-51996-4 (hbk)
ISBN: 978-0-367-51994-0 (pbk)
ISBN: 978-1-003-05598-3 (ebk)

Typeset in Times New Roman
by codeMantra

For Kim

Contents

Contributors

Jason C. Adelstone is an associate attorney in Vicente Sederberg's Denver office, where he focuses on cannabis corporate transactions and international cannabis trends and regulations.

Charles S. Alovisetti is a partner at Vicente Sederberg and chair of the firm's Corporate Practice Group, where he has focused his practice since 2015 on advising companies, investors, and other law firms on the nuances of executing financings, mergers and acquisitions, and other corporate transactions involving licensed and ancillary cannabis companies. Charlie has been recognized by Chambers & Partners as one of the top cannabis lawyers in the United States.

Charlie has worked on licensed transactions in all the major cannabis markets in the United States. He understands the state and local issues that commonly arise in stock and asset acquisitions as well as issues involved in management companies and other alternative structures. In addition to his specialized cannabis experience, Charlie has experience counseling companies through every stage of the corporate life cycle – from initial financing through acquisition – including advising on general corporate and commercial matters and compensation arrangements.

Charlie holds a Bachelor of Arts, with honors, from McGill University and a law degree from Columbia Law School, where he was a Harlan Fiske Stone Scholar. He is admitted to practice in Colorado, Massachusetts, and New York.

Sahar Ayinehsazian is an attorney in Vicente Sederberg's Los Angeles office, where she focuses on cannabis banking, corporate transactions, and regulations.

Matthew Bartling focuses his practice on corporate and business law, intellectual property, licensing, and regulatory compliance.

Michelle Bodian is a transactional attorney advising clients on hemp, environmental, and agricultural law.

Elliot Y. Choi is counsel at Vicente Sederberg and corporate chair of the firm's New York and Massachusetts offices.

Cassia Furman is a partner at Vicente Sederberg (VS) and managing attorney of the firm's California Practice Group based in Los Angeles. In addition to supporting the firm's policy and local government work in California and around the country, she counsels clients on a wide range of transactional, regulatory, and land-use issues related to the licensing and operation of California commercial cannabis ventures.

Before joining VS, Cassia worked with a noted public finance firm, where she oversaw the organization and operations of dozens of special districts in connection with complex public infrastructure projects, including the issuance of multi-million dollar debt issuances. Cassia also assisted in the representation of numerous Colorado municipalities, where her duties included the drafting and implementation of comprehensive medical cannabis ordinances.

Cassia specializes in the intersection of local and state regulation and private industry, having worked on both public and private sides of the negotiating table. Her background in public finance, land-use planning, local government law, and commercial real estate provides insight into all phases of permitting and licensed operations. She works extensively with cannabis operators across California, helping the firm's clients navigate the ever-changing regulatory and business landscape and anticipate new impacts and market forces before they occur. In addition to client advocacy, Cassia leads the Los Angeles office, plays an active role in multiple industry groups, and speaks frequently on California cannabis matters.

Andrea Golan is an associate attorney in Vicente Sederberg's Los Angeles office and a member of the firm's regulatory compliance and hemp practice groups.

Emily Hackman joined Vicente Sederberg in 2017 and is a Licensing Specialist on the California licensing team.

Shawn Hauser is a partner and chair of the Hemp and Cannabinoids Department at Vicente Sederberg.

Ben Leonard is an attorney at Vicente Sederberg focusing his practice in the areas of corporate and real estate.

Andrew Livingston first honed his skills as a drug policy activist in college at Colgate University and currently serves a unique role as an economist, business analyst, and general cannabis policy expert in Vicente Sederberg's Denver office.

Barine Majewska has experience working with clients in the cannabis space on corporate transactions, with a specific focus on negotiating and drafting intellectual property licensing, manufacturing, white label, services and brand agreements in a shifting regulatory framework.

Kelsey Middleton is a regulatory specialist in Vicente Sederberg's Los Angeles office, where she focuses on licensing and regulatory compliance.

Ilya Ross is a seasoned corporate and securities attorney and helps cannabis companies in all aspects of general corporate counseling and capital markets transactions, with a focus on public and private financing, corporate governance, securities law compliance, and strategic partnerships.

Jessica Scardina is a senior associate attorney and chair of Vicente Sederberg's Colorado regulatory law practice.

Phil Silverman serves as counsel at Vicente Sederberg in the Boston office assisting clients in developing strategies to create working relationships with municipalities to implement a practical and business-friendly approach to operations.

Carl Werner focuses his practice on several areas of law, including corporate and small business transactions, products liability, and international law.

Catie Wightman is a graduate of the University of Denver Sturm College of Law, where she was an associate editor of the Denver Law Review, and will be joining the Hemp & Cannabinoids Practice Group at Vicente Sederberg.

Acknowledgments

It is also an unfortunate fact that while many are making their fortunes in the cannabis industry, others remain in prison or are hampered by past drug convictions and unable to rebuild their lives. In acknowledgment of this unacceptable situation, the authors of this book are committed to donating all their profits to the Last Prisoner Project. This organization focuses on three key criminal justice reform initiatives: prisoner release, record clearing through clemency and expungement, and reentry programs.

We greatly appreciate the efforts of many Vicente Sederberg LLP colleagues and interns. Special thanks to Catie Wightman, Annie Mason, Jeremy Shaw, Courtney Barnes, Dane Chromzak, Aaron Tucker, Grant Hespeler, Abby Parker, Luke Stanton, David Kramer, Corey Cox, Scott Moskol, Matt Bewig, Keith Sealing, Catherine Norden, and Taylor Friedlander. Charlie would also like to thank Max and Susan Alovisetti for their constant encouragement and support. Finally, thank you to all the clients of Vicente Sederberg who have allowed us to pursue cannabis law as our profession.

A Note on Terminology
in the Cannabis Industry

There is a great deal of confusion, and political debate, over vocabulary in the cannabis space. In addition to disputes about semantics, there is also a debate about the scientific validity of terms like sativa and indica and how many species of cannabis exist. Scientific debates are beyond the scope of this book, which hopes merely to define terms clearly so we can discuss cannabis law.

A good place to begin is where everyone agrees – the scientific term cannabis. This refers to a genus of flowering plants in the family *Cannabaceae*. Other members of this family include hops, commonly used to flavor beer. Within the genus of *Cannabaceae*, scientists commonly identify three distinct species: *Cannabis sativa*, *Cannabis indica*, and *Cannabis ruderalis*. This is disputed and is a matter of controversy, however, as some believe all cannabis is *cannabis sativa*.

After this point, confusion begins. Non-scientific terms begin to make an appearance as legislators and operators need to differentiate crops. Hemp is often described as a separate plant from cannabis, but hemp is really a term used to designate specific *cultivars,* plant varieties produced by selective breeding, of cannabis that contain 0.3% or less of Tetrahydrocannabinol (THC) by dry weight (*i.e.*, not counting water). This threshold can vary by country. For example, in Switzerland, hemp refers to varieties of cannabis that contain 1% or less of THC. Hemp, then, is really defined by legal regulations rather than by botany or science.

Another designation based more on law than science is the term marijuana. This term is used to designate varieties of cannabis that contain more than 0.3% THC (again, by dry weight) or are otherwise grown pursuant to the regulations governing non-hemp cannabis plants. Many members of the cannabis industry do not like the term marijuana (or the antiquated spelling "marihuana" used in federal statute). The dislike of the term stems from the efforts of prohibitionists in the early 20th century, in particular Harry Anslinger, to use racist sentiment against Mexican immigrants – who were associated with the Spanish word marijuana – to drum up opposition to cannabis. Anslinger, and his ideological allies, successfully replaced the word cannabis (the term that was widely used at the time and associated with medical use) with marijuana in common use.

However, despite this prejudiced history, the term marijuana is used in so many statutes (Colorado has the Marijuana Enforcement Division) that it is difficult to avoid entirely. At the same time, there is a significant difference in how hemp is regulated from other varieties of cannabis. If you say you own a cannabis farm, what does that mean? It would be accurate to describe a hemp farm this way (since hemp is a cultivar of cannabis), and it would also be accurate to describe a marijuana farm this way (since marijuana is also a cultivar of cannabis). This confusion is why the antiquated term marijuana still has a use.

However, despite the advantages of retaining the use of the word marijuana, the authors of this book are sensitive to objections over the racist history of the term marijuana and have refrained from using it in this volume as much as possible. *The Business of Cannabis* will use the following naming convention to avoid confusion:

> *Cannabis* will be used to refer to all varieties of the cannabis plant, regardless of THC content or regulatory body, and it may also refer to varieties of the cannabis plant grown under state regulatory regimes for cannabis varieties over 0.3% in THC.
>
> *Hemp* will be used when the variety in question is regulated pursuant to hemp rules. (So, a plant would not be considered hemp, even if it had less than 0.3% THC content, if it was grown under a cannabis regulatory regime.)
>
> *Marijuana* will only be used where absolutely necessary to differentiate between hemp and non-hemp varietals of cannabis, and when quoting statutes.

Legal Disclaimer

This book is provided solely for educational purposes – it is not to be interpreted as a legal opinion, or legal advice, or tax advice. The laws and regulations governing cannabis continue to evolve rapidly, and, due to the timing challenges of publishing a book, the information provided herein was last updated on June 1, 2020, and should be considered out of date. Compliance with this book does not guarantee compliance with local, state, or federal law and does not insulate the recipient or any of its affiliates from enforcement actions by any governmental entity or third party against it. Cannabis remains federally illegal in the United States. Please consult with a legal advisor before taking any actions in the cannabis industry.

Abbreviations

BSA	Bank Secrecy Act
CBD	Cannabidiol
CBP	Customs and Border Protection
CSA	Controlled Substances Act
DEA	Drug Enforcement Administration
DOJ	Department of Justice
FCC	Federal Communications Commission
FDA	Food and Drug Administration
FDIC	Federal Deposit Insurance Corporation
FFDCA	Federal Food, Drug and Cosmetic Act
FinCEN	U.S. Department of the Treasury's Financial Crimes Enforcement Network
FTC	Federal Trade Commission
GRAS	Generally Recognized As Safe
IFR	Interim Final Rule
MCC	Merchant Category Code
MRB	Marijuana Related Business
NCUA	National Credit Union Association
NDI	New Dietary Ingredient
PVP	Plant Variety Protection
PVPO	Plant Variety Protection Office
RICO	Racketeer Influenced Corrupt Organizations
SAR	Suspicious Activity Report
THC	Tetrahydrocannabinol
USAM	United States Attorney's Manual
USDA	United States Department of Agriculture
USPTO	United States Patent and Trademark Office

Introduction

Charles S. Alovisetti

Everyone seems to think they are going to get rich in the cannabis industry. After all, it is a once-in-a-lifetime opportunity. A global, largely illicit market worth around $150 billion is slowly transitioning to a legal, regulated industry. The United States is at the forefront of that change as more and more states vote to legalize. But the "canna-curious" are finding that making a fortune in cannabis isn't as easy as some would hope. It is a challenging industry, made even more difficult by complexities and nuances of the law. While the number of states that have legalized medical and adult-use cannabis has grown, creating a patchwork of different laws, cannabis remains illegal at the federal level. And, to add to the confusion, hemp, but not cannabis, has become legal in the United States.

Entrepreneurs, investors, some 300,000 employees in the industry, and most Americans who support legalization need a reliable guide to understand the legal framework of this new industry. Legal knowledge is needed for anyone seeking to understand the industry: why the distinction between hemp and cannabis matters, why CBD isn't completely legal, and why you can only own so many licenses in Massachusetts but an unlimited number in Colorado. *The Business of Cannabis* has grown from our legal experience over the past five years working with cannabis clients (and ten years of cannabis work as a law firm), across a wide range of states and localities. We have worked closely with all types of cannabis clients, including licensed cannabis operators (cannabis and hemp), ancillary businesses, investors, and other law firms on a wide variety of regulatory and corporate matters. Our colleagues at Vicente Sederberg LLP helped write the laws in Colorado and Massachusetts and in many localities. Together we have represented over 1,000 cannabis clients. Named "the country's first powerhouse marijuana law firm" by Rolling Stone and ranked a Band 1 law firm by Chambers USA in its "Nationwide: Cannabis Law" practice category since its addition in 2019, Vicente Sederberg LLP is not just another law firm that decided to jump onto the cannabis bandwagon; rather, VS has been at the cutting edge of cannabis and hemp law and policy since the inception of the regulated cannabis industry.

In this book, we will provide a series of overviews of the major practical legal issues facing the cannabis industry. There is a tremendous amount of information available about the cannabis industry online, but it tends to be narrowly focused and is often unreliable since it is created by individuals with only a cursory knowledge of cannabis policy and operating conditions. This book is meant to serve as a broad introduction. While legal in focus, it will address complex issues in a practical manner, reflecting the authors' experiences in helping businesses navigate the constantly shifting cannabis legal landscape, and will aim at a broad audience.

Our book is far too short to be a comprehensive volume on the laws impacting the cannabis industry. The goal of *The Business of Cannabis* is not to provide a comprehensive review of each state and local law applicable to the cannabis industry in the United States. That is a far more ambitious book and such a publication would require a multi volume set of books and require the authors to retire from the practice of law to focus on writing. There is a tremendous variety among the cannabis regulatory systems of different states. More so than many industries, the cannabis sector is highly fragmented, and truly meaningful differences exist between state markets. That is why we consistently note that, in addition to the issues set forth herein, the final analysis of any cannabis law issue will require a careful review of all application-specific state and local rules and regulations.

Like Sisyphus, the authors of a book on cannabis law must expect no respite. Cannabis law changes so quickly that as soon as this book is published, it will already be out of date and will require substantial updates. While *The Business of Cannabis* cannot be fully up to date (to prepare this edition for publication, we decided to stop incorporating updates after June 1st), understanding any future updates will be easier with this book in hand.

The book falls into three parts: first, an introduction to the national legal landscape and federal legal risks associated with cannabis businesses; second, an overview of the assorted legal issues faced by cannabis companies; and finally, an introduction to the nuts and bolts of getting a cannabis deal done. *The Business of Cannabis* will provide you with a good grasp of the legal framework of the cannabis industry and will position you to succeed in your cannabis ventures. Reading this book will allow you to benefit from our hard-won experience dealing with new and rapidly evolving cannabis laws. We wish you the best of luck in whatever capacity you work, or hope to work, in the cannabis industry.

Part I

Understanding the National Landscape and Risks

1 Federal Law and Policy Overview – Cannabis

Charles S. Alovisetti and Carl Werner

Introduction

Before reviewing any of the issues unique to the practice of cannabis law, it is important to understand the current federal law landscape. In short, despite dramatic changes at the state and local levels that have occurred over the past decade, cannabis, with very few narrow exceptions, remains illegal at the federal level. Despite this illegality, however, federal law enforcement has largely followed a policy of non-enforcement with respect to businesses that are compliant with state law.

Federal Black Letter Law

The Controlled Substances Act

In the United States, 33 states and Washington, D.C. have legalized medical cannabis, and 11 states in addition to Washington, D.C. have legalized cannabis for recreational purposes or "adult-use." At the federal level, however, cannabis currently remains a Schedule I drug under the Controlled Substances Act of 1970 (CSA).[1] Under U.S. federal law, a Schedule I drug or substance is considered to have a high potential for abuse, no accepted medical use in the U.S., and no recognition of safety for its use under medical supervision. Thus, cannabis-related practices or activities including the importation, possession, use, cultivation, manufacture, sale, or distribution of cannabis remain illegal under U.S. federal law.

The CSA is an expansive piece of legislation, and its provisions go beyond merely criminalizing the production of cannabis. For example, under § 843(b) of the CSA, it is illegal to use a communication facility to facilitate a drug crime, and § 843(c) makes it illegal to place any advertisement that seeks to either sell or distribute a Schedule 1 substance. It is also illegal, under § 854(a), to invest the proceeds of drug crimes in any business engaged in interstate commerce. In addition, some activities that investors typically have viewed as ancillary, such as leasing property to a cannabis business, are a direct violation of the CSA under § 856, which makes it unlawful to lease, rent, use, or maintain any place, that has the purpose of manufacturing, distributing, or using any controlled substance.

Secondary Liability – Aiding and Abetting and Conspiracy

Because virtually all cannabis-related activities are illegal at the federal level, it is illegal to aid or abet such activities or to conspire or attempt to engage in the same. An individual may be liable for aiding, abetting, counseling, commanding, inducing, or procuring another person to commit a federal offense, or he may be punishable as a principal.[2] If an individual is charged with aiding and abetting a controlled substance possession or distribution offense, the government must prove that the defendant (1) had knowledge of the drugs, (2) had knowledge that the principal intended to distribute or possess drugs, and (3) purposefully intended to aid others in committing the crime alleged.[3]

Additionally, a person or entity may be liable under the CSA for attempting or conspiring to commit any offense.[4] Under a conspiracy theory, a corporation and participating individuals may be liable for conspiracy among multiple corporate officers, directors, or employees.[5] Even if corporate officials do not themselves commit the acts, they may be liable for foreseeable offenses committed by co-conspirators in furtherance of a common scheme.[6] In addition to aiding and abetting and conspiracy charges, an individual with an investment or business relationship with a cannabis company could also be charged with being an accessory after the fact. Under 18 U.S.C. § 3, someone who, after a federal crime has been committed, "receives, relieves, comforts or assists the offender in order to hinder or prevent his apprehension, trial or punishment" can be prosecuted as an accessory after the fact.[7]

Secondary Liability – Financial Crimes

U.S. federal money laundering laws, specifically 18 U.S.C. §§ 1956 and 1957, criminalize monetary transactions involving the proceeds of "Specified Unlawful Activity," which includes any violation of the CSA. The first of these statutes, 18 U.S.C. § 1956, criminalizes participation in financial transactions when the person or institution participating knows that the property or monetary instrument involved in the transaction is the proceeds of a "Specified Unlawful Activity;" and where the institution either intends to promote the specified unlawful activity or has knowledge that the transaction is designed to conceal elements of origin or ownership with respect to the proceeds of such specified unlawful activity.[8] Financial transactions between investors and regulated cannabis businesses would likely violate this provision.

The second money laundering statute, 18 U.S.C. § 1957, is a broader provision and criminalizes financial transactions over $10,000 conducted through financial institutions when the funds transferred are the proceeds of criminal activity.[9] Although § 1957 prosecutions carry a lower maximum potential sentence than § 1956, § 1957 is broad enough to encompass virtually all major financial transactions within the regulated cannabis industry. In summary, the use of financial institutions to conduct financial sanctions within the cannabis industry is usually a criminal act if the amount of the transaction exceeds $10,000.

The Bank Secrecy Act (BSA) sets out requirements for financial institutions that are meant to assist in the detection and prevention of money laundering.[10] Under the BSA, financial institutions must keep records of certain cash transactions, report suspicious activity, and file reports, called "Suspicious Activity Reports" (SARs), if they believe a transaction involves proceeds from illegal activity.

As a result of the federal money laundering statutes and the requirements of the BSA, banks and other financial institutions that provide a cannabis business with a checking account, debit or credit card, small business loan, or any other service could be found guilty of money laundering, aiding and abetting, or conspiracy.

Secondary Liability – RICO

Another potential violation of federal law that is linked to cannabis-related activities is the Racketeer Influenced Corrupt Organizations Act (RICO).[11] Under RICO, if a party commits at least 2 out of 35 specified predicate crimes, this constitutes a "pattern" and, therefore, a RICO violation. While RICO was intended to be used against organized crime, the list of predicate crimes includes dealing in a controlled substance and money laundering. Because of this, anyone who invests in, acquires, or maintains an interest in, conducts, or participates in the affairs of a cannabis company could be charged under RICO.

In addition to the criminal penalties under RICO, the statute creates a private right of action for anyone "injured in his business or property" because of a RICO violation. A successful civil RICO suit entitles a plaintiff to treble damages. There have been several high-profile civil RICO lawsuits largely driven by anti-cannabis advocates brought against ancillary service providers in the industry. Some of these cases have been dismissed,[12] some have settled,[13] and others have failed[14] due to an inability to prove damages, but the legal threat to ancillary and plant-touching companies remains.

If a prosecutor wanted to charge cannabis operators or investors or even businesses providing services to cannabis companies (including lawyers, bankers, and accountants), several statutes are available to be used as the basis for prosecution.

Secondary Liability – Immigration Law

Any non-U.S. citizen can be denied entry into the United States and may potentially receive a lifetime ban for direct or indirect involvement with the U.S. cannabis industry. A statement issued by the U.S. Customs and

Border Patrol (Customs) in October 2018 stated that in accordance with the U.S. Immigration and Nationality Act,

> [a] Canadian citizen working in or facilitating the proliferation of the legal cannabis industry in Canada, coming to the U.S. for reasons unrelated to the cannabis industry will generally be admissible to the U.S., however, if a traveler is found to be coming to the U.S. for reasons related to the cannabis industry, they may be deemed inadmissible.[15]

In fact, not long after releasing this statement, Customs placed a lifetime ban on entry into the U.S. on a Canadian national for admitting he was visiting the country to attend a cannabis business conference and tour a state-legal cannabis operation in which he had invested. While enforcement of the Immigration and Nationality Act has not been exceedingly strict with respect to cannabis, a very real possibility remains that a non-U.S. citizen attempting to enter the U.S. for cannabis-related activities may be denied entry or receive a lifetime ban, even if such activities are not directly plant-touching.[16] Applications for citizenship can also be affected by cannabis-related activities. A policy alert issued by U.S. Citizenship and Immigration Services in April 2019 states that "violations of federal controlled substance law, including violations involving cannabis, are generally a bar to establishing good moral character for naturalization, even where that conduct would not be an offense under state law."[17]

Secondary Liability – Asset Forfeiture

Asset forfeiture is the process by which the government seizes property that it suspects is involved in illegal activity.[18] Since cannabis is still illegal under federal law, real and personal property connected to cannabis-related activities are at risk of being seized. There are two main types of asset forfeiture: criminal and civil.[19] The most important criminal forfeiture statutes are RICO,[20] the Continuing Criminal Enterprise statute,[21] and the forfeiture sections of the CSA.[22] Under these statutes, the federal government can seize property used in drug-related activities as well as assets derived from drug sales. In civil forfeiture, unlike criminal forfeiture, no criminal charge against the property owner is necessary since the property itself is the defendant.[23] There only needs to be evidence linking the property to the drug activity. The standard of proof is the same for both civil and criminal forfeiture; however, the government must only prove that the asset or property was related to drug activity by a preponderance of the evidence.[24] The Supreme Court has held that both civil and criminal forfeitures are subject to the constraints of the Excessive Fines clause of the Eighth Amendment.[25]

Certain states, such as California, have adopted additional protections against asset forfeiture by local and state officials. Via passage of Senate Bill 443 (SB 443) in 2016, the California legislature established strict standards to protect the due process and property rights of California cannabis business owners, investors, and landlords. Under SB 443, state and local law enforcement agencies cannot transfer any property seized under state law to a federal agency. Further, a state agency must first obtain a criminal conviction for the illegal manufacturing or cultivation of cannabis to receive a share of federally seized property, including houses, vehicles, or cash under $40,000. A criminal conviction is also required for a state agency to recover any of it expenses for the seizure and destruction of cannabis. Finally, the bill raises the burden of proof for state agencies under existing law, requiring clear and convincing evidence to seize cash in the amount of $40,000 or more, and evidence beyond a reasonable doubt to seize cash of more than $25,000 but less than $40,000. Section 260302(b) of the state's Business & Professions Code now specifies that

> The actions of a person who, in good faith, allows his or her property to be used by a licensee, its employees, and its agents, as permitted pursuant to a state license and, if required by the applicable local ordinances, a local license or permit, are not unlawful under state law and shall not be an offense subject to arrest, prosecution, or other sanction under state law, or be subject to a civil fine or be a basis for seizure or forfeiture of assets under state law.

Two instances of the federal government unsuccessfully attempting to seize real property under the Controlled Substances Act are the Marin County and Harborside cases. Both arose out of circa 2011–2012 federal enforcement activity under California's previous Compassionate Use Act regulations and were decided in 2016. In the Marin County case, the Marin Alliance for Medical Marijuana (MAMM) successfully argued that the Rohrabacher-Farr Amendment prevented the DOJ from shutting down its state-law compliant medical cannabis business and seizing real property.[26] The DOJ later dropped a similar asset forfeiture case involving real property that was brought against Harborside in Oakland.[27] In light of the Rohrabacher-Blumenauer Amendment's ongoing renewals and, in some instances, attendant state law protections like California's SB 443, the threat of asset seizure to landowners who lease property to duly licensed and compliant cannabis businesses appears to have been diminished.

Constitutional Issues

A key issue in cannabis law is the tension between federal and state drug laws. Under the Supremacy Clause of Article VI, Clause 2, of the U.S.

Constitution, federal law is the supreme law of the land.[28] This means that state laws regulating cannabis and removing state-level criminal penalties for its possession and use have never actually "legalized" cannabis, nor could they. While there have been many constitutional challenges to federal prohibition over the years, all serious challenges, most notably *Gonzalez v. Raich*, were predicated on the notion that the federal government exceeded the limits of its own constitutional authority by criminalizing cannabis, and were never based on the argument that states may determine federal law.[29]

The federal government, however, cannot force state governments to criminalize an activity, and so both federal prohibition and state decriminalization persist in the law of each jurisdiction. This is likely also true of state regulation of cannabis businesses. While the issue has not been tried, the Supreme Court denied Nebraska and Oklahoma's motion for leave to file a complaint in *Nebraska and Oklahoma v. Colorado* in a 6-2 decision in 2016. The plaintiff states had attempted to enjoin Colorado from implementing cannabis regulation and decriminalization.[30] However, the federal prohibitions against engaging in cannabis-related activities (including aiding, abetting, conspiracy, and conspiracy to aid and abet those who do) do not create positive conflict with the laws of states that have ratified legal cannabis regulatory programs. Although such states have removed their own state-level prohibitions against certain cannabis-related activities and have regulated such activity under their own laws, and these activities remain illegal under U.S. federal law, the states do not require anyone to engage in cannabis-related activity – meaning there is no positive conflict with federal law.

The federal government may enforce its own criminal laws in any U.S. state. However, the Supreme Court has ruled, pursuant to the "anti-commandeering doctrine," that the federal government is generally prohibited from ordering state officials (law enforcement officers and administrative governing bodies) to enforce federal law via legislative or executive mandates. Put simply, the federal government cannot require state legislators to pass laws making cannabis illegal and cannot require state and local law enforcement agencies to enforce federal laws. Further, the ability of the federal government to enforce its laws concerning cannabis is limited by the financial resources allocated to enforcement, which creates budgetary issues for the U.S. Department of Justice (DOJ) in enforcing federal law without the cooperation of state authorities.

There is also at least one constitutional issue that has so far been avoided because of the tension between federal and state cannabis laws. Every state that has chosen to regulate cannabis has prohibited the importation and exportation of cannabis products, and many such states have also chosen to limit out-of-state investment or ownership in cannabis businesses. While the former prohibition is at least consonant with (and a result of) the federal government's desire to prevent interstate commerce of cannabis, as well as its authority to regulate interstate commerce, both the prohibition of imports and exports and limitations on out-of-state investment and ownership would likely run afoul of the "dormant Commerce Clause."

This unwritten doctrine is derived from Congress' Article I powers: Congress has been given power over interstate commerce, and so the states may not discriminate against interstate commerce or "unduly burden" interstate commerce, even in the absence of federal legislation regulating the activity. Interstate import and export bans have long been found to violate this doctrine and the recent Supreme Court case of *Tennessee Wine and Spirits Retailers Assn. v. Thomas*, which involved liquor licensing, strongly suggested that out-of-state investment restrictions would be overturned as well.[31] However, because cannabis businesses remain illegal under federal law, it is highly unlikely that federal courts would entertain a challenge to these state laws at this time.

Memos and Federal Policy

The U.S. government's approach to enforcement of federal cannabis laws has trended toward non-enforcement. On August 29, 2013, the DOJ issued a memorandum (Cole Memo) to all U.S. Attorneys' offices (federal prosecutors), directing U.S. Attorneys not to prioritize the enforcement of federal cannabis laws against individuals and businesses rigorously complying with strictly regulated state cannabis programs. While not legally binding, the Cole Memorandum laid a framework for managing the tension between state and federal laws concerning state-regulated cannabis businesses by laying out eight priorities for federal enforcement: distribution to minors, revenue going to criminal enterprises, diversion from states where cannabis is legal to states where it is illegal, use of state-authorized cannabis activity as a cover for other illegal drugs or activity, violence and the use of firearms, drugged driving or other adverse public health consequences, the use of public lands for cannabis production, and cannabis possession or use on federal property.[32]

On January 4, 2018, the Cole Memo was revoked by then-Attorney General Jeff Sessions. While this revocation did not create a change in federal law, it removed the DOJ's guidance to U.S. Attorneys that state-regulated cannabis industries substantively in compliance with the Cole Memo's guidelines should not be a prosecutorial priority. Nonetheless, cannabis industry prosecutions are not currently a priority for the DOJ. Sessions concurrently issued a one-page memorandum (Sessions Memorandum) explaining the Cole Memorandum was "unnecessary" due to existing general enforcement guidance adopted in the 1980s, as set forth in the U.S. Attorney's Manual (USAM). The USAM enforcement priorities are also based on the use of the federal government's limited resources and include "law enforcement priorities set by the Attorney

General," the "seriousness" of the alleged crimes, the "deterrent effect of criminal prosecution," and "the cumulative impact of particular crimes on the community."

Although the Sessions Memorandum reiterates "that marijuana activity is a serious crime," it explicitly describes itself as solely a guide to prosecutorial discretion. Such discretion is firmly in the hands of U.S. Attorneys in deciding whether to prosecute cannabis-related offenses. While numerous U.S. Attorneys across the country have stated that they will continue to exercise their discretion as they had under the Cole Memo's guidance, a few have displayed greater ambivalence. Nonetheless, cannabis remains a Schedule I controlled substance at the federal level, and the U.S. federal government continues to reserve the right to enforce federal law regarding cannabis-related activities, even if state law sanctions such conduct.

FinCEN Guidance

Additionally, the U.S. Department of the Treasury's Financial Crimes Enforcement Network (FinCEN) issued a memorandum on February 14, 2014 called "Guidance Regarding Marijuana Related Financial Crimes," (FinCEN Memo)[33] outlining pathways for financial institutions to service state-sanctioned cannabis businesses while fulfilling their BSA obligations. (The FinCEN Memo is discussed in Chapter 12.)

On the same day the FinCEN Memo was published, the DOJ issued a memorandum (2014 Cole Memo) directing prosecutors to apply the enforcement priorities of the Cole Memo in determining whether to charge individuals or institutions with crimes related to financial transactions involving cannabis-related proceeds. Like the original Cole Memo, the 2014 Cole Memo was rescinded on January 4, 2018. Rescission of the 2014 Cole Memo, however, has not affected the status of the FinCEN Memorandum. The Department of the Treasury has not given any indication that it intends to rescind the FinCEN Memorandum itself and continues to follow its guidance.

Although the Cole Memo and the 2014 Cole Memo have been rescinded, one legislative safeguard for the medical cannabis industry remains in place. Since 2015, Congress has used a rider provision in the FY 2015–2019 Consolidated Appropriations Acts (currently the Joyce Amendment, but previously called the Rohrabacher-Blumenauer Amendment, and before that the Rohrabacher-Farr Amendment) to prevent the federal government from using congressionally appropriated funds to enforce federal cannabis laws against state-compliant actors in jurisdictions that have legalized medical cannabis and cannabis-related activities. On February 15, 2019, the Joyce Amendment was renewed in the 2019 Consolidated Appropriations Act, which remained in effect until the end of FY 2019 (September 30, 2019). After the expiration of the 2019 Consolidated Appropriations

Act, President Donald J. Trump signed two budget continuing resolutions, which included the protections of the Joyce Amendment, to avoid government shutdown through December 20th. On December 20, President Trump signed the budget for FY 2020, which runs to September 30, 2020, and includes the Joyce Amendment.[34]

COVID-19 and Economic Aid

In spring 2020, the Federal Government adopted three landmark pieces of legislation in response to the coronavirus pandemic that provide relief for businesses and individuals, as well as critical protections for workers and assistance to states.

However, because the cultivation and sale of cannabis is illegal under federal law, cannabis businesses and certain ancillary businesses are not eligible to participate in many of these programs. In a March 22, 2020, Twitter post in response to a Washington-based cannabis business owner, the Small Business Administration (SBA) confirmed that cannabis businesses are not able to access the SBA-funded programs including the Economic Injury Disaster Loan Emergency Advance (EIDL) Program, even though cannabis businesses are as badly harmed by the coronavirus pandemic as other law-abiding, tax-paying small business operators.[35]

While SBA has not formally addressed the eligibility of cannabis businesses for the broader Paycheck Protection Program, it appears prior SBA regulation and policy guidance may prohibit access to this program by cannabis businesses and certain other types of businesses. In concert with passage of the 2018 Farm Bill, the SBA revised its lending policies in a 2019 Policy Notice to allow "hemp-related businesses" access to SBA financial assistance.[36] Notwithstanding this policy change, both "direct" and "indirect" "marijuana-related businesses" appear to remain potentially ineligible to receive SBA loans.[37]

Certain businesses that provide ancillary services to the cannabis and/or hemp industry may qualify for relief under the SBA, but eligibility must be assessed on a case by case basis. However, since many banks will not service the cannabis industry, even businesses indirectly involved in cannabis, that technically qualify for SBA loans could encounter challenges in obtaining SBA funds. In addition, businesses applying for SBA loans must certify that they do not violate federal law.

Politics

Despite the rescission of the Cole memos, there have been no publicly known federal criminal enforcement actions against state-legal cannabis companies during the Trump Administration. And although it is not possible to determine the future of the cannabis industry with certainty, many political commenters argue that a nationwide "crackdown" is unlikely. The sheer size of the cannabis industry, in addition to the participation by state and local governments and investors, suggests that a large-scale enforcement operation would more than likely create an unwanted political backlash for the DOJ and the Trump Administration.

Current Federal Cannabis Laws and Potential Legislative Changes

While there has been no material change to the law criminalizing cannabis since the passage of the CSA, there are several pieces of legislation at the federal level that, if passed, would have a major impact on the legal status of cannabis. The two major bills with the broadest legislative support are the "Strengthening the Tenth Amendment Through Entrusting States Act" (STATES Act) and the "Secure and Fair Enforcement Banking Act of 2019" (SAFE Banking Act), both of which have bipartisan sponsors in the House and Senate. This is key, as the Republican-held Senate is unlikely to take up cannabis reform measures without broad support from their side of the aisle.

The STATES Act

The STATES Act would resolve the tension between federal and state cannabis laws by deferring to state cannabis decisions. This would be accomplished by making the CSA inapplicable to operators who follow state cannabis laws. Because the STATES Act would remove federal criminal liability from state-compliant operators, this would remove issues around federal money laundering statutes, any issues related to aiding and abetting, conspiracy, RICO, and section 280E. The STATES Act has been introduced in both the House and the Senate with nine cosponsors in the Senate and 63 in the House, but the legislation has not passed out of committees in either chamber. Notably, Trump has stated he will "probably" support the STATES Act.[38]

The SAFE Banking Act

Discussed in Chapter 12.

The MORE Act

The Marijuana Opportunity Reinvestment and Expungement Act of 2019 (MORE Act) was introduced in the Senate by Sen. Kamala Harris on July 23, 2019, as S. 2227, and was referred to the Committee on Finance.[39] The bill has five cosponsors – Sens. Corey Booker, Jeff Merkley, Ron Wyden, Elizabeth Warren, and Ed Markey. On the same day, Rep. Jerrold Nadler introduced the same bill into the House as HR. 3884. This bill has 69 cosponsors, including one Republican, Rep. Matt Gaetz of Florida. That bill has been referred to eight committees, including the House Judiciary and House Small Business Committee. The bill was approved by the Judiciary Committee on November 20, 2019, on a bipartisan 24-10 vote.[40] More recently, on January 7, 2020, the House Small Business Committee waived its jurisdiction over the bill.[41]

Unlike the STATES Act, which has broader bipartisan support and is regarded as more likely to advance in the Republican-led Senate, the MORE Act has a strong social justice component. In addition to completely removing cannabis from the schedule of controlled substances under the CSA, which would fix a large measure of the cannabis industry's section 280E and banking issues, the MORE ACT[42] contains additional far-ranging provisions worth noting:

- Requires the Bureau of Labor Statistics to maintain demographic data on the cannabis industry, including owners and employees;
- Creates a 5% national excise tax on cannabis that is to be used, in part, to fund an opportunity trust fund;
- Creates the Community Reinvestment Grant Program to fund services for individuals most adversely impacted by the war on drugs (job training, reentry services, etc.);
- Creates a Cannabis Justice Office to administer the Community Reinvestment Grant Program;
- Directs the SBA to create an Equitable Licensing Grant Program to fund states to implement equitable cannabis licensing programs;
- Explicitly makes state-legal cannabis businesses eligible for SBA assistance;
- States that no person may be denied any Federal public benefit because of cannabis use or conviction for a cannabis offense;
- States that security clearances cannot be denied for cannabis use;
- Amends immigration laws so that immigration status will not be impacted by cannabis conviction or use; and
- Creates a federal expungement program and a process for sentencing review for individuals incarcerated for cannabis offenses.

As this bill moves through House subcommittees significant changes are possible. In addition to the STATES Act, the SAFE Banking Act, and the MORE Act, other bills have been introduced, including the Marijuana Justice Act of 2019, which has a social justice component like the MORE Act. This bill is unlikely to advance.

2020 Presidential Race as of June 1st

While Trump's opinions on the legalization of cannabis are hard to pin down, the Democratic Party's views have evolved to a point where Democratic presidential candidates can no longer publicly support the federal prohibition on cannabis. The official platform of the Democratic Party, last revised in 2016, calls for a number of changes to the current federal legal system: the removal of cannabis from the list of "Schedule 1" substances, a path towards future legalization, and freedom for states to adopt their own policies on cannabis.[43]

The presumptive Democratic nominee, Joseph Biden, has publicly walked back his statements supporting prohibition. He stated marijuana should be a misdemeanor and that no one should be in jail for nonviolent crimes and has advocated for decriminalization and further study before legalization.[44] It is instructive that Biden has been heavily criticized for his position on cannabis and his role in enacting the 1994 crime bill.[45]

Despite his history of anti-cannabis policies, if Biden, the current presumptive Democrat nominee, is elected to the White House in 2020, it is possible that we could see a further loosening of federal laws and policies regarding cannabis. However, as the status of the bills discussed above shows, if the Republicans and Senator Mitch McConnell retain control of the Senate, it will be difficult to pass major legislative changes to the current legal system. Nevertheless, due to the shifting support for cannabis legalization by U.S. citizens, whether a new President is elected, or Trump is re-elected, the existing policy of non-enforcement is likely to continue until a change in federal cannabis policy occurs.

Notes

1 Controlled Substances Act of 1970 § 202(c), 21 U.S.C. § 812(c) (2018).
2 18 U.S.C. § 2.
3 *U.S. v. Salmon*, 944 F.2d 1106 (3d Cir. 1991).
4 21 U.S.C. § 846.
5 *U.S. v. Hughes Aircraft Co.*, 20 F.3d 974 (9th Cir. 1994).
6 *U.S. v. Sain*, 141 F.3d 463 (3d Cir. 1998).
7 18 U.S.C. § 3.
8 18 U.S.C. § 1956.
9 18 U.S.C. § 1957.
10 Bank Secrecy Act of 1970, P.L. 91-508, 84 Stat. 1118 (codified as amended at various sections of Titles 12, 15, and 31 U.S.C.).
11 Racketeer Influenced and Corrupt Organizations Act, 18 U.S.C. §§ 1961–1968 (2018).
12 Robert Mikos, "Court Dismisses Civil RICO Suit against Marijuana Supplier, Tees Up Potential Circuit Split," *Marijuana Law, Policy and Authority*, Aug. 27, 2018, https://my.vanderbilt.edu/marijuanalaw/2018/08/court-dismisses-civil-rico-suit-against-marijuana-supplier-tees-up-potential-circuit-split/.
13 Ricardo Baca, "Anti-Pot Racketeering Suit Settles, Opens Door for Future RICO Claims," *Denver Post*, Dec. 30, 2015.
14 Robert Mikos, "Plaintiff Loses Colorado RICO Lawsuit (Safe Streets)," *Marijuana Law, Policy and Authority*, Nov. 1, 2018, https://my.vanderbilt.edu/marijuanalaw/2018/11/update-plaintiff-loses-colorado-rico-lawsuit-safe-streets/.
15 U.S. Customs and Border Patrol, "CBP Statement on Canada's Legalization of Marijuana and Crossing the Border," Sept. 21, 2018, https://www.cbp.gov/

newsroom/speeches-and-statements/cbp-statement-canadas-legalization-marijuana-and-crossing-border.

16 U.S. Citizenship and Immigration Services, "USCIS Issues Policy Guidance Clarifying How Federal Controlled Substances Law Applies to Naturalization Determinations," Apr. 19, 2019, https://www.uscis.gov/news/alerts/uscis-issues-policy-guidance-clarifying-how-federal-controlled-substances-law-applies-naturalization-determinations.

17 *Id.*

18 Brenda Grantland, "Federal Forfeiture Procedure," updated June 13, 2014, https://fear.org/1/pages/law-library/federal-forfeiture-statutes/federal-forfeiture-procedure.php; "Asset Forfeiture Rules and Procedures," uploaded June 15, 2011, https://www.scribd.com/document/57881988/Asset-Forfeiture-Rules-and-Procedures.

19 U.S. Department of Justice, "Types of Federal Forfeiture," Feb. 28, 2020, https://www.justice.gov/afp/types-federal-forfeiture.

20 18 U.S.C. § 1963.

21 21 U.S.C. § 848.

22 21 U.S.C. §§ 853, 881.

23 Ryan Reaves, "Civil Asset Forfeiture and Commercial Cannabis," *Canna-BusinessLaw*, Aug. 30, 2017, http://cannabusinesslaw.com/2017/08/civil-asset-forfeiture-and-commercial-cannabis/.

24 18 U.S.C. § 983.

25 *Austin v. U.S.*, 509 U.S. 602, 609 (1993).

26 An injunction can only be enforced if a business is violating state law. *United States v. Marin Alliance for Medical Marijuana*, 139 F.Supp.3d 1039 (N.D. Cal. 2015).

27 Elyce Kirchner, "U.S. Attorney Drops Oakland's Harborside Marijuana Dispensary Case," NBC Bay Area, May 3, 2016, https://www.nbcbayarea.com/new/local/us-attorney-drops-oaklands-harborside-marijuana-dispensary-case/90948/.

28 U.S. Const. Art. VI.

29 *Gonzales v. Raich*, 545 US 1 (2005).

30 *Nebraska and Oklahoma v. Colorado*, 577 U.S. ___ (2016).

31 *Tennessee Wine and Spirits Retailers Assn. v. Thomas*, 883 F. 3d 608 (6th Cir. 2019).

32 DOJ, "Guidance Regarding Marijuana Enforcement," Aug. 29, 2013, https://www.justice.gov/iso/opa/resources/3052013829132756857467.pdf.

33 U.S. Department of Justice, "Guidance Regarding Marijuana Related Financial Crimes," June 14, 2014, https://www.justice.gov/sites/default/files/usao-wdwa/legacy/2014/02/14/DAG%20Memo%20-%20Guidance%20Re-garding%20Marijuana%20Related%20Financial%20Crimes%202%2014%20 14%20%282%29.pdf.

34 Consolidated Appropriations Act of 2020, Pub. L. 116-93, § 531 (2019).

35 SBA Pacific NW (@SBAPacificNW) "With the exception of businesses that pro-duce or sell hemp and hemp-derived products (Agriculture Improvement Act of 2018, Public Law 115-334), marijuana-related businesses are not eligible for SBA-funded services (OMB, 2 C.F.R. § 200.300)." *Twitter*, Mar. 23, 2020, https://twitter.com/SBAPacificNW/status/1242227023302373377?ref_src=twsrc%5 Etfw%7Ctwcamp%5Etweetembed%7Ctwterm%5E1242227023302373377&ref_url=https%3A%2F%2F.

36 Small Business Administration, "SBA Information Notice," Feb. 15, 2019, https://www.sba.gov/sites/default/files/2019-02/Info%20Notice%20SOP%20 50%2010%205K%205000-19004.pdf.

37 Small Business Administration, "SBA Policy Notice," Apr. 3, 2018, https:// www.sba.gov/sites/default/files/resource_files/SBA_Policy_Notice_5000-17057_Revised_Guidance_on_Credit_Elsewhere_and_Other_Provisions.pdf.

38 John Wagner, "Trump Says He 'Probably' Will Support Bill to Protect States That Have Legalized Marijuana," *Washington Post*, June 8, 2018.

39 Marijuana Opportunity Reinvestment and Expungement Act of 2019, S.2227, 116th Congress (2019).

40 House Judiciary Committee, "Press Release: House Judiciary Passes MORE Act to Decriminalize Marijuana at Federal Level," Nov. 20, 2019, https:// judiciary.house.gov/news/documentsingle.aspx?DocumentID=2157.

41 NORML, "House Small Business Committee Moves Marijuana Bill Forward," Jan. 6, 2020, https://blog.norml.org/2020/01/06/house-small-business-committee-moves-marijuana-bill-forward/.

42 Marijuana Opportunity Reinvestment and Expungement Act of 2019, H.R.3884, 116th Congress (2019); the summary above pertains only to the text of the MORE Act as of May 26, 2020.

43 "The 2016 Democratic Party Platform," July 9, 2016, https://democrats.org/ wherewe-stand/party-platform/.

44 Catlin Oprysko, "Biden: 'Nobody Should Be in Jail for a Nonviolent Crime,'" *Politico*, Sept. 12, 2019, https://www.politico.com/story/2019/09/12/joe-biden-debate-nonviolent-crime-1493732; New York Times editorial board, "NYT Editorial Board Interview: Joe Biden," Jan. 17, 2020.

45 Kyle Jaeger, "Where Presidential Candidate Joe Biden Stands on Marijuana," *Marijuana Moment*, Apr. 25, 2019, https://www.marijuanamoment. net/where-presidential-candidate-joe-biden-stands-on-marijuana/.

2 Federal Law and Policy Overview – Hemp and CBD

Charles S. Alovisetti, Shawn Hauser, Michelle Bodian, and Catie Wightman

Introduction

Hemp is a variety of the plant *Cannabis sativa L*. Unlike cannabis, however, hemp contains only trace amounts of THC, the cannabinoid responsible for the plant's intoxicating effects. Hemp is cultivated for use in tens of thousands of consumer products, from human and animal nutritional foods and supplements to paper and construction materials, personal care and cosmetic products, and other industrial goods. In addition, Cannabidiol (CBD) can also be extracted from hemp (it can also be extracted from cannabis and synthesized).

There have been major changes to the laws governing hemp and CBD in the past few years. The two major pieces of federal legislation driving these changes have been the 2014 Agricultural Act (2014 Farm Bill) and the Agricultural Improvement Act of 2018 (2018 Farm Bill) and the implementing regulations for the 2018 Farm Bill. These laws and regulations govern the production of hemp in the US as an agricultural crop after decades of prohibition of hemp cultivation. However, as authority expressly reserved in the 2018 Farm Bill, the Food and Drug Administration (FDA) still governs the sale of consumable products.

Changes in Hemp Agricultural Laws

2014 Farm Bill

Until the passage of the 2014 Farm Bill, federal law did not distinguish between hemp and cannabis. Thus, all cultivation of hemp in the US was illegal (absent a schedule I registration from the Drug Enforcement Administration (DEA)). As a result, importation served as the only viable legal pathway for the use and distribution of products derived from "hemp." The 2014 Farm Bill established a limited research pilot program to cultivate hemp[1] (under certain conditions) administered by state departments of agriculture or institutes of higher education (territories and Indian tribes were ineligible).[2] The scope of the 2014 Farm

Bill was limited to cultivation that is: (i) for research purposes (inclusive of market research, which multiple federal agencies have confirmed includes commercial sales with a research purpose); (ii) part of an "agricultural pilot program" or other agricultural or academic research; and (iii) permitted by state law.[3] Further, the 2014 Farm Bill defined hemp as the plant *Cannabis sativa L.*, and any part of such plant, whether growing or not, with a THC concentration of not more than 0.3% on a dry weight basis.[4] Unlike the CSA – which distinguishes between "hemp" and "marijuana" based on the part of the plant from which a product is derived – the 2014 Farm Bill defined hemp to include all parts of the plant, and distinguished "hemp" from "marijuana" based solely on the concentration of THC present. Under the 2014 Farm Bill, cannabis plants that exceed the 0.3% THC limitation are considered marijuana under federal law. Despite these competing definitions, the U.S. Court of Appeals for the Ninth Circuit ruled that the 2014 Farm Bill preempts the CSA.[5]

While the 2014 Farm Bill mandates that hemp cultivation be for research purposes, it expressly allows such research to include the study of the "marketing of [I]ndustrial [H]emp," without further defining the term "marketing." The term "marketing" was commonly understood to include commercial sales of hemp and hemp-derived products. Several states implemented agricultural pilot programs permitting commercial sales creating debate as to the scope of commercial and interstate activity permitted under the 2014 Farm Bill. Federal policy guidance issued by the United States Department of Agriculture (USDA), DEA, and the FDA in 2016 (Statement of Principles) confirms that the 2014 Farm Bill, at a minimum, allows commercial activity in conjunction with market research and permits hemp-derived products to be transferred amongst states with agricultural pilot programs authorizing such activity.[6] Indeed, the Statement of Principles provides that hemp-derived products may be sold for "purposes of marketing research" …"but not for the purpose of general commercial activity."[7] While both informative and contested it is no longer materially relevant as under the 2018 Farm Bill, the DEA no longer has jurisdiction over "hemp."[8]

Activities determined to be 2014 Farm Bill compliant are protected from federal interference by language which has been included in federal appropriations riders and is currently included in H.R.1865 - Further Consolidated Appropriations Act, 2020. The language prohibits the use of funds to prevent the

> transportation, processing, sale, or use of [I]ndustrial [H]emp, or seeds of such plant, that is grown or cultivated in accordance with the [2014 Farm Bill], within or outside the State in which the [I]ndustrial [H]emp is grown or cultivated.[9]

The scope of activity permitted under the 2014 Farm Bill is limited and varies significantly from state to state. In addition, three federal agencies have taken the position that cultivation and production of hemp for the purpose of general commercial activity is not permitted under the 2014 Farm Bill,[10] and all cultivation, distribution, and sales of hemp and hemp products must still comply with other applicable federal and state law, which may include, but is not limited to, the Federal Food, Drug and Cosmetic Act (FFDCA).[11] The 2014 Farm Bill has now been succeeded by the 2018 Farm Bill and the 2014 Farm Bill will expire on October 31, 2020. Until that time, the 2014 Farm Bill will remain authoritative in states that have not received approval from the USDA for their 2018 Farm Bill plans.[12]

2018 Farm Bill

The passage of the 2018 Farm Bill materially altered the legal landscape governing hemp production in the US thus greatly expanding the scope of hemp and CBD production. Under the 2018 Farm Bill, hemp, previously regulated by the DEA as a Schedule I substance pursuant to the CSA (with certain limited exceptions), is regulated as an agricultural crop by the USDA in coordination with state departments of agriculture and tribal authorities.

First, the 2018 Farm Bill defines "hemp" as any part of the plant, "including the seeds thereof and all derivatives, extracts, cannabinoids, isomers, acids, salts, and salts of isomers, whether growing or not" with a THC concentration of not more than 0.3% THC on a dry weight basis[13] and amends the CSA to exclude "hemp" from the CSA definition of "marihuana."[14] This definition is a notable expansion from the limited definition of hemp in the 2014 Farm Bill, which only preempts from CSA control for hemp grown in accordance with state agricultural pilot programs. The 2018 Farm Bill also creates a specific exemption in the CSA for THC found in hemp.[15] These expanded definitions and corresponding exemptions from the CSA could also apply to imported hemp, if the definitional criteria are satisfied. (The exportation of hemp products would still be subject to laws of the receiving countries and potentially international treaty obligations.)

Second, the 2018 Farm Bill establishes a federal regulatory framework for hemp production in the US by making USDA, instead of DEA, the primary *federal* agency overseeing hemp production. However, any state,[16] US territory, or Indian tribe desiring to obtain primary regulatory authority over hemp production within their borders may do so by submitting, and receiving approval of, a plan to USDA for regulating hemp production.[17] State plans must be submitted by state's department of agriculture in consultation with the Governor and chief law enforcement officer of the state (or Tribal government, as applicable).[18] USDA is required to approve or disapprove any jurisdiction's plan within sixty (60) days of receiving it.[19]

Any jurisdiction plan must comply with certain minimum standards established by the USDA, including, among others: (i) a practice to maintain relevant information regarding land on which hemp is produced; (ii) a procedure for testing THC concentration levels of hemp produced; (iii) a procedure for the effective disposal of plants produced in violation of the statute; (iv) a procedure to comply with the statutory enforcement procedures; (v) a procedure for conducting annual inspections to verify that hemp is not produced in violation of the statute; (vi) a procedure for submitting important information regarding state hemp producers to the USDA in a timely manner; and (vii) a certification that the state or Indian tribe has the resources and personnel to carry out the practices and procedures described in (i) through (vi).[20] Nothing in the 2018 Farm Bill prohibits jurisdiction's plans from including "more stringent" requirements[21] or altogether prohibiting the production of hemp.[22]

Jurisdictions that receive USDA plan approval will be responsible for issuing licenses through their respective departments of agriculture.[23] Hemp production in jurisdictions that do not receive plan approval (and that do not otherwise prohibit hemp production) is governed by USDA regulation,[24] and USDA will issue licenses directly to applicants.[25] Thus, in jurisdictions *without* USDA-approved plans, it is unlawful to cultivate hemp in the jurisdiction without a license issued by the USDA.[26] By contrast, in jurisdictions with USDA-approved plans, it is unlawful to cultivate hemp in the jurisdiction without a license issued by that jurisdiction's department of agriculture (or tribal government).[27]

Third, the 2018 Farm Bill contemplates interstate transport of hemp and hemp products. Section 10114 of the 2018 Farm Bill states that "[n]o State or Indian Tribe shall prohibit the transportation or shipment of hemp or hemp products produced in accordance with Subtitle G of the [2018 Farm Bill]...through the State or the territory of the Indian Tribe, as applicable."[28] However, until the 2018 Farm Bill is fully implemented and the USDA approves jurisdiction's plans, transporting hemp grown pursuant to the 2014 Farm Bill remains risky – especially when such hemp is transported through states whose laws do not exclude hemp from their definitions of "marijuana," and/or which lack agricultural pilot programs pursuant to the 2014 Farm Bill.

The 2018 Farm Bill contains a number of limitations. For example, a jurisdiction is not required to authorize the production or sale of hemp or hemp products, and jurisdictions are afforded the express authority to adopt hemp regulations that are more stringent than federal regulations.

As a result, state hemp laws greatly vary and some states may continue to prohibit activities related to hemp (e.g., a state may permit cultivation but prohibit processing and/or the sale of certain products).[29] And the 2018 Farm Bill does not affect or modify FDA's authority under the FFDCA or Section 351 of the Public Health Service Act.[30] Any food, drug, device, or cosmetic marketed or sold in interstate commerce is subject to the FFDCA and applicable state laws.[31]

Interim Final Rule

Overview of the IFR

On October 29, 2019, the USDA released the hemp cultivation interim final rule (IFR), marking the first federal hemp farming regulations in the US since the crop was banned in 1937.[32] Effective October 31, 2019, the IFR implements provisions of the 2018 Farm Bill and will remain effective through November 1, 2021, at which point a final rule will replace the current regulations. USDA views the 2020 planting season as a test run of these rules.[33] The IFR includes provisions on state and tribal hemp production plan requirements and violations and audits of said plans. Within the plan requirements are the following topics: licensure, sampling and testing for THC, disposal of non-compliant plants, information sharing, reporting and recording keeping and enforcement. Notably, the IFR does not include provisions related to seed certification, transportation, or processing. The IFR does repeat the interstate transportation protection outlined in the 2018 Farm Bill, clarifying that states, tribes, and territories cannot prohibit the transfer of hemp across their borders.[34]

The hemp production standards under the IFR are identical regardless of which entity issues the hemp production licenses. For example, all individuals[35] with a felony conviction "relating to a controlled substance" are ineligible to participate in an authorized hemp program for ten years from the date of such conviction.[36] This "felony ban" applies regardless of whether a jurisdiction or USDA is issuing a license. If a jurisdiction has a USDA-approved hemp plan, a producer must receive a license from that jurisdiction.[37] However, if a jurisdiction does not prohibit the production of hemp or have their own hemp production plan (and has no intention of creating one), a producer can apply directly to USDA.[38]

A highly debated part of the IFR are the testing and "hot" hemp (i.e., hemp testing above the 0.3% THC threshold) requirements. Some of the more challenging elements include: (i) a requirement that hemp samples from all registered lots be tested by DEA certified laboratories within 15 days of harvest, (ii) an assessment of a negligent violation for farmers whose hemp tests above 0.5% THC, and (iii) a requirement that all hemp testing above 0.3% THC must be destroyed. To quantify the impact of these re-strictive provisions, officials in Colorado estimate that had the IFR been implemented in 2019, approximately 24,500 acres of hemp, with a value to farmers of $842.6 million, would have required destruction.[39] However, in February, 2020, USDA announced that it would delay enforcement of requirements (i) and (iii) starting with the 2020 crop year and continuing until October 31, 2021 or the publication of the final rules.[40] Some find the 0.3% THC threshold challenging; however, changing the threshold is beyond the scope of the USDA's authority and will require new legislation.

Importation of Hemp Seeds

As the 2018 Farm Bill removed hemp and hemp seed from the CSA, the USDA issued a bulletin titled "Importation of Hemp Seeds" which stated that the "DEA no longer has authority to require hemp seed permits for import purposes." The bulletin also made it clear that "hemp seeds can be imported into the US from Canada if accompanied by either:

1   a phytosanitary certification from Canada's national plant protection organization to verify the origin of the seed and confirm that no plant pests are detected; or
2   a Federal Seed Analysis Certificate (SAC, PPQ Form 925) for hemp seeds grown in Canada."[41]

The USDA Bulletin concluded that "hemp seed shipments may be inspected upon arrival at the first port of entry by Customs to ensure USDA regulations are met, including certification and freedom from plant pests."

COVID-19

The Coronavirus Aid, Relief, and Economic Security (CARES) Act passed into law by Congress on March 27, 2020, includes several emergency appropriations provisions to provide relief to the agricultural sector.[42] These relief programs are directed towards agricultural and rural businesses, and they are in addition to loans, tax relief provisions, and other benefits available to eligible businesses under the historic CARES Act legislation, including the Paycheck Protection Program and US Small Business Administration Emergency Economic Injury Disaster Loans. While cannabis businesses may not be eligible for certain programs under the CARES Act, hemp farmers and businesses are eligible to seek loans and direct aid to offset the immediate economic impacts of the virus.

Non-Agricultural Federal Law, FDA Regulations, and CBD

The FDA is responsible for ensuring public health and safety through regulation of food, dietary supplements, cosmetics, and drugs, among other products, pursuant to its enforcement authority under the FFDCA. A hemp product introduced into interstate commerce is subject to FDA regulation, provided it meets the definition of an FDA-regulated article (e.g., food, dietary supplement, cosmetic, drug). Before a product may be lawfully marketed, the FFDCA requires demonstration of the safety of particular uses of ingredients added to such products under provisions specific to each category. For example, a substance that will be added to food is subject to premarket approval by the FDA unless, among qualified experts, it is "generally recognized as safe" (GRAS) under the conditions of its intended use.[43] Although there are multiple approaches to obtaining FDA-approval for use of a new ingredient, the FDA currently takes the position that CBD cannot be added to food or marketed as a dietary supplement, for reasons explained in greater detail below.[44] The 2018 Farm Bill expressly makes no amendments to the FFDCA and accordingly does not have a direct impact on the FDA's position that CBD is precluded from use as a food ingredient and from being marketed as a dietary supplement. However, the 2018 Farm Bill will provide avenues for research as to the safety and efficacy of the plant that may cause the FDA to alter its position.

Regulation of Food Additives under the FFDCA

Pursuant to the FFDCA, a food additive may be marketed in the US under any of the following three alternative criteria: (i) if it was approved by the FDA or USDA between 1938 and 1958 for the intended use (commonly referred to as a "prior sanction"); (ii) if it is GRAS for its intended use; or (iii) pursuant to a food additive regulation promulgated by FDA. Prior-sanctioned substances are substances that the FDA or USDA had determined safe for use in food prior to 1958, whereas GRAS ingredients are those that are generally recognized by experts as safe, based on their extensive history of use in food before 1958 or based on published scientific evidence.[45] Prior sanction[46] and food additive regulations do not exist for new ingredients or new uses of old ingredients. Because of the significant cost and time associated with promulgation of a food additive regulation, most new uses of food ingredients occur under a determination of GRAS status.

Procedure for Issuance of a New Food Additive Regulation

In 1958, Congress enacted the Food Additives Amendment (1958 amendment) to the FFDCA. The 1958 amendment requires that, before a food additive may be used in food, the FDA must establish a regulation pre-scribing the conditions under which the additive may be safely used.[47] The 1958 amendment defined the term "food additive" and established a premarket approval process for food additives. Food additive is defined in the FFDCA as

> any substance the intended use of which results or may reasonably be expected to result — directly or indirectly — in its becoming a component or otherwise affecting the characteristics of any food ... *if such substance is not generally recognized, among experts qualified by scientific training and experience to evaluate its safety, as having been adequately shown through scientific procedures (or, in the case of a substance used in food prior to January 1, 1958, through either scien-tific procedures or experience based on common use in food) to be safe under the conditions of its intended use....*[48]

Thus, when a substance is not GRAS under the conditions of its intended use (or is not otherwise excepted from the definition of "food additive" in § 201(s) of the FFDCA),[49] that use of the substance is a food additive use subject to premarket review by the FDA.[50]

To market a new food additive (or before using an additive already ap-proved for one use in another manner not yet approved), a manufacturer or other sponsor must first petition the FDA for approval.[51] A petition must provide evidence that the substance is safe for the ways in which it is intended to be used. When the FDA evaluates the safety of a sub-stance to determine whether it should be approved, it considers: (i) the composition and properties of the substance; (ii) the amount that would typically be consumed; (iii) immediate and long-term health effects; and (iv) various safety factors.[52] In essence, the FDA determines, based on the best science available, whether there is a reasonable certainty of no harm to consumers when an additive is used as proposed.

If an additive is approved, the FDA issues regulations that may include the types of foods in which it can be used, the maximum amounts to be used, and how it should be identified on food labels.

> Federal officials then monitor the extent of Americans' consumption of the new additive and results of any new research on its safety to ensure its use continues to be within safe limits. If new evidence sug-gests that a product already in use may be unsafe, or if consumption levels have changed enough to require another look, federal authori-ties may prohibit its use or conduct further studies to determine if the use can still be considered safe.[53]

Based upon the above, more evidence must be submitted to the FDA on the safety and efficacy of CBD, as used in food, before the FDA could procedurally authorize its commercial use in such contexts. To date, studies evidencing the safety and efficacy of CBD oil in the US are limited, with most studies involving parental reporting of dosage and reduction of seizures.[54] Controlled, double-blind studies are imperative to assess the efficacy of CBD and to create guidelines for CBD concentrations and dosage instructions.[55] The 2018 Farm Bill's removal of hemp (and cannabinoids derived therefrom) from the CSA has greatly expanded opportunity for the needed research on CBD and other cannabinoids.

Procedures for Obtaining a GRAS Determination

As introduced above, there are two alternative bases on which a GRAS determination may be made: (1) common use in food prior to 1958; or (2) scientific "procedures" (i.e., data). General recognition of safety through scientific procedures requires the same quantity and quality of scientific evidence as is required to obtain approval of a food additive. It is based upon the application of generally available and accepted scientific data, information, principles, or methods, which ordinarily are published, and which may be corroborated by the application of unpublished scientific data or methods. A GRAS determination using scientific procedures can be made by a company internally or through the use of outside expert consultants or independent organizations. Manufacturers may request that the FDA review their self-determined GRAS status. FDA regulations state that any person may notify the FDA of a conclusion that a substance is GRAS under the conditions of its intended use. Broadly, the FDA's response to such notices is: (1) issuance of a "no questions" letter, meaning that the agency does not question the basis for the notifier's GRAS conclusion; (2) a determination that the notice does not provide a sufficient basis for a GRAS conclusion (e.g., because the notice does not include appropriate data and information or because the available data and information raise questions about the safety of the notified substance); or (3) a response letter stating that the agency has, at the notifier's request, ceased to evaluate the GRAS notice. It is the substance under the conditions of its intended use, rather than the substance itself, that is eligible for the GRAS determination. Thus, as introduced above, a substance added to food may be GRAS for one use but may not be GRAS for another.

For example, three GRAS notifications relating to hemp products received FDA validation (issuance of a "no questions" letter) upon FDA review on December 20, 2018 – one for hemp seed protein, one for hemp seed oil, and one for hulled hemp seed.[56] According to the FDA, the three aforementioned "GRAS conclusions can apply to ingredients from other companies, if they are manufactured in a way that is consistent with the notices and they meet the listed specifications."[57] A manufacturer could only rely on the existing GRAS determinations for hemp-derived ingredients, if it could ensure that the manufacture as well as the intended use of the GRAS ingredient falls within the conditions and specifications included in the applicable GRAS determination.

Notably, however, the FDA does not require agency confirmation of the GRAS status of an ingredient prior to marketing a product containing it, and recognizes that a company may use food ingredients based on a self-determination of GRAS status. If a company makes a self-determination of GRAS status and the FDA disagrees with that self-GRAS determination, the FDA has the right to bring regulatory action against the company on the grounds that the product is unsafe and therefore illegal. However, such an enforcement action is rare, and the agency has not apparently initiated any such action objecting to the safety of hemp or cannabinoid ingredients in any food product. While it may be possible to sell the aforementioned GRAS products or certain other hemp products that are the subject of a self-GRAS determination in compliance with Federal law, the current position of the FDA is that it is unlawful to sell consumable products to which CBD has been added in interstate commerce.

Regulation of Dietary Supplements under the FFDCA

The FDA regulates both finished dietary supplement products as well as dietary ingredients.[58] The FFDCA defines a dietary ingredient as a vitamin; mineral; herb or other botanical; amino acid; dietary substance for use by man to supplement the diet by increasing the total dietary intake; or a concentrate, metabolite, constituent, extract, or combination of the preceding substances.[59] Dietary supplements are commonly marketed in forms such as tablets, capsules, softgels, gelcaps, powders, and liquids; however, unlike drugs, supplements are *not* intended to treat, diagnose, prevent, or cure diseases.[60] Under the Dietary Supplement Health and Education Act of 1994 (DSHEA) manufacturers and distributors of dietary supplements and dietary ingredients are prohibited from marketing products that are adulterated or misbranded, and are responsible for evaluating the safety and labeling of their products before marketing to ensure that they satisfy all regulatory requirements.[61] Put simply, the DSHEA amended the FFDCA to define and regulate dietary supplement products as its own special category under the general umbrella of "foods" instead of under food additives or drugs – both of which require FDA's pre-market review and approval. While FDA premarket approval is not required for all dietary supplements, premarket approval *is* required for use of a new dietary ingredient or a dietary supplement that contains a new dietary ingredient. A new dietary ingredient (NDI) is defined as an ingredient that was not marketed in the US before October 15, 1994, and does not include any dietary ingredient which was marketed in the US before October 15, 1994.[62] Therefore, dietary ingredients marketed *prior* to October 15, 1994 (pre-DSHEA dietary ingredients) are not NDIs and, thus, do not require an NDI notification.

The manufacturer or distributor of an NDI or dietary supplement that contains an NDI must submit a notification to the FDA at least 75 days before introducing or delivering for introduction into interstate commerce a dietary supplement that contains the NDI.[63] Because the definition of "food additive" explicitly exempts "dietary ingredients in or intended for use in a dietary supplement," use of a substance as a dietary ingredient in a dietary supplement is not eligible for classification as GRAS.[64] Accordingly, an ingredient's use in a conventional food before October 15, 1994, does not establish the ingredient is not an NDI. What matters is whether the ingredient was marketed *as a dietary ingredient* – meaning that it was marketed in or as a dietary supplement, or for use in a dietary supplement – in the US before October 15, 1994.[65,66] There is an additional exception[67]; however, because the FDA has asserted that it has not received evidence proving that CBD was marketed as a food *or* dietary supplement prior to the early 2000s, it is unlikely that this exception would apply to CBD products.

Regulation of CBD under the FFDCA

The FDA has yet to approve an NDI notification involving CBD and takes the position that use of CBD as an ingredient in dietary supplements renders the product an adulterated and/or misbranded unapproved new drug, for the reasons explained below. Pursuant to the FFDCA[68] an article cannot be added to food or marketed as a dietary supplement if (among other things) such article has been approved by the FDA as a new drug,[69] or if such substance has been authorized for *investigation as a new drug* under an investigational new drug application (IND) for which: (1) substantial clinical investigations have been instituted; and (2) the existence of such investigations has been made public.[70] While there is an exception for articles that were marketed as a conventional food or dietary supplement before the new drug investigations were authorized (or the new drug was approved), the FDA has asserted that, based on available evidence, the exception does not apply to CBD.[71]

A company's IND application for Sativex, a cannabis-derived oral spray, was authorized by the FDA in 2006, triggering the preclusion. Although the IND application and clinical investigations for Sativex predate the initial IND authorization for Epidiolex, Sativex has not yet received final FDA approval. However, on June 25, 2018, the FDA announced its official approval of the company's application for its new drug, Epidiolex.[72] Although there are other FDA-approved drugs that contain synthetically produced THC, Epidiolex is the first FDA-approved drug that contains a purified drug substance derived from cannabis.[73] Potential arguments that certain CBD products may be exempt from this preclusion include (if provable) that CBD was marketed prior to the commencement of FDA-authorized IND clinical trials or that such IND preclusion would not apply if the particular CBD-containing food or dietary supplement product is a different "article" than Sativex or Epidiolex.

FDA Hearings and Potential Changes to Regulation of CBD

The 2018 Farm Bill removes federal barriers to research on cannabinoids (by legalizing hemp as an agricultural commodity) which will provide FDA with needed data. Despite the above described considerations of food and dietary supplements, the FDA has authority to issue a regulation allowing the use of a pharmaceutical ingredient in these products and has stated that it is taking new steps to evaluate whether the agency should pursue such a process. The agency announced that it is exploring pathways to consider whether there are circumstances in which certain cannabis-derived compounds might be permitted in a food or dietary supplement. The agency has established a working group to consider the best approach for regulating CBD.[74]

The FDA held a public hearing on May 31, 2019 in order to collect scientific data and other information related to products containing cannabis and cannabis-derived compounds.[75] During the public hearing, the FDA did not demonstrate any willingness to allow CBD at any level in food or dietary supplements, nor did the agency articulate any policy to differentiate their treatment of CBD isolate versus broad-spectrum extracts containing CBD. The agency seemed interested to understand the extent to which permitting the marketing of dietary supplements and foods containing CBD could impact the incentives for pharmaceutical companies to develop traditional pharmaceutical products containing CBD as an ingredient.

Multiple trade groups, industry organizations, and private companies requested that the FDA either expeditiously promulgate rules to authorize the marketing of CBD as a dietary supplement and/or its addition to food, or to exercise formal enforcement discretion. Either of these pathways would likely be accompanied by specific conditions for use established by the agency, which could potentially limit the concentration or dose of CBD (or THC) within a product category or could limit acceptable hemp-derived ingredients. For example, the FDA could allow use of broad-spectrum extract containing natural occurring CBD but not CBD isolate. The industry and FDA acknowledged the urgent need for regulatory clarification. Assuming the agency determines CBD can satisfy the safety criteria applicable to food and/or dietary supplements and pursues rulemaking, agency rulemaking is a lengthy process that can take over two to three years for unique or unprecedented issues.[76]

In the interim, it is possible that Congress could pass legislation to compel FDA to engage in accelerated rulemaking to authorize the marketing of CBD in dietary supplements and/or foods notwithstanding existing INDs; exempt CBD or other hemp-derived compounds from the IND preclusions of the FFDCA; or direct the FDA to issue revised public guidance that is more reflective of the nuances between CBD isolate and hemp-derived extracts or compounds that contain naturally occurring, non-standardized levels of CBD as a constituent.

Federal Policy Related to Unsubstantiated Claims: The FDA and FTC

The easiest way for a CBD company to get into trouble with federal regulators, including the FDA and the Federal Trade Commission (FTC), is to make unsubstantiated medical or therapeutic claims about its products.[77] A review of marketing and labeling practices is quite technical, but the central goal should be to avoid making any claims that establish the products are intended for use as a "drug," that the product is "intended to affect the structure or any function of the body of man," or is "intended for use in the diagnosis, cure, mitigation, treatment, or prevention of disease."[78] Examples of problematic claims would include suggesting CBD will cure all anxiety problems and provide lasting relief to chronic pain.

Additionally, regardless of the content of a given claim, it is critical that companies have adequate evidence to substantiate all claims made to mitigate risk of deceptive advertising claims from the FTC. It is unlawful under the FTC Act, 15 U.S.C. § 41 et seq., to advertise that a product can prevent, treat, or cure human disease unless you possess competent and reliable scientific evidence, including, when appropriate, well-controlled human clinical studies, substantiating that the claims are true at the time they are made.[79]

In April 2020, the FTC filed suit against a California-based marketer of a supplement (which did not contain CBD, only Vitamin C and herbal extracts) and a line of CBD-based products. The company made claims the non-CBD supplement was effective in treating COVID-19 and the CBD-based products were effective in treating cancer. In response to the complaint, the company agreed to preliminary order barring the company and its owner from making any efficacy claims regarding COVID-19 and cancer.[80]

Conclusion

In sum, certain hemp products may be legally marketed and sold in the US if such products are manufactured from hemp cultivated pursuant to a state agricultural pilot program established in accordance with the 2014 Farm Bill, and the products comply with other applicable state and federal law, including but not limited to the FFDCA. The 2018 Farm Bill, once fully implemented, will allow federal regulation of hemp as an agricultural commodity by, among other things, removing limitations on hemp production and interstate transfer, and allowing for a robust federally legal regulatory regime. The large and growing hemp-derived CBD market is still waiting on updated regulations. It is not clear when, and if, such regulations will emerge. For the time being, it is not possible to sell CBD, either as a supplement or a food ingredient, without violating federal law.

Notes

1 Note, the 2014 Farm Bill refers to "industrial hemp." The 2018 Farm Bill refers to "hemp." For purposes of this memo, "hemp" will be used to encompass both terms.
2 Agricultural Act of 2014, Pub. L. 113-79, § 7606, 128 Stat. 649, 912 (codified at 7 USC § 5940).
3 *Id.* The 2014 Farm Bill defines "agricultural pilot program" as a pilot program to study the growth, cultivation, or marketing of industrial hemp in states that allow the growing or cultivation of industrial hemp and in a manner that ensures only departments of agriculture and colleges/universities are used to grow or cultivate industrial hemp, requires the registration and certification of industrial hemp sites with the State department of agriculture, and authorizes State departments of agriculture to issue regulations to carry out the pilot program in accordance with the purposes of § 7606.
4 *Id.*
5 "Hemp Industries Association v. Drug Enforcement Administration," 720 Fed. Appx. 886, 887 (9th Cir. 2018).
6 Statement of Principles on Industrial Hemp, 81 Fed. Reg. 53395 (Aug. 12, 2016).
7 *Id.*
8 Brief for Members of United States Congress as Amici Curiae Supporting Petitioners, *Hemp Industries Association v. Drug Enforcement Administration*, 720 Fed. Appx. 886, 887 (9th Cir. 2018).
9 Further Consolidated Appropriations Act, 2020, H.R. 1865, 116th Cong. (2019).
10 Statement of Principles on Industrial Hemp, 81 Fed. Reg. 53395 (Aug. 12, 2016).
11 *Id.*
12 Pub. L. 115-334, Sec. 7605(b), 132 Stat 4490, 4829 (2018), codified at 7 USC 5940.
13 *Id.* (inserting § 297A(1)).
14 *Id.* at sec. 12619.
15 *Id.*

16 Consistent with the 2018 Farm Bill, the term "State" is defined herein to include: (A) a state; (B) the District of Columbia; (C) the Commonwealth of Puerto Rico; and (D) any other territory or possession of the United States.

17 Statement of Principles, 81 Fed. Reg. 53395 (inserting § 297B(a)(1)).

18 *Id.*

19 *Id.* (inserting § 297B(b)(1)).

20 *Id.*

21 *Id.* (inserting § 297B(a)(3)(A)(ii)).

22 *Id.* (inserting § 297B(f)(2)).

23 *Id.* (inserting § 297B(e)(2)(A)(ii)).

24 *Id.* (inserting § 297C(a)).

25 *Id.* (inserting § 297C(b)).

26 *Id.* (inserting § 297C(c)(1).

27 *Id.* (inserting § 297B(e)(2)(A)(ii)).

28 PL 115-334, 2018, 132 Stat 4490, Sec. 10114.

29 PL 115-334, 132 Stat 4490, sections 10113, 297B(a)(3)(A), 297B(f)(2); and "Joint Explanatory Statement of the Committee of Conference," at 738, in Agricultural Improvement Act of 2018 Conference Report, H.R. Rep. No. 115-1072 (2018) ("While states and Indian tribes may limit the production and sale of hemp and hemp products within their borders, the Managers, in Sec. 10112, agreed to not allow such states and Indian tribes to limit the transportation or shipment of hemp or hemp products through the state or Indian territory.")

30 Drug Export Amendments Act of 1986, Pub. L. 99-660, sec. 102, 100 Stat. 3743 (1986), codified at 42 U.S.C. § 262 (2019).

31 Federal Food, Drug, and Cosmetic Act of 1938, 21 U.S.C. § 301 (2019).

32 7 C.F.R. § 990 (2019).

33 "Establishment of a Domestic Hemp Production Program," U.S. Dep't of Agric., https://www.ams.usda.gov/rules-regulations/establishment-domestic-hemp-production-program (last visited June 14, 2020).

34 7 C.F.R. § 990.63 (2019).

35 After public advocacy, the applicability of the ban was limited to only, key participants (defined to include a sole proprietor, a partner in a partnership, or a person with executive managerial control in a corporation).

36 7 C.F.R § 990.6(e)(1) (2019).

37 *Id.* at § 990.2.

38 *Id.* at § 990.20(a).

39 "Comments in Response to USDA Establishment of a Domestic Hemp Production Program, Interim Final Rule (IFR)," State of Colo., Jan. 29, 2020, https://www.colorado.gov/pacific/sites/default/files/FinalIFRComments2020_0.pdf.

40 "USDA, DEA Provide Options for Labs, Disposal of Non-Compliant Hemp Plants," U.S. Dep't of Agric., Feb. 27, 2020, https://www.ams.usda.gov/press-release/usda-dea-provide-options-labs-disposal-non-compliant-hemp-plants.

41 "Importation of Hemp Seeds," U.S. Dep't of Agric., Apr. 18, 2019, https://www.ams.usda.gov/content/importation-hemp-seeds.

42 Coronavirus Aid, Relief, and Economic Security Act (CARES Act), Pub. L. 116-136 (2020).

43 "About the GRAS Notification Program," U.S. Food & Drug Admin., Oct. 2016, https://www.fda.gov/Food/IngredientsPackagingLabeling/GRAS/ucm2006851.htm.

44 21 U.S.C. § 321(ff)(3)(B)(ii) (2019).

45 Under the Food Additives Amendment to the FFDCA, two groups of ingredients were exempted from the regulation process.

46 GRAS determination based on common use in food requires evidence of a substantial history of consumption prior to January 1, 1958.
47 Draft Guidance for Industry: Best Practices for Convening a GRAS Panel, 82 Fed. Reg. 53433 (Nov. 16, 2017).
48 The definition of food additive also exempts "dietary ingredients in or intended for use in dietary supplements." "Overview of Food Ingredients, Additives, & Colors," U.S. Food & Drug Admin., revised Apr. 2010, https://www.fda.gov/Food/IngredientsPackagingLabeling/FoodAdditivesIngredients/ucm094211.htm.
49 According to the FDA, the purpose of the legal definition of "food additive," is

> to impose a premarket approval requirement. Therefore, this definition excludes ingredients whose use is generally recognized as safe (where government approval is not needed), those ingredients approved for use by FDA or the [USDA] prior to the food additives provisions of law, and color additives and pesticides where other legal premarket approval requirements apply.

> *Id.*

50 Under the Food Additives Amendment, two groups of ingredients were exempted from the regulation process: GROUP I – Prior-sanctioned substances – substances that FDA or USDA had determined safe for use in food prior to the 1958 amendment, and GROUP II – GRAS (generally recognized as safe) ingredients – those that are generally recognized by experts as safe, based on their extensive history of use in food before 1958 or based on published scientific evidence. *Id.*
51 *Id.*
52 *Id.*
53 *Id.*
54 Shelly B. DeAdder, "The Legal Status of Cannabidiol Oil and the Need for Congressional Action," 9 *Biotechnol. Pharm. L. Rev.* 68, 83 (2016).
55 *Id.*
56 "FDA Responds to Three GRAS Notices for Hemp Seed-Derived Ingredients for Use in Human Food," U.S. Food & Drug Admin., Dec. 20, 2018, https://www.fda.gov/food/cfsan-constituent-updates/fda-responds-three-gras-notices-hemp-seed-derived-ingredients-use-human-food.
57 *Id.*
58 "Dietary Supplements," U.S. Food & Drug Admin., Aug. 16, 2019, https://www.fda.gov/food/dietarysupplements/default.
59 21 U.S.C. 321(ff)(1) (2019).
60 *Id.*
61 Dietary Supplement Health and Education Act of 1994, Pub. L. 103-417, 108 Stat. 4325 (1994) (codified at scattered sections of Title 21 U.S.C.).
62 "Dietary Supplement Labeling Guide: Chapter VII. Premarket Notification of New Dietary Ingredients," U.S. Food & Drug Admin., Apr. 2005, https://www.fda.gov/Food/GuidanceRegulation/GuidanceDocumentsRegulatory-Information/DietarySupplements/ucm070614.htm.
63 *Id.*; 21 U.S.C. § 305b(a) (2019).
64 "Draft Guidance for Industry: Best Practices for Convening a GRAS Panel," U.S. Food & Drug Admin., Nov. 2017, https://www.fda.gov/regulatory-information/search-fda-guidance-documents/draft-guidance-industry-best-practices-convening-gras-panel.
65 *Id.*

66 Though the definitions of "dietary supplement" and "dietary ingredients" were added to the FFDCA after the October 15, 1994, cutoff, the FDA interprets the term "dietary ingredient" to refer to ingredients that: (1) if marketed today, would qualify as "dietary ingredients" under 21 U.S.C. 321(ff)(1); and (2) when marketed before October 15, 1994, were intended for use as or in a product that would now be a "dietary supplement" as defined in 21 U.S.C. 321(ff) and that would not also meet the definition of a drug. "Draft Guidance for Industry: Best Practices for Convening a GRAS Panel," U.S. Food & Drug Admin., Nov. 2017, https://www.fda.gov/regulatory-information/search-fda-guidance-documents/draft-guidance-industry-best-practices-convening-gras-panel.

67 There is an exception to the NDI notification requirement for dietary supplements that contain only dietary ingredients that have been present in the food supply as articles used for food in a form in which the food has not been chemically altered.

68 21 U.S.C. §§ 331(ll), 321(ff)(3)(B)(ii) (2019).

69 "FDA Approves First Drug Comprised of an Active Ingredient Derived from Marijuana to Treat Rare, Severe Forms of Epilepsy," U.S. Food & Drug Admin., June 25, 2018, https://www.fda.gov/newsevents/newsroom/pressannouncements/ucm611046.htm.

70 21 U.S.C. §§ 301(11), 201(ff)(3)(B)(ii) (2019) (GW's IND application for Sativex, a cannabis-derived oral spray, was authorized by the FDA in 2006. As part of the IND, the FDA agreed that GW could proceed directly into Phase III clinical trials in the US. This IND followed a pre-IND/end of Phase II meeting held with the FDA in June 2005, where the FDA reviewed extensive quality, safety, and efficacy data generated by GW on Sativex in Europe. Sativex contains naturally derived THC and CBD. Although the IND application and clinical investigations for Sativex predate the initial IND authorization for Epidiolex, Sativex has not yet received final FDA approval); "FDA Accepts Investigational New Drug Application for Sativex," GW Pharmaceuticals (2006), https://www.gwpharm.com/about/news/fda-accepts-investigational-new-drug-ind-application-sativexr.

71 "FDA Accepts Investigational New Drug Application for Sativex," GW Pharmaceuticals (2006) (Sativex contains a 1:1 THC:CBD ratio).

72 "FDA Approves First Drug Comprised of an Active Ingredient Derived from Marijuana to Treat Rare, Severe Forms of Epilepsy," U.S. Food & Drug Admin., June 25, 2018, https://www.fda.gov/newsevents/newsroom/pressannouncements/ucm611046.htm.

73 *Id.*

74 "Outgoing FDA Commissioner Scott Gottlieb on CBD," C-SPAN, Mar. 19, 2019, https://www.c-span.org/video/?c4786956/outgoing-fda-commissioner-scott-gottlieb-cbd&start=1759.

75 Scientific Data and Information about Products Containing Cannabis or Cannabis-Derived Compounds; Public Hearing; Request for Comments, 84 Fed. Reg. 6 12969, 12969–70 (Apr. 3, 2019).

76 "Outgoing FDA Commissioner Scott Gottlieb on CBD," C-SPAN, Mar. 19, 2019, https://www.c-span.org/video/?c4786956/outgoing-fda-commissioner-scott-gottlieb-cbd&start=1759.

77 "Warning Letters and Test Results for Cannabidiol-Related Products," U.S. Food & Drug Admin., Nov. 26, 2019, https://www.fda.gov/news-events/public-health-focus/warning-letters-and-test-results-cannabidiol-related-products.

78 These guidelines are derived from the FFDCA.

79 "Nutra Pure Warning Letter," U.S. Food & Drug Admin., Mar. 28, 2019, https://www.ftc.gov/system/files/attachments/press-releases/ftc-joins-fda-sending-warning-letters-companies-advertising-selling-products-containing-cannabidiol/nutra_pure_llc_warning_letter.pdf.
80 Lesley Fair, "What's at the Intersection of COVID-19, Cancer Claims, and CBD? This FTC Case," U.S. Fed. Trad Comm'n., Apr. 28, 2020, https://www.ftc.gov/news-events/blogs/business-blog/2020/04/whats-intersection-covid-19-cancer-claims-cbd-ftc-case.

3   State Law Overview – Cannabis

Charles S. Alovisetti and Andrew Livingston

Introduction

State laws vary tremendously when it comes to regulating cannabis – some maintain prohibitionist policies and penalize possession of even small amounts with jail time, while others create complex licensing regimes that permit adult-use and medical-use sales. For states with commercial cannabis regulatory structures, continued federal illegality in the United States puts applicable state governments in the role of primary industry regulator. At the state level, detailed rules and regulations govern almost every aspect of a cannabis business's operations and are enforced by dedicated administrative agencies. While states laws vary widely, there are some similarities. For example, at present, no states permit the transport or sale of cannabis across state lines.[1] Nor do any states permit the importation of cannabis products legally produced in other states. Each state's regulated system exists, to some extent, unto itself, with separate pricing mechanics, industry players (though numerous companies exist across multiple states), products, and regulatory guidelines. As such, studying state-level cannabis laws and their individual structural dynamics is essential to understanding the American national cannabis market.

Categories of State Laws

While state cannabis laws vary widely, it can be helpful to categorize the states into six broad descending categories of legalization: (i) commercial adult-use and commercial medical-use, (ii) adult-use and medical-use with commercial prohibitions, (iii) commercial medical-use, (iv) non-commercial medical-use, and (v) no permitted cannabis activities. This categorization does not consider state-level cannabis decriminalization measures,[2] which have advanced on a parallel track, and are not necessarily aligned with the cannabis operations permitted in each state.

Before assessing these six different state legal structures, it is important to clarify the meaning of the categorizing terms used in this section.

- "Commercial" means state laws that license cannabis businesses and allow for the sale of regulated cannabis products. On the medical side, there is a wide range of laws permitting commercial activity and some have attempted to distinguish between restrictive and comprehensive programs based on products allowed and permitted qualifying conditions. For purposes of this chapter, we have only noted the states where some believe the system is restrictive.
- "Non-commercial" means state laws that do not license cannabis businesses and allow individuals to access cannabis only through clinical trials or by either cultivating cannabis on their own or designating a caregiver to grow on their behalf.
- "Adult-use" means state laws permitting adults, designated as 21 years of age or older,[3] to possess and use cannabis.
- "Medical-use" means state laws that require individuals to obtain a recommendation (note that this is different from a prescription, which is only available for an FDA approved medicine) from an approved physician or other medical provider for a qualifying condition prior to possessing or using cannabis.[4] Medical conditions for which medical professionals can provide recommendations vary between different states.

Commercial Adult-Use and Commercial Medical-Use

States with both commercial medical and adult-use programs permit any individual 21 years of age or older to purchase from a licensed storefront where a wide variety of different cannabis and cannabis products are available for sale. Medical patients, who may be under the age of 21 or under 18 with a parental guardian, may purchase from these storefronts if they obtain a recommendation from a medical professional as well as a state-issued identification card. In some cases, medical and adult-use storefronts may be separate facilities, but typically states with both programs allow for a single facility to sell both medical and adult-use cannabis on the same premises using different sales floors or display cases.

Adult-Use and Medical-Use with Commercial Prohibitions

States with adult-use and medical-use programs with commercial prohibitions legalize the possession and consumption of cannabis by all individuals 21 and older and also permit medical-use with a qualifying recommendation but, unlike purely commercial systems, do not have licensing systems to regulate businesses to sell cannabis for adult-use or medical purposes or both. Instead, residents must rely on cannabis cultivated at home or provided by others for no remuneration.

Commercial Medical-Use Only

States with commercial medical-use programs establish a licensing and regulatory system for businesses to cultivate, process, and sell cannabis and cannabis products for medical purposes. To purchase, possess, and consume medical cannabis, patients must obtain a recommendation from a physician or other medical professional for a qualifying condition as established in state law. States with commercial medical-use programs differ in size, number of licensed businesses, permitted product forms, and qualifying conditions. A small number of states have commercial medical cannabis laws but enact regulations that so significantly limit THC potency and permitted forms of medical cannabis that they do not effectively serve patients. These states are customarily not included in the total count of medical cannabis programs nationally. However, due to the controversy around defining what states are considered restrictive or limited, we have lumped all commercial medical-use only states together, while noting those that some consider restrictive.

While it may be possible to access hemp-derived CBD in these states, as well as many states nationally, "low-THC"[5] medical cannabis products within these restrictive systems still come from federally unlawful high-THC cannabis plants while CBD-hemp products are sourced from federally legal hemp that contains no more than 0.3% THC. These states strictly limit product forms as well, often prohibiting vaporizable cannabis oils, confectionary edible products, and raw cannabis flower.

Non-Commercial Medical-Use Only

States with non-commercial medical-use laws are even more limited than those in states with commercial medical-use programs that are considered restrictive. These laws typically create an affirmative defense for medical patients with severe conditions to possess extracted cannabis oil products low in THC and high in CBD. In some states these restrictive programs authorize limited clinical trials, but do not allow for the legal production or sale of cannabis oils. It is common for these laws to be

Current Status of Cannabis Legality in the US* as of June 1, 2020

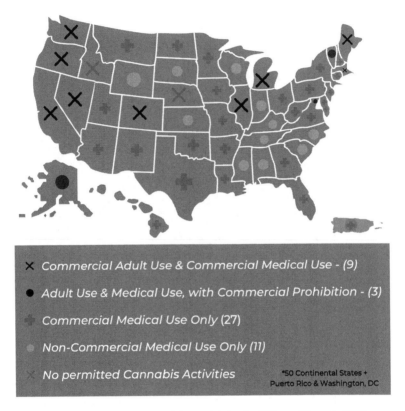

✕ *Commercial Adult Use & Commercial Medical Use - (9)*

● *Adult Use & Medical Use, with Commercial Prohibition - (3)*

✚ *Commercial Medical Use Only (27)*

● *Non-Commercial Medical Use Only (11)*

✕ *No permitted Cannabis Activities*   *50 Continental States + Puerto Rico & Washington, DC

Figure 3.1 Map of Legal Status of Cannabis in the US as of June 1, 2020.

named after a specific, sympathetic patient (e.g., South Carolina's law passed in 2014 is also known as "Julian's Law"). Figure 3.1 shows the current legality of cannabis in the US.

No permitted Cannabis Activities

While there are few states without any recognition cannabis for medical purposes, several states maintain harsh criminal penalties for possession of even small amounts of cannabis regardless of medical-use, physician recommendation, or qualifying condition. Table 3.1 shows the current legal status of cannabis at the state level in the US as of June 1, 2020.

Table 3.1 Current Status of Cannabis in the US as of June 1, 2020

Commercial Adult-Use and Commercial Medical-Use (9 states)
California
Colorado
Illinois
Maine
Massachusetts
Michigan
Nevada
Oregon
Washington

Adult-Use and Medical-Use, with Commercial Prohibitions (3)
Alaska (medical is non-commercial and adult-use is commercial)
Washington, D.C. (medical is commercial and adult-use is non-commercial)
Vermont (medical is commercial and adult-use is non-commercial)

Commercial Medical-Use Only (27)
Arizona
Arkansas
Connecticut
Delaware
Florida
Georgia (considered restrictive)
Hawaii
Iowa (considered restrictive)
Louisiana (considered restrictive)
Maryland
Minnesota
Missouri
Montana
New Hampshire
New Jersey
New Mexico
New York
North Dakota
Ohio
Oklahoma
Pennsylvania
Puerto Rico
Rhode Island
Texas (considered restrictive)
Utah
Virginia (considered restrictive)
West Virginia

Non-Commercial Medical-Use Only (11)
Alabama
Indiana
Kansas (restrictive even by non-commercial standards)
Kentucky
Mississippi (low THC CBD oil for intractable epilepsy only)
North Carolina
South Carolina
South Dakota (restrictive even by non-commercial standards)
Tennessee
Wisconsin
Wyoming

No permitted Cannabis Activities (2)
Idaho
Nebraska

Notes

1 Oregon has passed a bill that would permit transportation across state borders. Notably, however, the law requires federal law to change before such activities can take place (SB 582, 2019 Reg. Sess. (Or. 2019)).
2 Decriminalization is a policy whereby small-scale cannabis possession and use is no longer an offense punishable by jail time, which is typically replaced with a monetary fine.
3 While the legal age of adulthood is 18, adult-use cannabis laws in the United State mirror those regarding alcohol by establishing a threshold of 21 years of age to possess and use cannabis. Like alcohol, the legal age of cannabis possession, use, and purchase differs internationally.
4 The term is almost always recommendation, pursuant to the Clinton era court case that established the rights of physicians to recommend. *Conant v. Walters*, 309 F.3d 629 (9th Cir. 2002).
5 These programs often refer to "low-THC oil" and "low-THC oil products" that contain no more than 3% or 5% THC by weight. While these restrictions prevent the same type of intoxicating vaporizable products permitted in other commercial medical programs, the limitation still allows for capsules and other ingestible products with as much THC as often exists in adult-use edible products. This occurs because THC measured in percentages, even very small percentages, can still produce enough THC, typically measured in milligrams, to produce an intoxicating effect when consumed orally.

4 State Law Overview – Hemp and CBD

Charles S. Alovisetti, Shawn Hauser,
Michelle Bodian, and Catie Wightman

Introduction

While compliance with federal law is the baseline requirement for manufacturing and marketing hemp and CBD (for the purposes of this chapter CBD is hereinafter referred to as CBD) in interstate commerce, to lawfully manufacture and distribute such products, state and local law must be complied with as well. As discussed in Chapter 2, both the 2014 and 2018 Farm Bill permit jurisdictions to adopt "more stringent" requirements governing the production of hemp within their borders.[1] Jurisdictions may also opt to continue cultivating hemp under the 2014 Farm Bill or even prohibit the production of hemp entirely.[2] Further, many states have their own laws governing the sale of consumer products, particularly products marketed as containing CBD. Thus, in addition to the federal laws and regulations regarding hemp and CBD, there is also significant diversity in state-level regulation.

As outlined below, jurisdictions take varying approaches to regulating the production and sale of hemp and CBD under the 2014 Farm Bill, the 2018 Farm Bill, and state food and drug laws. The information contained in this chapter is valid as of June 1, 2020. While some states explicitly authorize and regulate the production and sale of CBD (or otherwise provide legal protection for authorized individuals to engage in commercial hemp activities), other states do not distinguish between cannabis, hemp, and/or CBD, resulting in hemp being classified as a controlled substance under state law. In these states, sale of any CBD product is either restricted to state medical or adult-use cannabis program licensees or remains otherwise unlawful under state criminal laws. Additionally, a number of states have product-type restriction. For example, some states prohibit the sale of ingestible CBD products based on the FDA's position that, pursuant to the FFDCA, it is unlawful to introduce food containing added CBD or THC into interstate commerce, or to market CBD or THC products as, or in, dietary supplements, regardless of whether the substances are hemp-derived.[3]

Status of State Hemp Programs as of June 1, 2020

The USDA has begun reviewing and approving hemp plans submitted by states, tribes, and territories that meet the minimum federal standards, giving those jurisdictions primary regulatory authority over hemp production with that jurisdiction. Some jurisdictions have already submitted, have been approved, or are in the process of developing a hemp plan. States may need to update their laws and hemp programs to conform to these new federal requirements. Jurisdictions that receive USDA approval for their hemp plans will be responsible for issuing licenses through their respective departments of agriculture. If a jurisdiction chooses not to submit a plan (and does not otherwise prohibit the cultivation of hemp), the USDA will control the production of hemp in that jurisdiction. A few states, like Idaho and Mississippi, may choose to prohibit any cultivation. Once a jurisdiction has submitted a plan, the USDA has 60 days to approve or disapprove that plan. The information contained in this chapter is based upon information posted on USDA's website and is valid as of June 1, 2020.[4] It is updated by USDA on a rolling basis based upon information submitted to USDA. States, territories, or Tribal Authorities which are not mentioned below have not yet self-reported to USDA.

States with Approved 2018 Farm Bill Plans as of June 1, 2020

Seventeen States have received USDA approval for their hemp production plans. States with approved plans include Delaware, Florida, Georgia, Iowa, Kansas, Louisiana, Massachusetts, Montana, Nebraska, New Jersey, Ohio, Pennsylvania, South Carolina, Texas, Washington, West Virginia, and Wyoming.[5]

States with 2018 Farm Bill Plans under Review or Pending Resubmission

In addition to states which have submitted initial drafts of their plans for USDA review within the last 60 days, this category also includes states that submit plans to USDA prior to the publication of the IFR. These plans were returned to the State for edits or amendments to ensure regulatory compliance and consistency. States with 2018 Farm Bill plans under review or pending resubmission include Arizona, Connecticut, Hawaii, and Tennessee.[6]

States Drafting 2018 Farm Bill Plans for USDA Review

Other states have announced their intention to submit a plan for USDA review but, for various reasons, have not yet done so. These states include California, Illinois, Nevada, and Oklahoma.[7]

States Maintaining 2014 Farm Bill Pilot Programs

As previously discussed, the 2014 Farm Bill will remain in effect until October 31, 2020 – one year after the USDA established regulations governing hemp production. Accordingly, 18 states have opted to continue regulating hemp production under their 2014 Farm Bill pilot programs for the 2020 planting season. These states include Alabama, Alaska, Arkansas, Colorado, Indiana, Kentucky, Maine, Maryland, Minnesota, Missouri, New Mexico, North Carolina, North Dakota, Oregon, Utah, Vermont, Virginia, and Wisconsin.[8]

USDA Hemp Producer Licenses

If a state, tribe, or territory chooses not to submit a plan and does not otherwise prohibit the cultivation of hemp, the USDA will control the production of hemp in that jurisdiction.[9] As of June 1, only New Hampshire has elected to defer to federal regulation of hemp production.[10] Accordingly, hemp growers in New Hampshire will have to apply directly to USDA for licensure.

States Where Hemp Alone Is Prohibited under State Criminal Laws

Finally, although the 2018 Farm Bill removed "hemp," including "cannabinoids derived from hemp" from the federal CSA definition of marijuana, not all jurisdictions have amended *state drug laws* to remove "hemp" from respective state definitions of marijuana. The CSA does not contain an overarching express preemption clause. Thus, states are permitted to enact prohibitions and restrictions on the cultivation, manufacture, and sale of controlled substances that are more restrictive than federal law and classify compounds as controlled substances even if such substances are not controlled at the federal level. A few states maintain laws that independently classify hemp as a controlled substance, and/or continue to define "marijuana" and/or "hashish" such that hemp could be classified as "marijuana" or "hashish" under state criminal law. Consequently, and although sporadically enforced, there is risk of criminal prosecution for the possession and sale of hemp in these states. These states include Idaho and Mississippi.[11]

Status of CBD under State Law as of June 1, 2020

States Where CBD Is Prohibited under State Criminal Laws

As stated above, a few states maintain laws that independently classify hemp as a controlled substance, and/or continue to define "marijuana" and/or "hashish" such that hemp could be classified as "marijuana" or "hashish" under state criminal law. By extension, CBD therefore could also be classified as "marijuana" or "hashish." These states include Idaho and Mississippi.[12]

States with Limited Protections for State Hemp Program Registrants

Some states have removed "industrial hemp" or "hemp" from the definition of "marijuana" under state law, but have amended such definitions to only include "hemp" or "industrial hemp" *that is possessed or handled by an approved grower or pilot program registrant under a particular state hemp program, or that was produced pursuant to a USDA-approved 2018 Farm Bill program.* While the production and possession of hemp by state hemp program registrants is protected under state law, these exemptions from state criminal codes do not apply to non-licensed businesses. Consequently, and although rarely enforced, there is risk of criminal prosecution for the possession and sale of hemp and CBD products by non-program registrants in these states, as such activity could be treated as the possession and sale of cannabis. These states include Alabama, Delaware, Iowa, Hawaii, New Hampshire, and North Carolina.

States with Otherwise Prohibitive Policies or Product-Type Restrictions

Other states have removed "industrial hemp" or "hemp" from the definition of marijuana under state law but either prohibit the sale of certain types of CBD products (i.e., food and dietary supplements) or explicitly require that the production and sale of hemp products comply with the FFDCA. In addition to complying with the FFDCA, states may impose additional production and/or licensing requirements for the sale of CBD products. States developing hemp programs that would authorize the commercial sale of CBD products, but which have not yet been implemented are also included in this categorization. These states include Arizona, California, Georgia, Kansas, Kentucky, Louisiana, Maryland, Massachusetts, Michigan, Minnesota, Missouri, Montana, Nebraska, Nevada, New York, North Dakota, Oklahoma, Pennsylvania, South Carolina, South Dakota, Washington, Wisconsin, and Wyoming.

States with No Specific Product-Type Restrictions or that Affirmatively Authorize the Sale of Certain CBD Products

Some states have removed "industrial hemp" or "hemp" from the definition of marijuana under state law and either: (a) do not have, or have only limited laws or policies restricting the types of CBD products that may be produced and sold; or (b) do not regulate the post-harvest processing and sale of CBD products. These states include Illinois, Indiana, and Tennessee.

States that Explicitly Permit CBD-Containing Ingestible Products

In an increasing number of states that have implemented robust commercial hemp programs the production and sale of hemp and CBD-containing ingestible products are expressly permitted in spite of FDA prohibition. Colorado became the first state to designate hemp as an approved food ingredient by amending its state Food and Drug Act to include hemp and dictate that a consumable product is not "adulterated" solely for containing hemp. Other states in this category include Connecticut, Florida, Maine, New Jersey, New Mexico, Ohio, Oklahoma, Rhode Island, Texas, Utah, Vermont, Virginia, West Virginia, and Wisconsin. It is critical to note that compliance with state law does not affect the FDA's determination of a product's compliance with Federal law and cannot prevent FDA enforcement actions for violations of the FFDCA. As FDA continues to evaluate potential regulations for CBD as a food and dietary supplements with minimal enforcement of its current prohibition, and the hemp and CBD market rapidly expands, more states have elected to fill the void and regulate the manufacture and sale of hemp products. As such, states have proceeded with enacting regulations governing the manufacture and sale of CBD products and including testing, packaging, labeling, and quality control requirements to ensure public health and safety.

Notes

1 Agriculture Improvement Act of 2018, Pub. L. 115-334, 132 Stat 4490, section 10113, 297B(a)(3)(A), 297B(f)(2); and "Joint Explanatory Statement of the Committee of Conference," at 738, in Agricultural Improvement Act of 2018 Conference Report, H.R. Rep. No. 115-1072 (2018)

> While states and Indian tribes may limit the production and sale of hemp and hemp products within their borders, the Managers, in Sec. 10112, agreed to not allow such states and Indian tribes to limit the transportation or shipment of hemp or hemp products through the state or Indian territory.

2 *Id.*
3 Scott Gottlieb, "U.S. Food & Drug Administration, Statement from FDA Commissioner Scott Gottlieb, M.D., on Signing of the Agriculture Improvement Act and the Agency's Regulation of Products Containing Cannabis and Cannabis-Derived Compounds," Dec. 20, 2018, https://www.fda.gov/NewsEvents/Newsroom/PressAnnouncements/ucm628988.htm.
4 https://www.ams.usda.gov/rules-regulations/hemp/state-and-tribal-plan-review.
5 U.S. Department of Agriculture, "Status of State and Tribal Hemp Production Plans for USDA Approval," updated Apr. 29, 2020, https://www.ams.usda.gov/rules-regulations/hemp/state-and-tribal-plan-review.
6 *Id.*

7 *Id.*

8 *Id.*

9 Agriculture Improvement Act of 2018, § 10113 (amending 7 U.S.C. 1621 by inserting § 297C (a)).

10 U.S. Department of Agriculture, "Status of State."

11 Idaho Code § 37-2701(t) (2019); Miss. Code Ann. § 41-29-136 (2019).

12 *Id.*

5 Risks of Cannabis Investments

Charles S. Alovisetti, Ben Leonard,
and Sahar Ayinehsazian

Introduction

Federal laws that involve cannabis are broad and, as a result, almost any investment in a cannabis company in the United States, whether a direct investment in a licensed plant-touching entity, or an indirect investment in an ancillary company, will involve the violation of federal law. Consequently, there are risks involved when making such an investment that should be considered in advance of any transaction, regardless of the type of target or the structure of the transaction, if the underlying company is involved in the cannabis industry.

Representations and Covenants

If a company, or an individual investor, is required to make representations about compliance with laws in connection with a cannabis investment, it is important to review these well in advance. For example, most companies that have lines of credit are subject to an affirmative covenant to remain in compliance with U.S. federal law. A potential investor should consider whether a cannabis investment may trigger a violation of any such covenants.

Exchanges

Making cannabis investments can also create potential issues for planned public listings. Most major North American exchanges expect issuers to be compliant with the law of the jurisdictions in which they operate. Holding cannabis investments can impede the ability to meet this requirement. While it is true that some listed companies on major exchanges are, arguably, in violation of the CSA, exchanges may not always view issuers applying to be listed for the first time in the same lenient manner. The details of these kinds of arrangements can matter, and this is another instance where obtaining legal counsel is advisable.

Banking

Investors should not assume that they will not face any practical issues wiring money to, and receiving money from, a cannabis company. As explored in depth in Chapter 12, providing funds to a cannabis company will involve an investor in the challenges related to accessing banking as a marijuana-related business (MRB), implicating Bank Secrecy Act concerns. Some banks will balk at wiring money to a cannabis business simply as a business decision. And if international wires are involved, the matter can become even more complex.

Insurance

As discussed in detail in Chapter 13, many insurance policies, even those used for plant-touching businesses, have carve-outs for damages related to violations of the CSA. It is thus unlikely that an investor's existing insurance policies would provide any protection for possible negative outcomes from a cannabis investment.

Federal Bankruptcy

Another area where investors may find themselves facing a surprise is the unavailability of federal bankruptcy law in the event an investment goes south. As explored in Chapter 8, salvaging the value of an insolvent cannabis company may prove challenging and investors are likely to be forced to rely on state law remedies.

Criminal Charges

Moving from the realm of practical issues to theoretical ones, any investment in an MRB will expose investors to some level of risk of criminal or civil sanctions, including the possibility of facing private RICO claims.[1] As discussed in Chapter 1, federal authorities have not pursued enforcement against investors in state-legal cannabis business in some time. However, the risk is always present, and while it can be mitigated to some degree, there is no way to eliminate it entirely.

Asset Forfeiture

The other major theoretical risk of cannabis investments is the possibility of asset forfeiture. As discussed in Chapter 1, the CSA subjects a wide range of property to possible forfeiture, including real estate, personal property, and all proceeds traceable to the exchange of a controlled substance in violation of the CSA.[2]

Indirect Cannabis Investments

When people talk about indirect cannabis investments, they often use the terms "ancillary" or "non-planting touching" to describe the companies in which they are investing. These companies do not hold commercial cannabis licenses or directly engage in cannabis operations. Examples include real estate investments, technology companies, third-party service providers, and intellectual property licensing companies.

Investments in ancillary businesses are seen by many as less risky than direct investments in plant-touching operators, because indirect investment structures are additional steps removed from any criminal activity that may be imputed to the plant-touching operator. The relative risk level accompanying various types of investment structures involving the cannabis industry may be based on the likelihood of being identified by a prosecutor as a potential target and a potential prosecution's estimated difficulty, expense, and likelihood of success. For example, if an investor knowingly provides capital or services to an ancillary cannabis business who then sells its products to plant-touching cannabis businesses, a direct charge of a CSA violation and a charge of aiding and abetting are unlikely. Nonetheless, an investor's knowledge that the intended use of the capital provided was to enable the ancillary company to service the cannabis industry could potentially subject the investor to liability in connection with a conspiracy to violate federal law. Additionally, the risk of prosecution for money laundering could be greater in equity investments, such as the purchase of shares or units, than non-equity investments, like debt financing, because the profits from the specified unlawful activity may be more easily traced to an investor with equity in a direct violation of federal law.

The preceding risk analysis remains an uncertain theory as there is limited data to study in order to determine the exact risk of different investments due to the current federal policy of non-enforcement. The limited information that exists comes from the enforcement actions seen during the first term of the Obama administration. During that brief bout of federal enforcement, prosecutors focused their attention on the operators of direct plant-touching cannabis businesses.[3] However, this is an imprecise analogy as many of the current ancillary players in the cannabis industry did not exist at the time (e.g., there were little to no technology companies focused on the space), so it is hard to say prosecutors would have no interest in these operations or would simply focus on the easier cases against equity holders and managers of licensed operations.

Direct Cannabis Investments

Direct ownership in a licensed cannabis operator is generally viewed as the highest risk cannabis investment structure. Although investors who own equity in a company that engages in cannabis operations activities may not themselves be directly engaging in cannabis-related activities, such investors may still face prosecution for aiding and abetting or conspiring to aid and abet the violation of the CSA, among other federal statutes.[4] As discussed above, based on previous patterns of prosecution, U.S. Attorneys would be more likely to bring charges against a direct plant-touching business, and perhaps its equity holders, than those engaged in other types of non-equity investment structures involving cannabis industry operators. In addition to the higher theoretical risk of prosecution, there are practical differences involved with direct cannabis investments that investors should consider.

Regulatory Jurisdiction

Investors in plant-touching businesses will be subject to the jurisdiction of cannabis regulators. This is in contrast to ancillary companies, where the jurisdiction of cannabis regulators is not at all clear. There have been some public disputes around whether regulators can direct the behavior of such non-licensed companies.[5] But it is very clear that cannabis regulators can exercise jurisdiction over the companies that they actually license. This provides a range of practical concerns for investors, the most prevalent of which are explored below.

Background Checks

Any investment in a licensed business, whether structured as a debt or equity, could require a background check of an investor. This check can extend up the chain so far as to include all individuals that own part of the investor (e.g., all of an LPs of fund investors). In the experience of the authors, cannabis ownership background checks only rarely cause problems, mostly due to criminal issues. Issues arise far more because investors, or their investors in the case of a fund, simply balk at providing the required information to regulators. Regulators generally retain broad authority to request information related to a licensed cannabis business at any time while the business retains its license, which could mean that individuals who were initially able to bypass undergoing a background check may be required to undergo one at a later time, such as when the MRB's license is renewed. While rare, it is important to note that if regulators are not satisfied with the information provided, they can simply deny, suspend, or even revoke a license.

Violations and Ownership

Responsibility for any compliance issues related to a license falls on the owners of the licensed company. That means an equity investor in a licensed cannabis company could potentially face civil or even criminal sanctions from a regulator for violations occurring at the operational level. It would, however, be unusual for an investor who has not been involved in the operational violations to face criminal charges. This is far more likely in an instance where the owners/investors were clearly responsible for the issues.[6] In addition, if an investor is considered responsible for a regulatory violation, the violation may require disclosure to other regulatory bodies in certain instances. For example, in most licensing applications any past violations (on the part of the applicant or any equity holder of the applicant) must be disclosed, which can negatively impact the chances of being awarded a license, particularly in a competitive licensing environment.

280E

Finally, as discussed in detail in Chapter 7, most licensed cannabis companies are subject to Internal Revenue Code Section 280E. If an MRB is audited and the IRS challenges its tax position (which is a frequent occurrence in the cannabis industry), the company may end up owing a significant amount of back taxes.[7]

Practical Risk Mitigation Steps

Many of the risks attendant to investing in a cannabis company, particularly the theoretical risks of criminal prosecution and asset forfeiture, must be accepted at some level. At least in the short term, there is no way to change the federal illegality of cannabis. However, many of the practical risks of cannabis investments, as well as the risks related to federal illegality, can be reduced and managed.

Unique Situations

For some investors in unique situations, the best risk mitigation strategy may be to simply avoid making any cannabis investments. Two categories of investors that should proceed carefully are federal contractors and those applying for asylum or in other vulnerable immigration scenarios. Because of cannabis's federal illegality, federal employees and contractors who own stock in cannabis-related companies may face difficulties in maintaining their necessary level of security clearance.[8] The issue of immigration and cannabis-related activities has become especially concerning given the April 2019 United States Citizen and Immigration Services policy guidelines, clarifying that "violation of federal controlled substance law, including for marijuana, established by a conviction or admission, is generally a bar to establishing [good moral character] for naturalization even where the conduct would not be a violation of state law."[9]

Proper Disclosure and LPs

Investors who have raised funds via a private equity or a venture capital fund should also be especially mindful of the degree to which they may violate federal law pursuant to the documents related to the fund. While a majority of fund formation documents include some form of a covenant to remain compliant with federal laws, the degree to which a cannabis investment may violate these covenants depends on the particular documents at play. It is also important to consider whether proper disclosures regarding any investments in cannabis-related businesses have been made to the fund's investors.

State and Local Compliance and Due Diligence

For cannabis industry investors looking to mitigate their risk, due diligence and compliance should be top priorities. Given the highly regulated nature of the cannabis industry, a commercial cannabis business' compliance with state and local law remains critical. In most, but not all cases, state officials have confirmed their commitment to uphold state laws and other regulatory regimes governing cannabis businesses. Investors should seek assurances that the businesses in which they invest are operating, and will continue to operate, in compliance with state and local laws and be wary of investing in businesses that are operating in unsettled areas of law. One of the ways investors can ensure the compliance of the companies in which they invest is by conducting comprehensive due diligence to ensure that any investment business is compliant with applicable local and state laws (including tax laws) and that it has processes in place to ensure continued compliance.

Investors should be wary of investing in businesses that appear to be operating outside of state law or in areas of unsettled state. In addition, the location of a cannabis business, and the policies of U.S. Attorneys in the area should be considered in determining the risk of any investment, as enforcement policies have been largely left to individual U.S. Attorneys to set.

International Investments

Investors who must strictly comply with federal laws, and cannot, therefore, invest in MRBs in the United States, may consider investing in MRBs in foreign counties, such as Canada. Section 841(a) of the CSA makes it unlawful for any person to "knowingly or intentionally... manufacture, distribute, or dispense, or possess with intent to manufacture, distribute, or dispense, a controlled substance." By contrast, section 841 does not on its face state whether it applies to the manufacture, distribution, or dispensation of cannabis *outside* of the United States.

As a preliminary matter, the U.S. Supreme Court has held that, in general, federal statutes are presumed to have domestic, not extraterritorial, application.[10] Moreover, several federal Courts have specifically considered the extraterritorial application of section 841 of the CSA and concluded that it does not apply to conduct outside the U.S. where there is a lack of intent to possess or distribute a controlled substance inside the U.S.[11]

Pursuant to section 959(a) of the CSA, it is unlawful to manufacture or distribute a Schedule I controlled substance "intending, knowing, or having reasonable cause to believe that such substance ... will be unlawfully imported into the United States or into waters within a distance of 12 miles of the coast of the United States." Unlike section 841 of the CSA, which is silent about its extraterritorial application, section 959 explicitly states that it is "intended to reach acts of manufacture or distribution committed outside the territorial jurisdiction of the United States."[12] Notwithstanding its extraterritorial application, section 959 does not apply to a company that is investing in a foreign entity that manufactures or distributes cannabis outside the U.S., unless that entity imports, or intends to import, cannabis into the U.S.

Deal Structuring

Under the theory that the riskiest investments involve directly owning license-holding cannabis companies, it is possible to structure deals to position investors further away from the hypothetical bullseye of a potential federal enforcement action. One such way to accomplish this would be by making a loan to a cannabis operator, rather than a direct investment into the business, as a loan would allow the investor to stay off of the cannabis business' cap table.[13] This method may not always work in keeping an investor from being disclosed, as certain states' cannabis regulations require the disclosure or background check of those who provide loans to a licensed cannabis business.

Investors may also consider purchasing options in a cannabis business that can only be exercised upon the federal legalization of cannabis. However, investors should be aware when paying for these options, as the business' use of such funds for cannabis-related operations could be viewed as promotional money laundering.[14]

Those with non-equity investments may be viewed as having less control over the decision-making and day-to-day operations of a direct federal law violator, making it harder to build a conspiracy charge against them. While accepting interest income from debt investments or royalty payments from licensing agreements could still subject an investor to money laundering violations, it is far more likely that a prosecutor would go after the plant-touching industry players themselves, rather than an investor two steps or more removed.

Notes

1 RICO Act, 18 U.S.C. 1961(1) (The definition of "racketeering activity" in RICO includes "any act or threat involving... dealing in a controlled substance or listed chemical[as defined in §102 of the Controlled Substances Act], which is chargeable under State law and punishable by imprisonment for more than one year") and 18 U.S.C. § 1962(a)

> It shall be unlawful for any person who has received any income derived, directly or indirectly, from a pattern of racketeering activity ... to use or invest, directly or indirectly, any part of such income, or the proceeds of such income, in acquisition of any interest in, or the establishment or operation of, any enterprise which is engaged in, or the activities of which affect, interstate or foreign commerce.

2 21 U.S.C. § 881(a)(6)-(7)

> The following shall be subject to forfeiture to the United States and no property right shall exist in them... All moneys, negotiable instruments, securities, or other things of value furnished or intended to be furnished by any person in exchange for a controlled substance or listed chemical in violation of this subchapter, all proceeds traceable to such an exchange, and all moneys, negotiable instruments, and securities used or intended to be used to facilitate any violation of this subchapter [and] All real property, including any right, title, and interest (including any leasehold interest) in the whole of any lot or tract of land and any appurtenances or improvements, which is used, or intended to be used, in any manner or part, to commit, or to facilitate the commission of, a violation of this subchapter punishable by more than one year's imprisonment.

3 Keith Coffman, "Attorney Tells More Colorado Medical Pot Centers to Close," *Reuters*, Mar. 23, 2012, https://www.reuters.com/article/us-marijuana-centers-colorado/attorney-tells-more-colorado-medical-pot-centers-to-close-idUSBRE82N00T20120324 (John Walsh, U.S. Attorney for the District of Colorado, sent letters to 25 dispensaries in 2012, requiring them to close within 45 days); Melinda Haag, "Warning Letter," Sept. 28, 2011, https://cdn.kqed.org/wp-content/uploads/sites/10/2011/10/US-Attorney-marijuana-letter.pdf (Haag, U.S. Attorney for the Northern District of California, sent numerous closure letters to cannabis operators and pursued the prosecution of Harborside Health Center until her resignation in 2015).

4 18 U.S.C. § 2(a) ("Whoever commits an offense against the United States or aids, abets, counsels, commands, induces or procures its commission, is punishable as a principal.")

5 Lori Ajax, California Board of Cannabis Control, "Warning Letter," Feb. 16, 2018, https://mjbizdaily.com/wp-content/uploads/2018/03/Letter-Re-Weed maps1.pdf (letter directing Weedmaps to stop advertising unlicensed operators on its platform).

6 "Owners of Colorado Marijuana Retailer Sweet Leaf Sentenced to Prison in Landmark Case," *Marijuana Business Daily*, Jan. 25, 2019, https://mjbizdaily.com/owners-of-colorado-marijuana-retailer-sweet-leaf-sentenced-to-prison-in-landmark-case/.

7 John Schroyer, "Cannabis Firm Harborside Owes $11 million under 280E, US Tax Court Rules," *Marijuana Business Daily*, Oct. 21, 2019, https://mjbizdaily.com/cannabis-firm-harborside-owes-11-million-under-280e-us-tax-court-rules/ (Harborside Health Center found to owe the IRS approximately $11 million in back taxes.)

8 Leslie Albrecht, "Investing in Cannabis Companies Can Threaten Federal Employees' Security Clearances," *MarketWatch*, June 10, 2019, https://www.marketwatch.com/story/forget-elon-musks-marijuana-smoking-security-clearance-troubles-just-investing-in-cannabis-stocks-can-cause-you-problems-2019-03-11.

9 U.S. Citizenship and Immigration Services, "Controlled Substance-Related Activity and Good Moral Character Determinations," Apr. 19, 2019, https://www.uscis.gov/sites/default/files/policymanual/updates/20190419-Controlled SubstanceViolations.pdf.

10 *Small v. United States*, 544 U.S. 385, 388–89 (2005).

11 *United States v. Lopez-Vanegas* (493 F.3d 1305 (11th Cir. 2007)) (in a case involving an alleged conspiracy to purchase cocaine in Colombia and ship it to France, the United States Court of Appeals for the Eleventh Circuit explicitly held that where "the object of the conspiracy was to possess controlled substances outside the United States with the intent to distribute outside the United States, there is no violation of § 841(a)(1).") *See also Small,* 544 U.S. at 388–89 (2005).

12 21 U.S.C. Ch. 13, § 959(d).

13 Ciara Linnane, "Canadian Cannabis Company Canopy Growth Completes C$80.5 Million Loan Financing with TerrAscend," *MarketWatch*, Mar. 11, 2020, https://www.marketwatch.com/story/canadian-cannabis-company-canopy-growth-completes-c805-million-loan-financing-with-terrascend-2020-03-11 (Canopy Growth's C$80.5 million equity sale to TerrAscend Corp.)

14 18 U.S.C § 1965(a)(1)(A).

6 Risks of Cannabis Investments – Hemp and CBD

Charles S. Alovisetti, Michelle Bodian, and Catie Wightman

Introduction

The 2018 Farm Bill removed hemp and the cannabinoids within it (such as hemp-derived CBD) from the list of federal controlled substances[1] and, as a result, many businesses and individuals are looking to invest in this burgeoning new industry. While these changes to federal law have certainly lessened the risk associated with investing in hemp and CBD businesses, there are still some small risks that the prudent investor should be aware of. These risks vary depending on the type of business in which one invests.

While unlikely, it is theoretically possible that an investor in a hemp or CBD business could be held liable for aiding and abetting criminal violations of federal or state law. In general, to be liable for aiding and abetting a criminal violation, the investor must (1) intend to facilitate the commission of the crime by another; (2) participate in the commission of the underlying substantive offense; and (3) someone must have committed the underlying substantive offense.[2] This chapter discusses the potential risks associated with investing in hemp and CBD businesses and also outlines steps that investors can take to reduce those risks.

Hemp Only Transactions

There are many companies that could be considered "hemp only" businesses. These are businesses that cultivate hemp and sell it to a processor that turns the raw hemp into a marketable product. There are several considerations that investors should take into account before investing in hemp only businesses.

Under the 2018 Farm Bill, states that wish to have primary regulatory authority over hemp must develop a state plan that meets certain minimum criteria and submit that plan to the USDA for approval.[3] The 2018 Farm Bill also established a federal hemp plan under which farmers in states that do not have an approved state plan may cultivate hemp with the USDA retaining primarily regulatory authority.[4] In addition, the 2014 Farm Bill allowed for states to establish hemp pilot programs under which farmers

can cultivate hemp for research purposes, and many states are still operating under these pilot programs. The 2014 Farm Bill will be repealed on
October 31, 2020. State programs conducted under the 2018 Farm Bill or the
2014 Farm Bill will have varying regulations. Investors should ensure that
hemp only businesses are compliant with all applicable state and federal
regulations.

There are theoretical risks to investors if a cultivator grows hemp with
more THC than is allowed under federal law, regardless of whether that
hemp is grown under the 2018 Farm Bill or 2014 Farm Bill. Under federal
law, hemp is defined as

> the plant Cannabis sativa L. and any part of that plant, including the
> seeds thereof and all derivatives, extracts, cannabinoids, isomers, ac-
> ids, salts, and salts of isomers, whether growing or not, with a delta-9
> tetrahydrocannabinol concentration of not more than 0.3 percent on
> a dry weight basis.[5]

Any cannabis with a THC concentration of greater than 0.3% is considered
marijuana, a schedule I controlled substance. The Interim Final Rule establishing the USDA hemp regulations lists producing hemp that exceeds
the 0.3% THC threshold as a "negligent violation" if (1) the producer made
reasonable efforts to grow hemp and not marijuana; and (2) the THC concentration does not exceed 0.5%.[6] Those that commit a negligent violation are not subject to any federal criminal enforcement.[7] However, if the
THC concentration exceeds 0.5%, this is no longer a negligent violation
and the producer will be reported to the Attorney General and the chief
law enforcement officer of the state where the crop was grown.[8] It is important to note that the protection from criminal enforcement for crops
that do not exceed 0.5% THC only applies to hemp that is grown under
a 2018 Farm Bill state plan approved by the USDA or a USDA producer
license. Many states still operate hemp pilot programs under the 2014
Farm Bill, and any hemp grown under these programs would not receive
the same protection. However, states operating 2014 Farm Bill pilot programs may have enacted similar state-level protections.

If the investor, with knowledge of the company's operations, invests in
a company that cultivates cannabis that tests above 0.3% THC, the hemp
is considered marijuana, and if this is not considered a negligent violation under the applicable hemp program, it is in violation of the CSA
and potentially a violation of state controlled drug laws.[9] If an individual
is charged with aiding and abetting a controlled substance possession
or distribution offense, the government must prove that the defendant
(1) had knowledge of the controlled substance, (2) had knowledge that
the principal intended to distribute or possess the controlled substance,
or (3) purposefully intended to aid others in committing the crime alleged.[10] As a result, it is unlikely, albeit not impossible, that an investor

in a non-compliant hemp business could be held liable for aiding and abetting, or conspiring to aid and abet, a violation of the CSA if she was aware of such non-compliance and the company's intent to violate the CSA, and purposely invested to aid the company in committing the crime alleged.

CBD Transactions

Since the 2018 Farm Bill became law, hemp and hemp-derived cannabinoids are no longer controlled substances under federal law; however, this does not mean that CBD products are legal in all circumstances or jurisdictions. The production and distribution of CBD products are regulated by various federal, state, and local agencies. Additionally, the 2018 Farm Bill does not require states to legalize hemp, leaving it up to each state whether to sanction the production of hemp and permit sale of hemp-related products in its jurisdiction.[11] Additional legal barriers applicable to producing and selling hemp and hemp-derived CBD products result from a number of factors, including the fact that both hemp and cannabis are derived from the same plant species, the rapidly changing patchwork of state laws governing hemp and hemp-derived CBD, and the FDA's position that CBD cannot be added food or marketed as a dietary supplement.[12] As a result, it is important for businesses and investors to fully understand the legal risks that may accompany an investment in a CBD business.

The primary risk investors face when investing in a CBD business is that an investor could be held liable for the intentional non-compliance of its investee, provided certain conditions are met. Put simply, an investor that is held liable for aiding and abetting violations of federal law (or most state laws) is punishable as a principal.[13] This means that even though you didn't do the illegal act – if you participated in it and helped to facilitate it (e.g., by providing funding or capital), with the knowledge that the capital would be used to further that illegal act, you can be punished as if you committed the act yourself. While unlikely, it is theoretically possible that an investor in a CBD business could be held liable for aiding and abetting criminal violations of federal or state law.

Federal Law Violations

Because the FDA takes the position that it is unlawful to market or sell food or dietary supplements that contain CBD in interstate commerce, it is possible, albeit unlikely, that an investor could be held liable for aiding and abetting a violation of the FFDCA by virtue of investing in a CBD business that markets or sells food or dietary supplements containing CBD. Principal liability for FFDCA violations typically requires a person to be in a position with authority to implement adequate procedures to prevent any violations of the FFDCA.[14] While an investor in a CBD business may not be in a position of authority to prevent FFDCA violations, she could still theoretically be held criminally liable under the federal aiding and abetting statute if she was aware of the violation before investing, and aware that the investment would help the company continue to violate the FFDCA.

There are also potential violations of the CSA to consider. Plants that exceed the 0.3% THC limitation are considered marijuana, and therefore, a schedule I drug under the CSA. As a result, if a company sources hemp, manufactures, or sells products that test above 0.3% THC, the company would be considered to be possessing and distributing marijuana in violation of the CSA. To convict an individual with aiding and abetting a controlled substance possession or distribution offense in this scenario, the government must prove that the defendant (1) had knowledge that the company was distributing cannabis; (2) intended to facilitate the company's distribution of cannabis; (3) assisted with such distribution (i.e., by providing capital); and (4) the company must actually have engaged in illegal possession or distribution. As a result, it is unlikely, albeit not impossible, that an investor in a non-compliant CBD business could be held liable for aiding and abetting a violation of the CSA if she was aware of such non-compliance and the company's intent to violate the CSA, and purposely invested to aid the company in committing the crime alleged.

State Law Violations

Although the 2018 Farm Bill removed "hemp," including "cannabinoids derived from hemp" from the federal definition of marijuana,[15] not all jurisdictions have amended state drug laws to remove "hemp" from state definitions of marijuana. The 2018 Farm Bill does not require states to change state law or permit the production and sale of hemp or hemp products. As a result, certain states continue to classify hemp and/or CBD as a controlled substance. Additionally, even if a state does not consider hemp-derived CBD to be a controlled substance, many states prohibit the sale of certain types of CBD products (e.g., food and dietary supplements) or explicitly require that the production and sale of hemp products comply with the FFDCA. In these states, the sale of hemp-derived CBD food and dietary supplements would be considered the unlawful sale of adulterated or misbranded food. Potential aiding and abetting liability for violations of state food and drug laws likely varies on a state by state basis.

If a CBD business sells hemp-derived CBD products in a state that still considers hemp and/or CBD to be a controlled substance, an investor in the CBD business could theoretically be held liable for aiding and abetting the violation, and could be punished as the principal. Liability would depend on that state's aiding and abetting statutes and on the investor's intent (i.e., whether she had a culpable mental state as determined by state statute).

Although potentially a relatively short-term issue, an investor in a CBD business could also theoretically be held liable for aiding and abetting a violation of a state's controlled substances laws if the investor knows that the CBD or hemp is going to be transported through a state that considers it to be a controlled substance. Potential investor liability in this scenario would likewise depend on that state's aiding and abetting statutes and on the investor's intent (i.e., whether she had a culpable mental state as determined by state statute). Notably, the 2018 Farm Bill explicitly prevents states from prohibiting the transportation of hemp or hemp products through other states, even those where hemp may remain a controlled substance, so long as the hemp or hemp product was produced in accordance with a federal or state cultivation plan approved by the USDA.[16] However, to date, many state hemp programs are still operating under the 2014 Farm Bill, and the hemp grown under these programs arguably is not granted the same transport protections. Once a state hemp program is approved by the USDA pursuant to the 2018 Farm Bill and hemp is cultivated under the new program, there will be protection for transportation of lawfully produced hemp and hemp products. In addition, there is not currently a uniform system whereby businesses can document that their hemp or hemp products are lawful. As a result, there have been multiple enforcement actions commenced against transporters of hemp.

There is also potential liability for investors under state food and drug laws. Sale of adulterated food or dietary supplements is unlawful under state law. An investor could theoretically be held liable for the sale of an adulterated food product under state law if the state where such products are sold considers hemp or CBD to be an unlawful food ingredient (i.e., an adulterant) or dietary supplement and the applicable state's laws provide for aiding and abetting violation of the state's food and drug laws. Potential investor exposure for such violations must be determined on a state-by-state basis.

RICO Violations

Lastly, under the RICO federal statute, an investor in a CBD business could theoretically be held liable for participating in, or aiding and abetting, a racketeering activity. The definition of racketeering activity includes "dealing in a controlled substance or listed chemical ..., which is chargeable under state law and punishable by imprisonment for more than one year."[17] Although unlikely, if a CBD business has violated state controlled drug laws that provided for penalties of imprisonment of more than one year, and an investor aided and abetted such violations, the investor could theoretically be liable for that violation under the RICO statute as well as under the state's drug control statutes. Although we are unaware of an investor being held liable under RICO in such a scenario, it is technically possible.

Conclusion

There are several ways that investors in hemp and CBD businesses could theoretically be held liable for criminal law violations. These risks will depend on the specific type of business. However, there are things that investors can do to mitigate potential legal risks. Due diligence should be completed to ensure that the hemp or CBD business is properly licensed, operating in compliance with all state laws, and has procedures in place to promote continued compliance. Investors should also require the company to represent and warrant past and continued compliance with all laws and regulations as a condition of investment and include terms for breach and indemnification in the event non-compliance is identified.

Notes

1 21 U.S.C. § 802(16) (2018).
2 18 U.S.C. § 2 (2018).
3 7 U.S.C. § 1639p (2018).
4 *Id.* at § 1639q(a) (2018).
5 *Id.* at § 1639o(1) (2018).
6 7 C.F.R. § 990.29(a)(3) (2019).
7 *Id.* at § 990.29(c).
8 *Id.* at § 990.29(f) (2018).
9 21 U.S.C. § 802(16) (2018).
10 *United States v. Salmon*, 944 F.2d 1106, 1114 (3d Cir. 1991).
11 7 U.S.C. 1639p(a)(3), (f) (2018).
12 Amy Abernethy and Lowell Schiller, "FDA Is Committed to Sound, Science-based Policy on CBD," U.S. Food & Drug Administration, July 17, 2019, https://www.fda.gov/news-events/fda-voices-perspectives-fda-leadership-and-experts/fda-committed-sound-science-based-policy-cbd.
13 18 U.S.C. § 2 (2018).
14 *U.S. v. Torigian Labs., Inc.*, 577 F.Supp. 1514, 1529 (E.D.N.Y. 1984)

> The evidence presented at trial demonstrates beyond a reasonable doubt that Puzant Torigian was in a position of authority in the corporation to implement adequate procedures to insure that violations of the Act did not occur, but that he did not do so, and that he failed to take adequate measures to determine the cause of and to eliminate an obvious problem when it did occur.
>
> (judgment aff'd, 751 F.2d 373 (2d Cir. 1984)

15 21 U.S.C. § 802(16) (2018).
16 7 U.S.C. § 1639o (2018) (provision is contained in a note titled Rules of Construction).
17 18 U.S.C. § 1961(1) (2018).

Part II
Practical Legal Issues

7 Introduction to Cannabis and Tax Law

Charles S. Alovisetti and Andrew Livingston

Introduction

Even more so than in other sections of this book, it is important to point out that this chapter is not meant to be an exhaustive description of the tax issues involved in the cannabis industry, and nothing in this chapter can substitute for professional tax advice. Instead, this chapter is meant as a very broad and simplified overview of the unique tax issues faced by cannabis companies (much of which does not apply to hemp businesses). Cannabis companies face two major areas of taxation that do not apply to other industries: the increased tax burden posed by section 280E of the Internal Revenue Code and the state-level sales and/or excise taxes specific to cannabis.

Federal Taxation

Taxable Profits

As a general rule, both the profits gained by federally illegal and legal activity are taxable.[1] This principal was clearly set out in *James v. United States* where an embezzler was convicted of "willfully" attempting to evade federal income tax by not reporting the funds he had embezzled as gross income on his federal income tax returns.[2] The court found that, with respect to the Income Tax Act of 1913 (which was enacted shortly after the Sixteenth Amendment was ratified and created a new federal income tax), it was "the obvious intent of the Congress to tax income derived from both legal and illegal sources, to remove the incongruity of having the gains of the honest laborer taxed and the gains of the dishonest immune."[3]

Until the passage of section 280E, section 162(c) of the Internal Revenue Code, which disallowed deductions for illegal expenditures, was the primary provision dealing with cannabis businesses. The problem – from the viewpoint of Congress – with section 162(c) was that it only prohibited illegal expenditures from being deducted and did not prevent an illegal drug business from taking deductions for its legal expenses. This was demonstrated by *Edmondson v. Commissioner* in 1981.[4] In *Edmonson*, a drug trafficker (who sold amphetamines and cocaine in addition to cannabis) was permitted to deduct the legal expenses (e.g., office rent) of his business. Congress, eager to be seen as tough on crime, passed the Tax Equity and Fiscal Responsibility Act of 1982, which included the new section 280E of the Internal Revenue Code.

The relevant language in section 280E of the Internal Revenue Code states

> [n]o deduction or credit shall be allowed for any amount paid or in-curred during the taxable year in carrying on any trade or business if such trade or business (or the activities which comprise such trade or business) consists of trafficking in controlled substances (within the meaning of Schedule I and II of the CSA) which is prohibited by Federal law or the law of any State in which such trade or business is conducted.[5]

Thus, pursuant to section 280E, it is not just illegal expenditures that cannot be deducted, but both legal and illegal expenditures for businesses engaged in federally unlawful trafficking of a Schedule I or II substance. However, despite this blanket prohibition on deductions and credits, the Supreme Court has determined that, as a constitutional matter, all tax-payers, even drug traffickers, should pay tax only on their gross income (which is gross receipts less the cost of goods sold (COGS)).[6]

Hemp and CBD

The 2018 Farm Bill removed hemp and its extracts from the CSA.[7] Be-cause hemp and its extracts (e.g., CBD) are no longer controlled sub-stances, selling these substances will not subject a business to section 280E. For that reason, this chapter is focused on the tax issues affecting federally unlawful cannabis businesses.

280E Caselaw and Guidance

When section 280E was enacted in 1981 it was, in many respects, a sym-bolic law meant to signal the tough on crime attitude of Congress.[8] At the time, most cannabis businesses operated completely in the illegal marketplace and did not file any taxes. If a tax issue arose, it was only after a business had been charged and then audited by the IRS. Almost 40 years later, the situation is very different. State-legal cannabis busi-nesses file taxes like any other business. And as a result of this change in circumstance we now have a range of caselaw related to section 280E that provides some additional guidance on the effects and parameters of the provision. In addition, the IRS has provided some interpretive guidance on the rules (sections 471 and 263A) governing determination of COGS for cannabis businesses.[9]

Californians Helping to Alleviate Medical Problems v. Commissioner (CHAMP)[10]

CHAMP operated a facility where sick individuals could receive caregiving services, including being provided with medical cannabis. In order to benefit from these services, one needed to be a member of CHAMP and pay a monthly fee.[11] On examination, the IRS determined CHAMP was trafficking cannabis, and therefore, was subject to section 280E which precluded it from deducting all of its otherwise permissible business expenses.[12] The IRS then assessed a deficiency reflecting the disallowance of business expense deductions which had been taken. CHAMP argued that it was in fact engaged in two separate businesses – supplying medical cannabis (subject to section 280E) and caregiving services (which did not involve trafficking cannabis and hence was not subject to section 280E). The Tax Court agreed with CHAMP, finding that the caregiving service was CHAMP's primary business and was a separate trade or business from the trafficking of cannabis. Part of the holding of the court was that Congress' intent in enacting section 230E was to disallow only expense deductions associated with a trade or business of trafficking in schedule I or II controlled substances.

Olive v. Commissioner[13]

While *CHAMP* was a Tax Court case, *Olive v. Commissioner*, decided seven years later, was a United States Court of Appeals for the Ninth Circuit case. Thus, on one hand it "outranked" the Tax Court's, but it only applies to the Ninth Circuit. However, the Ninth Circuit encompasses all of California, where many cannabis-related cases arise. The *Olive holding* is generally cited as diverging from *CHAMP* in that it limits the ability of a business to bifurcate its operations into trafficking and non-trafficking operations and deduct business expenses from its tax liability associated with its non-trafficking operations. To engage in a "trade or business" separate from trafficking, the non-trafficking operations must be a real business – something that is undertaken with the principal goal of realizing a profit.

In *Olive*, a dispensary (the Vapor Room Herbal Center in San Francisco) provided vaporizers and games and held activities, including yoga and movie showings, all free of charge, to customers of its dispensary. The court noted that "[t]he test for determining whether an activity constitutes a 'trade or business' is whether the activity was entered into with the dominant hope and intent of realizing a profit."[14] In applying the test, the court found the only "trade or business" of Vapor Room was selling medical cannabis – since this was the only income-generating activity of the enterprise. Unlike *CHAMP*, the court noted, Vapor Room "d[id] not provide counseling, caregiving, snacks, and so forth for a separate fee; the only 'business' in which [it] engages is selling medical marijuana."[15]

Patients Mutual Assistance Collective Corporation v. Commissioner[16]

In *Patients Mutual Assistance Collective Corporation d/b/a Harborside Health Center v. Commissioner*, the operators of Harborside, a large California dispensary, raised several issues previously addressed as well as some new issues. In particular, the plaintiffs argued: (i) Harborside's business was not subject to section 280E since this provision contained the words "consists of" which meant it only applied to a trade or business that was engaged exclusively or solely in trafficking controlled substances; (ii) even if section 280E applied to its cannabis sales, Harborside should be able to deduct its expenses for any separate, non-trafficking trade or business (e.g., its sale of non-cannabis products and therapeutic services); and (iii) they could follow a somewhat more expansive determination of what constitutes COGS (the argument is fairly technical and outside the scope of this chapter).

The Tax Court found the following: (i) it rejected the argument regarding the meaning of "consists of" and concluded that section 280E denies any deduction for businesses expenses of a trade or business trafficking in controlled substances, even if the trade or business undertook other activities; (ii) relying on *CHAMP* and *Olive*, the Tax Court held that Harborside really only had a single trade or business (selling cannabis) since these sales accounted for over 99.5% of its revenue; and (iii) it rejected Harborside's arguments about the calculation of COGS and found that it must calculate its COGS according to section 471 of the Internal Revenue Code and may not use the capitalization rules of 263A.[17]

Alternative Health Care Advocates v. Commissioner[18]

In *Alternative Health Care Advocates v. Commissioner*, several legal issues were presented, but the most important question was whether 280E applied to a management company (Wellness Management Group, Inc., which was taxed as an S corporation) which did not hold a cannabis license. The management company was set up to provide employees to dispensaries and took several business expense deductions, including compensation, rent, and advertising.

The court found that, while the management company never took legal title to cannabis, as this would have been impermissible under state law because it did not hold a license, its employees were engaged in the purchase and sale of cannabis (albeit on behalf of the licensed entity). The court did not find "trafficking" to require taking title to cannabis. This important case was the first finding that section 280E applied to a non-licensed taxpayer.[19]

General Challenges to 280E

The cases outlined above also included challenges to the 280E regime itself, none of which have been successful. For example, in *Olive*, the court rejected the argument that section 538 of the Consolidated and Further Continuing Appropriations Act of 2015 (what was called the Rohrabacher-Farr Amendment at the time), which prohibited federal funds from being used to prevent states from implementing their medical cannabis laws, prevented the government from pursuing Tax Court litigation.[20] Many companies have made other legal arguments to attempt to avoid the impact of section 280E, including claiming the provision is unconstitutional.[21] These arguments have not been persuasive to courts.[22] However, there is some judicial agreement with these arguments, as one dissent found that section 280E

> transforms the ... income tax into something that is not an income tax at all, but rather a tax on an amount greater than a taxpayer's 'income' within the meaning of the Sixteenth Amendment ... I would hold that the Sixteenth Amendment does not permit Congress to impose such a tax and that Section 280E is therefore unconstitutional.[23]

State Cannabis Taxes

Overview of State Cannabis Specific Taxes

In addition to the challenges state-licensed cannabis businesses face with respect to federal taxation, they must also contend with state taxation regimes specific to the industry. States often tax cannabis with general state-level retail sales taxes as well as a cannabis-specific retail tax, cannabis-specific excise tax, or both. Statewide cannabis excise taxes are typically levied higher up the supply chain on cultivators or distributors while retail taxes apply to stores that directly sell cannabis to patients or consumers. Depending on the jurisdiction, cannabis excise taxes may come in the form of a tax on physical cultivation area, volume of production, wholesale value of products transferred, or an average market value applied to specific forms of cannabis. In addition to statewide taxes, many states permit local governments to apply general local sales taxes as well as additional cannabis-specific local sales and excise taxes. In Massachusetts, for example, localities may add up to a 3% tax on adult-use sales, but not medical sales, within the community. This last example highlights an additional nuance with respect to state cannabis specific taxes – the tax rates and methods of collection often differ between adult-use and medical-use cannabis.

Sales Tax

Sales taxes applied to the retail price of cannabis are the simplest form of cannabis taxation. These cannabis-specific sales taxes are typically levied in addition to general sales tax applied at the state or local level. Sales tax revenue generated at the storefront level is then remitted to the state by the retailer monthly or quarterly depending on the jurisdiction.

While sales taxes are the simplest for states and businesses to administer, they may be difficult to physically collect as banking and payment processing roadblocks often force consumers to pay for cannabis products with cash. While this issue also occurs with business to business excise taxes, it is more likely for a cannabis business to have a commercial bank account than it is for that same business to have non-cash payment options for customers. This forces states, and even the IRS, to institute security-centered cash handling, counting, and intake processes that themselves require revenues to implement.

Unlike taxes on all cannabis cultivated or harvested; sales taxes only collect revenues from cannabis products that are sold to consumers. All else being equal, this will reduce tax collections in instances where cannabis or cannabis products are destroyed or otherwise turned to waste before they are sold to consumers.

Excise Tax

Excise taxes on cannabis differ depending on state and local law and can be quite complicated. Cannabis businesses should engage with local tax and regulatory counsel to ensure they are paying their excise taxes appropriately. Typically, state cannabis excise taxes are imposed on cultivation facilities based on weight of production. Different tax rates are then established for different forms of usable cannabis, typically cannabis flower, trim (leaves surrounding the flowers used for oil extraction), as well as seeds and immature plants. In some states, including California and Alaska, these taxes are determined by establishing a set price per pound, ounce, seed, or clone and then adjusting that rate over time to account for inflation and price changes. In other states, such as Colorado and Nevada, excise tax rates are based on a percentage of the average or fair market value for that product category. For instance, Colorado establishes a 15% excise tax on cannabis trim based on an average market rate of $350 per pound (the average market rate for cannabis trim in January 2020). This means that, in Colorado, if a cultivation facility transferred five pounds of cannabis trim to a commonly owned products manufacturing facility during that time, they would pay 15% of $350 per pound across five pounds (15% times $350 times five pounds = $262.50 in tax). This tax structure enables the state to establish a taxable rate using actual data from seed to sale tracking systems for instances when there is not a fair-market contract price established from a non-commonly owned financial transaction (i.e., arms-length). Because the average market rate is continually adjusted, quarterly in Colorado and biannually in Nevada, state regulators do not need to establish new weight-based excise taxes to account for price shifts and inflation.

Even without the need to continually adjust weight-based excise taxes or apply different average market rates for commonly owned and non-commonly owned financial transactions, excise taxes levied on cultivators are complicated by the various forms of wholesale cannabis. In Nevada, as of January 2020, the state has established eight different excise tax rates which include: Flower, Small Bud, Trim, Wet Whole Plants, Immature Plants, Pre-Rolls, Unsalable Flower Approved for Extraction, and Unsalable Trim Approved for Extraction.[24] State tax regulations and guidance documents further detail this complex categorization. For instance,

> Cannabis Wet Whole Plant[s] must be weighed within 2 hours of the batch being harvested and without any further processing, including any artificial drying such as increasing the ambient temperature of the room or any other form of drying, curing, or trimming.[25]

Adult-Use v. Medical-Use

Many states tax adult-use cannabis differently from medical cannabis. In some states, such as Colorado, cannabis-specific excise and sales taxes do not apply to medical cannabis or medical cannabis products. In other states regulations do not differentiate between medical and adult-use cannabis until later in the supply chain when the products reach retailers, so the cultivation-based excise taxes apply to both medical and adult-use, while cannabis-specific sales taxes only apply to adult-use cannabis. Further, some states have medical cannabis discount or donation programs for low-income medical patients in need. In California, lawmakers passed Senate Bill 34 and established a system where medical cannabis products could be donated to patients free of charge without the cultivation tax being applied.

As additional states pass adult-use laws, the tax structures governing medical and adult-use sales will continue to change. To ensure businesses remain in compliance with their tax remittance obligations it is essential that state and local tax laws are complied with closely. Not only can tax collection processes differ between states and between medical and adult-use programs, tax remittance requirements may differ as well. While many states require taxes to be remitted monthly, some states only require remittance quarterly. For those operating cannabis businesses in multiple states, these differences require careful record keeping and cash management schedules to ensure that taxes are paid on time to the appropriate state collections agency.

Notes

1 James v. U.S., 366 U.S. 213 (1961).
2 *Id.*
3 *Id.*
4 Edmonson v. Comm'r, 42 T.C.M. (CCH) 1533 (1981).
5 26 U.S.C. § 280E (2019).
6 James v. U.S., 336 U.S. 213 (1961); Feinberg v. Comm'r., 916 F.3d 1330 (10th Cir. 2019); Alternative Health Care Advocates v. Comm'r., 151 T.C. No. 13 (2018).
7 21 U.S.C. § 802(16) (2019).
8 Mark Osbeck and Howard Bromberg, *Marijuana Law in a Nutshell* (West Acad. 2017).
9 Office of Chief Counsel Internal Revenue Service Memorandum Number: 201504011, Jan. 23, 2015, https://www.irs.gov/pub/irs-wd/201504011.pdf.
10 Californians Helping to Relieve Medical Problems v. Comm'r., 128 T.C. 173 (2007).
11 *Id.*
12 Rodney Bedow, "Making Sense of Internal Revenue Code Section 280E - Part I," Lexology, Aug. 22, 2018, https://www.lexology.com/library/detail.aspx?g=3cad3a73-4015-4632-81e9-18c4fe96a62f.
13 Olive v. Comm'r., 792 F.3d 1146 (9th Cir. 2015).
14 *Internal Revenue Code--Medical Marijuana--Ninth Circuit Holds Medical Marijuana Dispensary Ineligible for Federal Tax Deductions--Olive V. Commissioner*, 792 F.3d 1146 (9th Cir. 2015), 129 Harv. L. Rev. 1444 (2016).
15 Olive v. Comm'r., 792 F.3d 1146 (9th Cir. 2015).
16 Patients Mutual Assistance Collective Corp. v. Comm'r., 151 T.C. 176 (2018).
17 The court follows the interpretation of the IRS in the memo issued in 2015. Office of Chief Counsel Internal Revenue Service Memorandum Number: 201504011, Jan. 23, 2015, https://www.irs.gov/pub/irs-wd/201504011.pdf.
18 Alternative Health Care Advocates v. Comm'r., 151 T.C. No. 13 (2018).
19 *Id.*
20 *Id.*
21 Alpenglow Botanicals v. U.S., 894 F. 3d 1187 (10th Cir. 2018); Jeff Smith, "US Supreme Court Declines to Hear 280E Marijuana Tax Case," *Marijuana Business Daily*, June 28, 2019, https://mjbizdaily.com/us-supreme-court-declines-to-hear-280e-marijuana-tax-case/; Cheryl Miller, "The IRS Keeps Winning Marijuana Cases in US Appeals Courts," *National Law Journal*, Mar. 5, 2019, https://www.law.com/nationallawjournal/2019/03/05/the-irs-keeps-winning-marijuana-cases-in-us-appeals-courts/.
22 Aysha Bagchi, "Medical Marijuana Business Deduction Ban Upheld by Tax Court (2)," Bloomberg Tax, Oct. 23, 2019, https://news.bloombergtax.

com/daily-tax-report/medical-marijuana-business-deduction-ban-upheld-by-tax-court.

23 "In Cannabis Case, Tax Court Dissent Concludes Section 280E Is Unconstitutional," Duane Morris, Oct. 24, 2019, https://www.duanemorris.com/alerts/cannabis_case_tax_court_dissent_concludes_section280e_unconstitutional_1019.html.

24 "Fair Market Value at Wholesale of Marijuana," Nev. Dep't. of Tax'n, https://tax.nv.gov/uploadedFiles/taxnvgov/Content/Forms/Fair%20Market%20Value%20at%20Wholesale%20Summary%20Jan%2020%20(Final%20Draft).pdf (last visited May 1, 2020).

25 "Wholesale Cannabis Tax Return Cultivation Facility," Nev. Dep't. of Tax'n, https://tax.nv.gov/uploadedFiles/taxnvgov/Content/Forms/WMT%20RETURN-%20%20JAN20-JUNE20(2).pdf.

8 Introduction to Cannabis and Bankruptcy Law

Charles S. Alovisetti, Phil Silverman, and Jason C. Adelstone

Introduction

One of the many issues arising out of the tension between state and federal law in the cannabis industry is whether cannabis companies can access the protections of the U.S. Bankruptcy Code. Almost all bankruptcy courts faced with this question have clearly stated that cannabis companies cannot access the federal bankruptcy system. (Hemp companies do not have the same issues.) Without access to federal bankruptcy protection, cannabis companies must turn to out-of-court restructurings and state law insolvency proceedings.

Cannabis Companies and Access to Federal Bankruptcy Courts

Caselaw Regarding Access to Federal Bankruptcy Courts

Plant Touching Businesses

Courts uniformly agree that businesses growing or selling cannabis may not take advantage of federal bankruptcy laws, even in the cases of liquidation. As a bankruptcy court in Colorado stated, "a federal court cannot be asked to enforce the protections of the Bankruptcy Code in aid of a Debtor whose activities constitute a continuing federal crime."[1] That court further noted that the debtor was barred from bankruptcy protections by the equitable doctrine of unclean hands.[2] Other cases have been dismissed because a trustee or debtor-in-possession cannot take control of a debtor's property, or liquidate the cannabis company's inventory, without violating federal law.

When faced with a Chapter 11 protection petition in *Mother Earth's Alternative Healing Coop. Inc.*, the Southern District of California Bankruptcy Court held that since the debtor's only means of "funding Chapter 11 protection would be by cultivating and distributing a federal prohibited substance, that the debtor could not qualify for Chapter 11 protection due to his violation of the CSA."[3] The inherent bad faith of the proposal required the court to dismiss the case, rather than convert it.[4]

The United States Court of Appeals for the Tenth Circuit has also adopted this view. The Bankruptcy Appellate Panel of the 10th Circuit held in *In Re Frank Anthony Arenas*, that despite the legal classification of cannabis in Colorado, a cannabis grower is not eligible for bankruptcy protection because "neither a Chapter 7 nor 13 trustee can administer the most valuable assets in this estate. Without those assets or the cannabis-based income stream, the debtors cannot fund a plan without breaking the law."[5]

There was some hope throughout the cannabis industry when the United States Court of Appeals for the Ninth Circuit affirmed *Garvin v. Cook Invs. NW, SPNWY, LLC, and the cannabis-business debtor's proposed Chapter 11 bankruptcy plan*.[6] However, a closer review of the case indicates that the decision was based on procedural rather than substantive grounds, and the result was largely due to mistakes by the U.S Trustee. In *Garvin*, the District Court, and the Ninth Circuit, affirmed a Bankruptcy Court ruling that while the plan proposed by the debtor depended on an illegal substantive provision, the court could still affirm that plan because Section 1129 "directs courts to look only to the proposal of a plan, not the terms of the plan."[7] However, the Ninth Circuit confirmed that a plan of bankruptcy "does not insulate debtors from prosecution for criminal activity, even if that activity is part of the plan itself."[8] This decision has subsequently faced harsh criticism from other bankruptcy courts. Both a Colorado and a Michigan bankruptcy court declined to follow the Ninth Circuit's position, with the Michigan court stating, in a footnote, that it disagreed with the Ninth Circuit and that the court should have dismissed the case rather than setting a precedent which allows a federal court to confirm a Chapter 11 plan that permits a debtor to violate federal criminal law.[9]

Ancillary Businesses

It is not just licensed cannabis companies that are barred from bankruptcy courts. Judges have also barred landlords (renting to a cannabis company is prohibited by Section 856(a) of the CSA) and sellers of hydroponic growing equipment (it is a crime to distribute equipment used to manufacture a controlled substance under Section 843(a)(7) of the CSA). Leasing space to cannabis businesses has proved to be fatal to debtors seeking Chapters 11 or 13 bankruptcy protection. However, unlike plant touching businesses, ancillary businesses appear to have more of an opportunity to convert to Chapter 7 protection, rather than face a dismissal.

For example, in *In Rent-Rite Super Kegs Ltd.*, the Colorado Bankruptcy Court ruled that it would dismiss the debtor's Chapter 11 or convert it to Chapter 7 because the debtor derived 25% of its revenues from leasing warehouse space to a cultivator of cannabis.[10]

Likewise, in *Arm Ventures, LLC*, a debtor, owning 48.8% of a commercial property, intended to lease part of the property to a state legal medical cannabis facility but was denied Chapter 11 protection by the Southern District of Florida Bankruptcy Court.[11] The court demanded that the debtor provide a plan that did not depend on cannabis as a source of income, or the case would be converted to a Chapter 7 proceeding.[12] In *In re Basrah Custom Design*, the judge dismissed a Michigan bankruptcy case because the debtor business had leased property to a medical cannabis dispensary.[13] The court found that the debtor's status as a landlord put it in direct violation of Section 856(a) of the CSA, and thus, the debtor had unclean hands and the court could not provide assistance in violation of the CSA.

Landlords are not the only ancillary businesses being denied protection. Sellers of products used by state-legal cannabis businesses are also being denied bankruptcy-protection. In *In re Way to Grow*, the court faced a decision regarding whether to provide bankruptcy protection to a company that knowingly sold hydroponic supplies to both the general public and cannabis businesses. The court analyzed a debtor's access to bankruptcy protection by assessing whether a business must directly and aggressively market to, or aid and abet, cannabis consumers in violation of the CSA. The court in *Way to Grow* determined that a company selling hydroponic equipment to cannabis growers could not hide behind the fact that legal growers also purchased their products. However, focusing on Section 843(a)(6) and (7), the court determined that the debtors did not aid and abet the manufacture of cannabis because a "court would need to conclude [that] Debtors share the same intent as their customers to violate the CSA and willfully associate themselves with their customers' criminal ventures."[14] But, even though debtors did not share this intent, the fact that they knew they were selling their products to customers who will, and do, violate the CSA was enough to prevent debtors from obtaining federal bankruptcy protections.[15]

U.S. Trustee

Finally, beyond the separate decisions of bankruptcy courts, the U.S. Trustee, a division within the Department of Justice that is responsible for overseeing the administration of bankruptcy cases and private trustees, has taken a very public and clear position that cannabis assets may not be administered in federal bankruptcy.[16] This policy position, combined with the weight of precedent, strongly indicates that cannabis companies should not expect any access to U.S. Bankruptcy courts until a change in federal law occurs.

Chapter 15

Chapter 15 cases are meant to address cases of cross-border insolvencies and provide many of the same protections as Chapters 7 or 11 cases. It may be possible for a Canadian-based cannabis company to begin insolvency proceedings in Canada and then seek recognition in the U.S. However, if the company has any US-based cannabis assets it appears likely that the filing would be disputed as against public policy for the same reasons as other purely U.S. federal bankruptcy filings.[17]

Alternatives to Federal Bankruptcy Protections

Out-of-Court Restructurings

An out-of-court restructuring is any transaction in which a contract arrangement is reached outside of bankruptcy court or state receivership proceedings to recapitalize or reorganize the capital structure of a company. There is no legal reason why an out-of-court restructuring could not be used in a cannabis transaction. The difference, however, with respect to cannabis transactions, is that the lenders will know that the debtor does not have access to federal bankruptcy protection, and, thus, will be in a stronger negotiating position.

State Receiverships

A state court receivership provides for the court appointment of a third party to act on behalf of all interested parties (i.e., not merely as an agent of the lenders). (Note, that in addition to state receiverships, there are also federal receiverships, but cannabis companies will have limited access to them for the same reasons they are limited regarding bankruptcy protection.) As receiverships have become more common, many states have recently enacted comprehensive receivership statutes.[18]

Appointments typically occur in one of four situations:

1   A receiver is appointed to oversee commercial real estate and collect rent.
2   A receiver is requested by the senior secured (or, occasionally, just the unsecured) lenders of a company.
3   A receiver is requested by the company, i.e., the debtor, itself.
4   A receivership is instituted to protect the health and safety of the public (e.g., an Attorney General requests receivership over a mismanaged nursing home).

Courts do not freely grant receiverships and generally require evidence of insolvency or a need to preserve a company's assets from being dissipated.[19] And most states grant judges broad latitude in determining whether to appoint a receiver.

Unlike assignments for the benefit of creditors (ABCs), discussed below, a receivership is always court supervised. The court order appointing the receiver will place the company's property under the control of the receiver and set forth the scope of the receiver's authority, which can vary significantly.[20]

Assignments for the Benefit of Creditors (ABCs)

Another alternative is an ABC. An ABC is generally a non-judicial (although there are also judicial ABCs, which are becoming more common), state common law-governed process. Increasingly, however, states are codifying the process by statute and allowing insolvent companies to voluntarily assign their assets to a third party, who then holds these assets in a fiduciary capacity for the benefit of the company's creditors.[21] This process typically requires approval of the board of directors and shareholders of the company, which may delay the process (in contrast to a federal bankruptcy petition where shareholder approval is not necessary). The ABC is started by executing a deed of assignment, or assignment agreement, transferring all of the assets of the company to the third party.[22] As noted above, an ABC is not necessarily court supervised.

An ABC has the advantages of possibly being faster and cheaper than a Chapter 7 or liquidating Chapter 11 case, but it is ultimately a dissolution of the company and does not contemplate the restructuring of an insolvent business into a going concern. In addition, an ABC cannot take advantage of the powers provided to a trustee in a federal bankruptcy court, such as the ability to assign executory contracts without the consent of a counter party or the ability to sell assets free and clear of liens.[23]

Transfers of state licenses can also be more difficult in an ABC than in a state receivership. It will depend on both the cannabis and ABC regulations of the applicable state, which need to be looked at holistically. One question is whether the cannabis regulations require the process to be judicially overseen or if any assignment for the benefit of creditors will suffice. For example, California's cannabis regulations contemplate a procedure for the transfer of a license under both an ABC and receivership.[24] Colorado, on the other hand, only has expedited license procedures in the case of court appointees.[25] The other question is the nature of an ABC within a jurisdiction. ABCs vary considerably between states and range from being purely a creature of common law to being heavily regulated and overseen judicially. Participants in ABCs will need to review the laws governing both cannabis licenses and ABCs in their jurisdiction in order to determine if a license transfer will be practical. There is limited precedent in this area, and it is difficult to predict exactly how it will play out in practice.

Remedies for State Creditors under the UCC

Under Article 9 of the Uniform Commercial Code (UCC), upon a default, a secured creditor can repossess and dispose of its collateral. Article 9 governs the terms of the repossession and subsequent sale of the collateral. These rules include obligations to provide reasonable notice to the debtor and other parties of interest of the intent to sell the collateral, the use of reasonable efforts to maximize the proceeds of the sale, and the requirement that they properly apply the proceeds of the sale.[26] If the assets secured are subject to cannabis regulations, however, any state and local cannabis regulatory requirements must be followed in addition to the UCC procedures. For example, if an all-assets lien has been filed on the debtor's property, a lender cannot repossess cannabis or cannabis products.[27] All state regulatory regimes have concluded that only a licensed business can possess and sell cannabis and unless the lender holds the requisite licenses, any attempt to repossess the collateral would be illegal.

Winding Up under State Statutes

Finally, a cannabis company can simply wind up pursuant to the rules of its state of formation. In winding up, the company directors, or members, will dissolve the business, signifying the termination of business operations. Treatment of business debt, and whether it needs to be paid prior to dissolution, needs to be evaluated considering the applicable state laws.

Cannabis Licenses and Insolvency

One area of law that is still unsettled is how cannabis licenses will be treated in an insolvency. Since cannabis companies are typically prevented from transferring licenses without regulatory approval, the issue of insolvency creates a unique predicament for cannabis companies. There are typically no rules that prohibit an insolvent company from transferring a license – a licensee would need to follow the normal process. However, following a typical transfer process may not be possible – it would require initial approval to put a third party in charge of the insolvent company and then a separate approval to sell the license to another party. Given the timeline to close a change of control, this may not be practical. However, some states have adopted regulations that provide for the transfer of licenses in an insolvency scenario.

Colorado

Section 2–275 of Colorado's Marijuana Rules, which became effective on January 1, 2020, was added to clarify procedures and requirements for court-appointed receivers, trustees, and other court appointees.[28] The regulations permit court appointees to accept an appointment prior to licensure from the state licensing authority so long as they file an application within 14 days of their appointment.[29] While the court appointees will not be able to establish an independent license, they are authorized to exercise the privileges of a temporary licensee and the license will expire upon the conclusion of the court's appointment.[30] If necessary, the temporary license remains valid for one year and can be renewed annually in accordance with Colorado's Marijuana Code.

Washington

One instance where a cannabis license has been successfully transferred through a receivership occurred in Washington.[31] Under state law, the Washington State Liquor and Cannabis Board (WSLCB) is explicitly empowered to approve receiverships over cannabis businesses.[32] Further, the cannabis regulations state that a receiver appointed over a licensee must notify the WSLCB's licensing and regulation division in the event of the receivership of any license, and receive approval from the WSLCB unless the receiver is a pre-approved receiver.[33]

California

At this writing, at least one publicly traded company has begun an insolvency proceeding in California. DionyMed, a multi-state operator listed on the CSA, recently defaulted on over $24.81 million after a creditor demanded immediate payment of its approximately $19 million loan.[34] DionyMed then failed to restructure its debt or find a strategic buyer to acquire its assets, triggering the Supreme Court of British Columbia to appoint FTI Consulting Canada Inc. as receiver of the company's properties and assets. At present the contemplated asset sale has been sealed so it is not possible to determine if any of the state cannabis licenses will be transferred.[35]

Hemp and CBD Companies and Access to Federal Bankruptcy Courts

Caselaw

With the passage of the 2018 Farm Bill, will bankruptcy courts view violations of the FFDCA the same way they have viewed violations of the CSA? Two recent bankruptcy court rulings appear to suggest that courts will focus on the CSA and not the FFDCA, but this issue has not been dealt with in enough detail to provide much guidance.

In *In re Way to Grow*, the Appellants filed a motion to stay a pending appeal in which they argued that, with the passage of the 2018 Farm Bill, they could pivot their business to focus on commercial and industrial hemp to avoid violating the CSA.[36] The court, however, did not consider this argument persuasive and noted that the business had historically advertised as a cannabis business and there was no way the company could ensure that new customers were buying its hydroponic equipment only for legal hemp operations.

On June 3, 2019, the United States Bankruptcy Court for the District of Nevada addressed, albeit in dicta, the question of whether a hemp company could avail itself of the federal bankruptcy court system, stating that a "Debtor's CBD Business... may no longer be prohibited under federal law as a result of the [2018 Farm Bill]."[37] The court continued by highlighting the importance of hemp's removal from the CSA in the 2018 Farm Bill and noted that the FDA had been placed in the position to regulate such products. The court thought it was important that the Debtor's CBD business might not be in violation of the CSA (assuming the CBD was derived from hemp). But the court did not address the FFDCA at all, and there was no discussion of whether a violation of the FFDCA would bar a company from the federal bankruptcy system.

On February 6, 2020, GenCanna Global USA Inc. (GenCanna), a large Kentucky vertically integrated producer of hemp and hemp-derived CBD products, filed for bankruptcy.[38] GenCanna noted that it was hurt by a "dramatic plunge" in the price of CBD products. On May 19, 2020, the bankruptcy court approved the sale of the bulk of GenCanna's assets for $77 million to MGG Investment Group, one of GenCanna's creditors.[39] This is a positive indication for the ability of hemp and CBD companies to access the protections of U.S. bankruptcy courts.

Insolvency and Licenses

Unlike the case with cannabis regulatory regimes, it does not appear as though hemp licensing contemplates the possibility of license transfers in receivership or other insolvency scenarios.[40] The IFR (which only governs licenses issued by the USDA directly) notes that "[l]icenses may not be sold, assigned, transferred, pledged, or otherwise disposed of, alienated or encumbered."[41] So unless a state insolvency proceeding involves a change of ownership, as opposed to a transfer of assets, as is common, there is no possibility of transferring USDA-issued licenses. Practically, this may not be a material concern because the process of obtaining USDA licenses is very different from the process of obtaining state cannabis licenses. USDA licenses are not limited in number and are generally far easier to obtain, so the inability to transfer the licenses in an insolvency proceeding may not matter because a new license could be obtained easily.

Notes

1 *In re: Way to Grow, Inc.*, 597 B.R. 111, 117 (Bankr. D. Colo. 2018) (quoting *In re Rent-Rite Super Kegs West Ltd.*, 484 B.R. 799, 805 (Bankr. D. Colo. 2012).
2 597 B.R. 111 at 117 (quoting 484 B.R. 799, 807).
3 Law360, "Bankruptcy Court's Buzzkill of the Marijuana Industry," Aug. 1, 2019 (*citing* In re Mother Earth's Alternative Healing Coop. Inc.); Chapter 11

Voluntary Petition, In re: Mother Earth's Alt. Healing Coop., Inc., No. 12-10223-11 (Bankr. S.D. Ca. dismissed Oct. 23, 2012).
4 *Id.*
5 *In re Frank Anthony Arenas*, 535 B.R. 845, 854 (B.A.P. 10th Cir. 2015).
6 *Garvin v. Cook Invs. NW*, No. 18-35119, 2019 WL 1945280 (9th Cir. 2019).
7 *Id.*
8 *Id.*
9 *In re Basrah Custom Design*, 2019 WL 2202742 fn. 38 (Bankr. E.D. Mich. 2019).
10 *In re Rent-Rite Super Kegs West Ltd.*, 484 B.R. 799, 811 (Bankr. D. Colo. 2012).
11 *Arm Ventures, LLC*, 564 B.R. 77, 86-87 (Bankr. S.D. Florida 2017).
12 *Id.*
13 *In re Basrah Custom Design*, 2019 WL 2202742.
14 *In re: Way to Grow, Inc.*, 597 B.R. 111, 126.
15 *Id.*, at 131.
16 Clifford J. White III and John Sheahan, "Why Marijuana Assets May Not Be Administered in Bankruptcy," *U.S. Department of Justice*, https://www.justice.gov/ust/file/abi_201712.pdf/download.
17 Jason Rosell, "Will U.S. Cannabis Companies Find Grass Is Greener in Canada for Restructuring?" *Turnaround Management Association*, Jan. 2019, http://www.pszjlaw.com/media/publication/552_Will%20US%20Cannabis%20 Companies%20find%20Grass%20Is%20Greener%20in%20Canada%20 for%20Restructuring.pdf.
18 Joyce Kuhns, "Receiverships 2019: The Bankruptcy Option Revisited," *I95 Business*, Mar. 31, 2019, https://i95business.com/articles/content/receiverships-2019-the-bankruptcy-option-revisited-785.
19 *Id.*
20 Keri L. Wintle, "State Receivership: An Alternative to Bankruptcy," *abfjournal*, Apr. 2018, https://www.abfjournal.com/%3Fpost_type%3Darticles%26 p%3D72054.
21 David S. Kupetz, "Assignment for the Benefit of Creditors: Effective Tool for Acquiring and Winding Up Distressed Businesses," *Business Law Today*, Nov. 15, 2015, https://www.americanbar.org/groups/business_law/publications/ blt/2015/11/05_kupetz/.
22 *Id.*
23 *Id.*
24 Bureau of Cannabis Control, "Death, Incapacity, or Insolvency of a Licensee," Cal. Code Regs. Tit. 16, § 5024 (2020), https://bcc.ca.gov/law_regs/ cannabis_order_of_adoption.pdf.
25 *Id.*
26 Garry M. Graber and Steven W. Wells, "UCC Article 9 Secured Party Sales," *Practical Law*, Nov. 2017, Resource I.D.: w-008-7326, https://www.hodgson russ.com/media/publication/1758_UCC%20Article%209%20Secured%20 Party%20Sales%20_w-008-7326_.pdf.
27 Note that it is somewhat of an open question whether a lien can be placed on assets (e.g., cannabis or a cannabis license) subject to cannabis regulations.
28 Colorado Marijuana Rules, 1 Colo. Code Regs. 212-3, § 2-275 (2020), https:// www.sos.state.co.us/CCR/GenerateRulePdf.do?ruleVersionId=8737&file Name=1%20CCR%20212-3.
29 *Id.*
30 *Id.*
31 Dominique R. Scalia, "Washington's First Marijuana Receivership Reaches a Successful Conclusion," *NWLawyer* 36 (July–Aug. 2017), http://wabarnews. wsba.org/wabarnews/july_august_2017/MobilePagedReplica.action?pm=2& folio=36#pg38.

32 Wash. Admin. Code § 314-55-137 (2018).
33 *Id.*
34 Kristine Owram and Olivia Rockeman, "Pot Firms Face a Cash Crunch and No Access to U.S. Bankruptcy Protection," *Los Angeles Times*, Dec. 17, 2019, https://www.latimes.com/business/story/2019-12-17/pot-firms-cash-crunch-no-us-bankruptcy-protection; Jayson Derrick, "DionyMed Fails to Restructure Debt, Heads for Receivership," *Benzinga*, Oct. 29, 2019, https://www.msn.com/en-us/money/news/dionymed-fails-to-restructure-debt-heads-for-receivership/ar-AAJy8pH; Dionymed, "DionyMed Announces appointment of Receiver, Resignation of Directors, and Update Regarding OTCQB Listing," *Business Wire*, Nov. 1, 2019, https://www.businesswire.com/news/home/20191101005337/en/DionyMed-Announces-Appointment-Receiver-Resignation-Directors-Update.
35 FTI Consulting, "DionyMed - Court Orders," http://cfcanada.fticonsulting.com/DionyMed/courtOrders.htm.
36 *In re: Way to Grow, Inc.*, C.A. No. 18-cv-3245-WJM, Bankr. No. 18-14333-MER, Order Denying Stay Pending Appeal, 2019 WL 669795 (Bankr. D. Colo. Jan. 18, 2019).
37 *In re: CW Nevada LLC*, 602 B.R. 717, 724 (Bankr. D. Nev. 2019).
38 Jonathan Randles, "CBD Producer GenCanna Files for Bankruptcy," *Wall Street Journal*, Feb. 6, 2020, https://www.wsj.com/articles/cbd-producer-gencanna-files-for-bankruptcy-11581029308.
39 "Judge OKs $77 Million Sale of GenCanna Global Assets Out of Bankruptcy," *Hemp Industry Daily*, May 20, 2020, https://hempindustrydaily.com/bankruptcy-judge-approves-77-million-sale-of-gencanna-global-assets-out-of-bankruptcy/.
40 It should be noted, however, that the authors may not be aware of a smaller licensing regime and these regimes could change in the future.
41 7 C.F.R § 990.22(b)(3) (Oct. 31, 2020).

9   Introduction to Cannabis and Intellectual Property Law

Charles S. Alovisetti, Matthew Bartling, Barine Majewska, and Michelle Bodian

Introduction

Like many other areas of cannabis law, the federal illegality of canna-bis and the human consumption of hemp-derived CBD present chal-lenges for obtaining full intellectual property (IP) rights in the United States. There are five fundamental types of IP protection relevant to the cannabis industry: copyrights, trademarks and service marks, trade se-crets, patents, and plant variety rights.

Copyrights

Copyright Law Basics

Copyright law, governed by the Copyright Act of 1976 (Copyright Act), protects original works of authorship fixed in any tangible medium of expression from which they can be perceived, reproduced, or otherwise communicated.[1] Examples of works of authorship that can be protected under copyright law include literary and musical works, as well as artistic expressions such as songs, movies, and novels. Copyright law protects the *expression* of an idea or fact, but it does not protect the underlying idea or fact. It also cannot protect names, brands, or slogans.

Is Registration Necessary and What Benefits Does It Bring?

It is possible, but not necessary, to obtain copyright registration with the United States Copyright Office. All original, qualifying works automati-cally obtain some copyright protection when published or made public.[2] All copyright registration is federal; there are no state-level equivalents of the United States Copyright Office. Formally registering a copyright will place on record a clearly verifiable account of the date and content of work in question. This helps in the event of a claim, infringement, or pla-giarism. Perhaps the most important benefit of registering a copyright is the ability to file a lawsuit for copyright infringement. Unless a copyright is registered, or in some jurisdictions while an application is pending, a copy-right owner cannot file a lawsuit to enforce or protect the owner's rights.

Unlike certain other areas of IP law, there is no legality requirement to access copyright law protection. Instead, the Copyright Act focuses on the originality of a work. To qualify as original, the work must be created independently and must have "at least a modicum" of creativity. As the Supreme Court explicitly ruled, in *Feist Pubs., Inc. v. Rural Tel. Svc. Co., Inc.*, "the requisite level of creativity is extremely low; even a slight amount will suffice."[3] Because of this, there should be no obstacle to a cannabis company obtaining copyright protection.

How Long Does Copyright Protection Last?

The length of copyright protection depends on several factors, including whether the copyrighted item at issue has been published and the date of its publication. Generally, for cannabis copyrights, almost all of which were created after January 1, 1978, the protection lasts for the life of the author, plus an additional 70 years. The length of protection for works created anonymously or before January 1, 1978 varies based on other factors. No renewal registration is necessary for works created after January 1, 1978.[4]

Unique Considerations for Cannabis Companies

Under the Copyright Act, federal courts have exclusive subject matter jurisdiction over infringement claims.[5] Potentially, the federal illegality of cannabis could lead to a federal court declining to enforce the rights of a cannabis company.[6] There are also copyright issues that arise in contractual relationships between a company and third parties. "Work for hire" is a statutory concept that creates an exception to the general rule that the person who actually creates a work is the legally recognized author of that work. Under the work for hire doctrine, when a work is "made for hire," the employer, and not the individual creating the work, is considered the legal author. It is common for companies in the cannabis space to hire consultants, contractors, or employees to create a variety of work product for the company, such as branding materials, cultivation processes, and employee handbooks. It is important that these companies ensure that any agreement anticipating the creation of work product is drafted in consideration of the applicable copyright and work for hire issues to obtain the desired outcome with respect to IP ownership.

Trademarks and Service Marks

Trademark and Service Mark Basics

A trademark is any word, name, symbol, or design used in commerce to identify and distinguish the goods of one manufacturer or seller from those of another, and to indicate the source of the goods.[7] A service mark is a word, name, symbol, or design used in commerce that identifies and distinguishes a service rather than products or goods. The term "trademark" is often used in a general sense to refer to both trademarks and service marks.[8] Generally, brand names, slogans, and logos are the most common types of trademarks used by businesses.

In the United States, trademarks are governed at both the federal and state levels. Federal trademark law is generally governed by the Lanham Act, codified at 15 U.S.C. § 1051 (known as the Trademark Act of 1946). The precise definition offered by the United States Patent and Trademark Office (USPTO) is: "[a] trademark is a word, phrase, symbol and/or design that identifies and distinguishes the source of the goods of one party from those of others."[9] This definition sets forth the three elements of a trademark: (i) it must be a "tangible symbol" (this may be either a word or a logo), (ii) the symbol must be in use or there must be a bona fide intent to use the mark, and (iii) the symbol must distinguish and identify the goods in question from those of other sellers. Unless a trademark is determined to have become "generic" through common use, a party has the exclusive right to use its trademark.

In addition to federal trademark law, each state has similar laws protecting trademarks and maintains its own registry of approved trademarks. Registering a trademark with a state provides rights within the borders of that specific state and prevents local competitors from using similar branding, but it will not protect against out of state operations.[10]

Is Registration Necessary and What Benefits Does It Bring?

Registration is not necessary to benefit from the protection of trademark law. "Common law" rights can be established in a mark based solely on use of the mark in commerce, without registration. However, registration with the USPTO has several advantages. For example, without federal registration, common law rights may be limited to the geographic region where a mark has been used. Additionally, registration gives notice to the public of the registrant's claim of ownership of the mark, a legal presumption of ownership nationwide, the exclusive right to use the mark on or in connection with the goods or services set forth in the registration, and use of the ® registered trademark symbol.

Compared to filing a federal trademark with the USPTO, registering a trademark at the state level is relatively quick and inexpensive. Additionally, state-level trademark registration is a viable alternative to the hurdles of federal trademark registration, especially for "plant-touching" cannabis businesses that cannot seek federal registration for goods and services, which are illegal under the CSA. Registration of cannabis-related trademarks is allowed in all states where recreational use of cannabis is legal, and in most states where medical use is permitted.[11]

Note that unregistered trademarks are subject to the same exclusions as registered trademarks. The Supreme Court has stated, "the general principals qualifying a mark for registration under Section 2 of the Lanham Act are for the most part applicable in determining whether an unregistered mark is entitled to protection."[12]

How Long Does Trademark Protection Last?

Trademark rights derive from actual "use" and can last forever if the mark is used in commerce to indicate the source of goods or services. A federal trademark registration lasts for ten years, with theoretically unlimited ten-year renewal terms that can be filed if the trademark is still being used in commerce. Between the fifth and sixth year of registration, an affidavit must be filed stating the trademark is still in use. If the affidavit is not filed, the registration is cancelled.[13]

Unique Considerations for Cannabis Companies

The USPTO takes the position that "[u]se of a mark in commerce must be lawful under federal law to be the basis for federal registration under the U.S. Trademark Act."[14] This statement is based on court cases that have interpreted the requirement that a trademark be used in commerce to mean lawful use of the trademark in interstate commerce. These cases are the grounds under which the USPTO will deny an application for a trademark to a cannabis business. The Trademark Manual of Examining Procedure § 907 notes the following: "[E]vidence indicating that the identified goods or services involve the sale or transportation of a controlled substance or drug paraphernalia in violation of the CSA, would be a basis for issuing an inquiry or refusal."[15]

While a cannabis company cannot register marks used in connection with its core products and services with the USPTO, as these will be denied for violating federal law, it may be possible to register ancillary trademarks in connection with non-cannabis–based products and services such as an informational website, blog, or apparel. In fact, this is common practice among many cannabis industry brands to gain some federal protection and to ensure they appear in the USPTO records. A company's application could be denied because of the company's other illegal activities and the USPTO may shift the burden to the company to prove the trademark is in lawful use.

Even if registration were obtained, the scope of such registration would only apply to the non-cannabis goods and services identified in the application. The registered trademark would not protect activities that were not sufficiently related such that consumers might believe there was an affiliation.[16] Despite these limitations, an ancillary cannabis trademark may still provide some benefits. The registered trademark symbol could still be used, the registration number could be used in demand letters, and in the event of federal legalization, the ownership of ancillary registrations might strengthen the claim of a brand owner's priority of use.[17]

With the passage of the 2018 Farm Bill, the ability of hemp companies to obtain federal trademarks has drastically expanded. The USPTO has come out with clear guidance (Examination Guide 1–19) that permits hemp companies to obtain federal trademarks. However, the USPTO notes that because the FDA does not permit the inclusion of CBD as a food ingredient or dietary supplement, such use of CBD remains illegal and cannot be federally trademarked.[18]

Trade Secrets

Trade Secret Basics

Trade secrets are a form of IP traditionally governed by state law. Trade secrets may consist of an idea, process, pattern, formula, physical device, or compilation of information that: (i) provides a competitive advantage and (ii) is treated in a way that can reasonably be expected to prevent the public or competitors from learning about it.[19]

Is Registration Necessary and What Benefits Does It Bring?

Registration is not necessary or even possible for a trade secret, which is protected through court action to enjoin misappropriation. Trade secret protection depends on the information being held confidential; if information is openly disclosed or independently developed, there will be no protection for information under trade secret law. Unlike a patent holder, a trade secret holder is only protected from misappropriation or unauthorized disclosure and use.[20]

How Long Does Trade Secret Protection Last?

Protection lasts as long as the trade secret remains a secret, potentially indefinitely. A trade secret holder must take reasonable measures to protect information that it considers a trade secret. If such protective precautions were not taken to protect the information, courts would likely rule that the information was not a trade secret, and thus, the holder would not have grounds for legal action against the person who disclosed the secret.

Unique Considerations for Cannabis Companies

Due to the unavailability of other types of IP protection, properly using the protections of trade secrets may take on greater importance for a cannabis company.

Patents

Patent Law Basics

There are three general types of patents: (1) utility patents, (2) design patents, and (3) plant patents. Utility patents are the most common and provide protection for "any new and useful process, machine, manufacture, or composition of matter, or any new and useful improvement thereof."[21] The four categories listed above (process, machine, manufacture, and composition of matter) are the universe of patentable subject matter for utility patents. A utility patent requires (1) novelty, (2) utility, and (3) nonobviousness.

Design patents and plant patents are specialty patents that are less common than utility patents. A design patent protects "any new, original, and ornamental design for an article of manufacture."[22] It effectively protects the decorative and nonfunctional aspects of an object. It's possible to obtain a design and utility patent for the same invention. A design patent requires (1) novelty, (2) originality, and (3) nonfunctionality.

Finally, a plant patent protects "any distinct and new variety of plant" that the investor has "asexually reproduced," meaning that fertilization of seeds is not involved.[23] Instead other methods of reproduction are used, such as taking cuttings or cloning. It is not possible to patent a plant found in a wild or uncultivated state. A plant patent requires (1) novelty, (2) distinctness (defined by the Supreme Court as "the aggregate of the plant's distinguishing characteristics"), (3) nonobviousness, and (4) asexual production.[24]

The United States Patent Act of 1952 and its subsequent amendments (most recently the Leahy-Smith America Invents Act) are the governing patent statutes. Generally, U.S. patent laws have been codified in Title 35 of the U.S. Code. Section 35 U.S.C. § 161 originated as an amendment to the preexisting patent statute with the Plant Patent Act of 1930. As enacted, the "invents or discovers" requirement limited patent protection to plants "that were created as a result of plant breeding or other agricultural and horticultural efforts and that were created by the inventor."[25] The plant patent provisions were separated from the utility patent provisions in the Patent Act of 1952 to create 35 U.S.C. § 161. Section 161 was amended in 1954 to extend protection to "newly found seedlings," provided they were found in a cultivated state, but did not otherwise alter the scope of plant patent protection.

Grant of a plant patent precludes others from asexually reproducing, selling, offering for sale, or using the patented plant or any of its parts in the United States or importing them. A plant patent is regarded as limited to one plant, or genome (complete genomic sequence of a plant species). A plant derived from a spore or a mutant is unlikely of the same genotype as the original plant, and thus would not be covered by the plant patent of the original plant. Such a plant derived from a spore or such mutant may itself be protected under a separate plant patent, subject to meeting the requirements of patentability.

Is Registration Necessary and What Benefits Does It Bring?

There are no patent protections available until a patent is issued by the USPTO. However, the date of a patent application is still important with respect to determining who can claim ownership of an invention. Holding a patent provides the exclusive right to certain activities – selling, making, using, or importing the patented invention. Obtaining a patent is a lengthy process and typically takes between two and three years.[26]

How Long Does Patent Protection Last?

There are nuances around potential extension or adjustment of length, but typically a patent will last 20 years (14 for design patents) from the date the patent application was filed.[27]

Unique Considerations for Cannabis Companies

Unlike a federal trademark, there is no legality requirement to obtain a patent; the USPTO has issued almost 250 cannabis patents in 2017 and 2018.[28] Courts have repudiated a previous requirement that an invention "should not be frivolous or injurious to the well-being, good policy or sound morals of society."[29] In fact, the federal government itself owns a cannabis patent – U.S. Patent No. 6.630,507 – which relates to the use of cannabinoids in treating neurodegenerative disease.[30]

Both plant and utility patents have been issued for cannabis strains. On July 2, 2019, Charlotte's Web obtained the first U.S. patent for a cultivar of hemp, CW2A.[31] As discussed above, cannabis is sometimes clonally propagated, and plant or utility patents are an effective way to protect new cannabis strains. Until recently, however, it was a criminal act to cultivate or even possess cannabis. As a result, most cannabis growers did not publicly disclose the traits of their strains. This has caused confusion because it limits the ability of the USPTO to determine whether strains of cannabis are new, which can lead to wrongfully granted patents.[32]

While this might seem like an opportunity for breeders, it also poses a threat to anyone in the cannabis industry. If the USPTO grants a patent on an old strain of the plant, those who have already been using the strain could incur liability. The fear of frivolous litigation has the potential to create uncertainty in the industry. Ultimately, one would expect patents for old strains to be invalidated in court. Nevertheless, evidence of invalidity could be hard to obtain, and litigation is costly even for the prevailing party. Many would be inclined to give up using the strain or settle the matter out of court, even when the case involves an invalid patent.[33]

However, utility patents are potentially far broader in scope than plant patents, since the applicant is not limited to a single claim covering the entire plant (as would be the case for a plant patent).[34] A utility patent may, instead, claim a strain based on ranges of chemical composition instead of specific amounts of cannabinoids. This allows a far broader range of protection for the patent holder and could present concerns for the wider industry (as those in the industry would be at risk for patent infringement claims).

There are also questions about the viability of enforcing cannabis patents in federal court. (State courts do not have jurisdiction over matters of patents.)[35] Federal courts have, in some instances, declined to rule on cases involving cannabis, given that they would be aiding a party engaged in a federally illegal act. This has not yet become an issue, as there has only been one case testing a cannabis patent – the United Cannabis Corp's lawsuit. To date, in this case the legal status of cannabis has not been an issue.[36]

The federally illegal nature of cannabis also creates challenges for the patent system itself. There is a comparatively limited amount of information and scientific study on the field. This presents challenges for USPTO, as examiners need to review prior works when determining the novelty of a patent. The absence of good information could lead to issuing overly broad patents, since the USPTO may not be aware of prior existing plants.[37]

Plant Breeders' or Plant Variety Rights

Plant Variety Rights Basics

In addition to the ability to protect IP through patents, breeders can obtain protection for new plant varieties through plant variety protection (PVP). Plant variety rights are sometimes also referred to as plant breeder rights. These protections are issued pursuant to the Plant Variety Protection Act of 1970,[38] (PVPA), which provides legal rights to breeders of new varieties of plants which are sexually reproduced (i.e., by seed) or tuber-propagated.[39] The USDA's Plant Variety Protection Office (PVPO) administers the PVPA by delivering Certificates of Protection.[40]

The 2018 Farm Bill amended the PVPA to permit protection for asexually propagation (i.e., taking a part of one parent plant and causing it to regenerate itself into a new plant) plants. The amendment also included a change that would make asexual propagation of a protected variety an act of infringement. As of June 1, 2020, proposed rules for asexually propagated plants were still being developed so no applications are currently permitted. However, on April 24, 2019, the PVPO began accepting applications of seed-propagated hemp for plant variety protection.[41]

The PVPO provides three significant exemptions to the rights of an owner of a certificate. First, a research exemption exists that excludes the use and reproduction of a protected variety for breeding purposes or other bona fide research. Second, there is a farmer's exemption that permits the saving of seed for the sole use of replanting on the farmer's land. Finally, regulators are permitted to declare a protected variety open to the public for policy reasons – though they must provide the owner of the variety appropriate notice and an opportunity to present its views.

Is Registration Necessary and What Benefits Does It Bring?

Registration is necessary to benefit from the protections of the PVPA. It is necessary to apply for and obtain a Certificate of Projection from the PVPO. While obtaining a certificate is necessary for plant variety rights protections to apply, provisional protection is available upon receipt of the application by the PVPO.[42] Additionally, obtaining plant variety protection comes with a number of benefits, including the exclusive legal rights to market the variety, the right to exclude others from selling the protected variety, and the ability to expedite foreign plan variety protection application filings.

How Long Do Plant Variety Rights Last?

Protection lasts 20 years from the date of issue of a Certificate of Protection (25 years in the case of a tree or vine). As noted above, provisional protection is also available upon the receipt of the application.

Unique Considerations for Cannabis Companies

As noted above, after the passage of the 2018 Farm Bill, hemp plants became entitled to the protections of the PVPA. The status of cannabis plants remains questionable. It appears that the seed deposit requirements of the PVPA would prevent the PVPO from issuing a certificate (taking possession of a viable seed of cannabis would put the PVPO in violation of the CSA).[43] Historically this may have been a moot point since, until the 2018 Farm Bill, asexual propagation was not covered, which tends to be the main method of growing cannabis. However, now that asexually reproduced plants may be protected, the question may arise as to whether the PVPO will protect cannabis plant varieties.

Closing Remarks

The best solution to the problems faced by the cannabis industry, from an IP standpoint, is for the federal government to legalize cannabis. Federal legalization would allow industry participants to apply for national IP rights and, in turn, immediately eliminate many barriers to protection that the industry currently faces.

Notes

1 Copyright Act of 1976, Pub. L. No. 94-553, 90 Stat. 2541 (1976).
2 "Copyright in General," U.S. Copyright Off., https://www.copyright.gov/help/faq/faq-general.html.
3 Feist Pubs., Inc. v. Rural Tel. Serv. Co., Inc., 499 U.S. 340 (1991).
4 "How Long Does Copyright Protection Last?" U.S. Copyright Off., https://www.copyright.gov/help/faq/faq-duration.html.
5 Copyright Act of 1976, Pub. L. No. 94-553, 90 Stat. 2541 (1976).
6 Nathalie Bougenies, "Protecting Your Cannabis Copyrights (Yes, You Have Them)," Harris Bricken, June 21, 2018, https://harrisbricken.com/cannalawblog/protecting-your-cannabis-copyrights-yes-you-have-them/.
7 15 U.S.C. § 1127 (1946).
8 "Trademark, Patent, or Copyright?" U.S. Pat. & Trademark Off., https://www.uspto.gov/trademarks-getting-started/trademark-basics/trademark-patent-or-copyright.
9 *Id.*
10 "Protecting Your Trademark," U.S. Pat. & Trademark Off., https://www.uspto.gov/sites/default/files/documents/BasicFacts.pdf.
11 Russell Jacobs, "Cannabis Trademarks: A State Registration Consortium Solution," 74 *Wash. Lee L. Rev.* 159 (2017).
12 Cravath Swaine and Moore LLP, *Intellectual Property Law Answer Book* 265 (2015).
13 *Id.* at 320.
14 "Examination Guide 1-19, Examination of Marks for Cannabis and Cannabis-Related Goods and Services after Enactment of the 2018 Farm Bill," U.S. Pat. & Trademark Off., May 2, 2019, https://www.uspto.gov/sites/default/files/documents/Exam%20Guide%201-19.pdf.
15 *In re* JJ206, LLC, 120 USPQ2d 1568, 1569-70 (TTAB 2016); *In re* Brown, 119 USPQ2d 1350, 1351-53 (TTAB 2017).
16 Christopher McElwain, "High Stakes: Cannabis Brands and the USPTO's "[Lawful] Use" Registration Criterion," Int'l Trademark Ass'n, 2016, http://www.inta.org/Academics/Documents/2016/McElwain.pdf.
17 "Trademark Manual of Examining Procedure October 2018, § 1207.01(a)(v)," U.S. Pat. & Trademark Off., https://tmep.uspto.gov/RDMS/TMEP/current#/current/TMEP-1200d1e5353.html.
18 "Examination Guide 1-19, Examination of Marks for Cannabis and Cannabis-Related Goods and Services after Enactment of the 2018 Farm Bill," U.S. Pat. & Trademark Off., May 2, 2019, https://www.uspto.gov/sites/default/files/documents/Exam%20Guide%201-19.pdf.
19 "Trade Secret Policy," U.S. Pat. & Trademark Off., https://www.uspto.gov/ip-policy/trade-secret-policy.
20 *Id.*
21 Cravath Swaine & Moore LLP, *Intellectual Property Law Answer Book* 8 (2015).
22 *Id.*
23 *Id.*
24 "General Information about 35 U.S.C. 161 Plant Patents," U.S. Pat. & Trademark Off., https://www.uspto.gov/patents-getting-started/patent-basics/types-patent-applications/general-information-about-35-usc-161.

25 *In re* Beineke, 103 USPQ2d 1872, 1877; 690 F.3d 1344, 1352 (Fed. Cir. 2012).
26 Cravath Swaine and Moore LLP, *Intellectual Property Law Answer Book* 61 (2015).
27 "Trade Secret Policy," U.S. Pat. & Trademark Off., https://www.uspto.gov/ip-policy/trade-secret-policy.
28 Ryan Davis, "4 Burning Legal Questions About Cannabis Patents," Lexis Nexis Law 360, Nov. 4, 2019, https://www.law360.com/cannabis/articles/1209779/4-burning-legal-questions-about-cannabis-patents?nl_pk=f1e37ba6-85b9-46ea-9422-; Matthew Bultman, *Cannabis Activity Surges Amid Industry Gold Rush*, LexisNexis Law 360, Oct. 16, 2019, https://www.law360.com/articles/1203746/cannabis-patent-activity-surges-amid-industry-gold-rush.
29 *Id.*
30 Brett Schuman, Cynthia Hardman, Olivia Uitto, and David Simson, "Emerging Patent Issues in the Cannabis Industry," LexisNexis Law 360, Feb. 20, 2018, https://www.law360.com/articles/1013575/emerging-patent-issues-in-the-cannabis-industry.
31 Chris Roberts, "This Is the First Hemp Strain to be Awarded a U.S. Patent," Leafly, Sept. 13, 2019, https://www.leafly.com/news/industry/this-is-the-first-hemp-strain-patented-in-the-us.
32 Nicholas Landau and James Wright Jr., 31-7 Intel. Prop. & Tech. L. J. 9 (2019).
33 *Id.*
34 Allison Butler, Brittany Butler, and Nicole Grimm, "Protecting Cannabis – Are Plant Patents Cool Now?" JD Supra, Dec. 6, 2017, https://www.jdsupra.com/legalnews/protecting-cannabis-are-plant-patents-34919/.
35 "Areas of Exclusive Federal Jurisdiction," U.S. Legal, https://civilprocedure.uslegal.com/jurisdiction/areas-of-exclusive-federal-jurisdiction/.
36 Matthew Bultman, "Cannabis Activity Surges Amid Industry Gold Rush," LexisNexis Law 360, Oct. 16, 2019, https://www.law360.com/articles/1203746/cannabis-patent-activity-surges-amid-industry-gold-rush.
37 Brett Schuman, Cynthia Hardman, Olivia Uitto, and David Simson, "Emerging Patent Issues in the Cannabis Industry," LexisNexis Law 360, Feb. 20, 2018, https://www.law360.com/articles/1013575/emerging-patent-issues-in-the-cannabis-industry.
38 7 U.S.C. § 2321-2582.
39 7 U.S.C. Ch. 57; *Plant Variety Protection Act*, U.S. Dep't of Agric., https://www.ams.usda.gov/rules-regulations/pvpa.
40 *Id.*
41 "USDA Now Accepting Applications of Seed-Propagated Hemp for Plant Variety Protection," U.S. Dep't of Agric., Apr. 24, 2019, https://www.ams.usda.gov/content/usda-now-accepting-applications-seed-propagated-hemp-plant-variety-protection.
42 "Plant Variety Protection Marketing New Plant Varieties by Protecting Plant Breeders' Innovations," U.S. Dep't of Agric., Feb. 2016, https://www.ams.usda.gov/sites/default/files/media/Plant%20Variety%20Protection%20factsheet.pdf.
43 Allison Butler, Brittany Butler, and Nicole Grimm, "Protecting Cannabis – Are Plant Patents Cool Now?" JD Supra, Dec. 6, 2017, https://www.jdsupra.com/legalnews/protecting-cannabis-are-plant-patents-34919/; RJ Vogt, "Should Pot Be Patented? Inside A Pending IP War," LexisNexis Law 360, Aug. 31, 2018, https://www.law360.com/articles/1078515/should-pot-be-patented-inside-a-pending-ip-war.

10 Introduction to Cannabis and Real Estate Law

Cassia Furman and Charles S. Alovisetti

Introduction

Along with financing, access to real estate – either by lease or acquisition – is a threshold issue facing cannabis operators, posing a significant hurdle to establishing a successful venture in the space. In many states, including California,[1] a cannabis business must first obtain approval to operate a cannabis business from its locality (and obtaining this approval requires proof of control of an appropriate physical location) and then obtain a cannabis business license from the state. This structure heightens the importance of locating real estate suitable for licensing as a first step in starting a cannabis business. This step is also a costly one, as real estate is often one of the largest expenses in getting to market. It can be exceptionally difficult to find a suitable location for a cannabis (and sometimes hemp) business given the plethora of zoning restrictions, building code classifications, and restrictive covenants impacting cannabis businesses. Many would-be cannabis companies are deterred from entry and subsequent expansion due to lack of available, and often affordable, real estate. Because of this, traditional real estate due diligence is of heightened importance to the cannabis industry.

Once an operator finds an area or a building that meets regulatory requirements, negotiating favorable terms with landlords is the next test, as expectations frequently fail to align. Landlords, particularly those new to cannabis, are often skittish of cannabis tenants and attempt to mitigate perceived risk with above-market rents and personal guarantees. Landlord concerns are well-founded, given both the specter of asset forfeiture and current restrictions on commercial lending when the rent roll includes cannabis tenants. Tenants and buyers frequently overextend on lease or acquisition price or fail to build in an adequate cushion to obtain full licensing (which often takes far longer than anticipated), leading to a risk of default on a lease or seller leaseback instrument.

Augmenting these challenges, it can be difficult to move a cannabis business's location. Typically, regulatory approval is required to change the location of a licensed premise, and new locations are often in short supply. Some regulators further impose an obligation for a business to remain active for a license to stay in good standing, so being caught without a new location while attempting to relocate from a prior location can present an existential threat. Taken together, these conditions underscore the importance of selecting a viable location for the business at the onset and negotiating terms that will enable the business to open and grow. In this vein, this chapter explores issues facing cannabis landlords as well as tenants and purchasers, including an overview of market conditions.

Cannabis Landlord/Tenant Relationships

Risks and Opportunities

Commercial landlords may benefit in numerous ways by renting to cannabis businesses. Cannabis businesses must often make significant tenant improvement upgrades to comply with the strict regulations that guide the industry and to provide a safe and professional environment for their staff and customers. These improvements may significantly increase the value of the property and, in blighted areas, improve the market value of an entire neighborhood. Landlords can often command higher rents from cannabis tenants and further mitigate the threat of loss by imposing strong protective clauses in their leases. For a savvy landlord, renting to a cannabis tenant is an opportunity to revitalize an underutilized asset in a manner not typically available to a Class C property, for example.[2] Leasing to a cannabis tenant, however, is not without complications. While commercial cannabis activity may be lawful at the local and state level if conducted in compliance with license requirements, it remains federally illegal. And Section 856(a) of the CSA makes it a crime to lease or rent any place for the purpose of manufacturing, distributing, or using a controlled substance.[3] This reality has the potential to impact landlords in several ways, including criminally and financially.

Commercial Lending

Standard real estate contracts, such as those adopted by statewide associations of realtors, include as a default provision the covenant that a tenant's occupancy of a leasehold will not violate federal law. If a tenant signs a standard contract without requesting waivers of these clauses, they may unwittingly be operating in breach of the lease for the entire lease term. This is an additional consideration for prospective landlords. Institutional lenders impose similar, broadly drafted federal law compliance clauses in commercial loans. Federal law also makes it a felony to lease or rent any place for the purpose of manufacturing, distributing, or using any controlled substance, including cannabis. If the lender knows that cannabis activity is occurring on the mortgaged property, they will typically threaten to declare the borrower/landlord in default. We have seen this pattern play out many times over the years, typically when the commercial landlord attempts to refinance the loan. For commercial mortgages, this typically occurs at five-year intervals. As part of its re-financing diligence, the lender will review documents for all tenants on the rent roll. Due to commercial lending restrictions, a property owner should only consider leasing to a tenant if the property is unencumbered or is leveraged through non-traditional sources, such as private equity.

Asset Forfeiture

A frequent concern raised by landlords is the threat of asset forfeiture based on past attempts by the federal government to seize real and personal property assets, which is covered in Chapter 1.

Bankruptcy

As described in Chapter 8, licensed cannabis companies are barred from bankruptcy courts and protections. Judges have also barred landlords from bankruptcy protection, under the theory that renting to a cannabis company is prohibited by Section 856(a) of the CSA. Although leasing space to cannabis businesses has proved to be fatal to debtors seeking Chapter 11 or 13 bankruptcy protection, property owners may be able to convert to Chapter 7 protection rather than face a dismissal.

Best Practices: Know Your Tenant

Commercial cannabis remains a new and dynamic industry. A typical commercial lease term of five years may be equivalent to five decades for a cannabis operator, so quickly does the industry move. It is the unfortunate reality that the significant constraints faced by cannabis operators – e.g., punitive tax treatment, complex regulatory environment, lack of "vested" property rights, and lack of commercial financing, to name a few – may increase the risk of tenant default. Similarly, while many licensed cannabis companies have access to basic banking services, it remains a heavily cash-dependent industry, which increases the risk of theft and criminal activity. Added to these pressures, the scarcity of available licenses sometimes contributes to "shotgun" partnership dynamics in which principals without much prior history form business ventures to maximize the potential for profit. In this environment, property owners should take every reasonable step to safeguard lease revenues.

As noted above, the absence of federal prosecution only applies to state-legal businesses. Federal and state prosecutions of illegal cannabis businesses are ongoing. While charges are not frequently brought against landlords, if the tenant business owners are arrested or otherwise forced to stop operating their business, this would have a negative financial impact on the landlord. To reduce this risk, property owners should spend the time to vet their potential and existing tenants. Fortunately, some of this work can be outsourced to state and local regulators. Landlords can request copies of licenses and, in some states, confirm the status of those licenses online. Other states may permit verification of licenses by the regulators, with the permission of the licensed business. Full verification of a tenant's compliance, however, does involve more detailed legal due diligence.

Savvy cannabis landlords conduct a version of "Know Your Customer" diligence common in the banking world to vet potential tenants. Typically, commercial landlords already require evidence of solvency and run background checks on prospective tenants.

In addition to standard diligence on the tenant entity and its principals, cannabis landlords should consider requesting evidence of the following:

- Evidence that the proposed cannabis use is authorized by the local government.
- Copies of the company's policies, plans, and operating procedures, with emphasis on such items as security plans (including cash handling and storage) and anti-diversion protocols.
- Copies of any enforcement actions taken against the principals of the tenant by a cannabis regulatory agency or other government agency.
- If the principals hold other cannabis licenses, evidence that those licenses are in good standing.
- Description of the tenant's corporate structure, including affiliates and any outside companies or persons with control over the daily operations of the facility.
- Evidence of zoning clearance from local government or evidence that the building meets all required cannabis "sensitive use" setbacks, as required by local and state governments.
- Prior to commercial cannabis operations commencing, copies of all applicable state and local licenses, permits, zoning clearances, business licenses, inspections, and similar government approvals required to operate. The tenant should further be required to maintain all required approvals on an ongoing basis and alert the landlord immediately if any such approvals are suspended or terminated.

Additionally, cannabis landlords should be aware that holding a cannabis license is a privilege, not a right. Unlike most uses, the right to participate in the cannabis industry typically does not become "vested." Cannabis tenants are typically required to show evidence of a lease or other evidence of a possessory right to real property as a condition of licensure. Thus, the prospective tenant may be negotiating the lease prior to receiving local and state authorization to operate as a cannabis business. Landlords should consider a custom lease term allowing the parties to terminate the lease early if the tenant fails to secure a commercial cannabis permit or license or if the permit or license is rescinded.

Security and Collateral

As an additional protection against the threat of default, cannabis landlords frequently require personal guarantees. Beyond this level of protection, landlords sometimes seek to collateralize the cannabis license for the facility by building in lease clauses that would authorize the landlord to demand its transfer in the event of default. Collateralization of cannabis licenses is addressed in Chapter 18 of this text. In brief, the ability of a landlord to secure lease payments in this matter may be constrained by local or state law. Many states and localities prohibit the transfer of licenses from one entity to another, and states and localities rarely explicitly allow the collateralization of a cannabis license. A third option for securing lease payments – the so-called "landlord's lien" security interest available under Article 9 of the Uniform Commercial Code – is also more complicated when cannabis is present. This is because to the extent the inventory includes cannabis products, such products cannot be possessed or sold by a non-licensee.

Site Selection and Regulatory Issues

Site Selection

In any jurisdiction, sourcing a compliant commercial cannabis property requires careful analysis and vetting of both local and state regulations. A holistic approach should encompass not just local zoning and any specific state requirements for siting cannabis facilities, but also an understanding of any special restrictions on landlord/tenant relationships, profit sharing, co-location, and related issues. For example, some states (California being one) prohibit the co-location of cannabis and industrial hemp operations. This restriction has stymied plans for many operators who assumed that a large warehouse could support both operations on the same floor. In cases of leased real estate, it is important to assess the landlord's relationship with the regulatory compliance of any leases. As an example, cannabis leases that contain participation rent can constitute ownership, raising regulatory approval and suitability issues. An incorrectly located or managed facility could be subject to sanctions and could be unusable.

Local Control and Zoning

Many states have laws that allow localities to prohibit cannabis businesses, even when those activities have been legalized at the state level. The California Supreme Court has upheld many cities' right to ban medical cannabis dispensaries, and under corresponding adult-use regulations, municipalities have the explicit right to prohibit the presence of such businesses. As of January 2020, approximately two-thirds of California municipalities prohibit adult-use cannabis businesses despite widespread acceptance of cannabis use and culture statewide. Likewise in Colorado, where state law permits a city or township to ban cannabis businesses, the geographical majority of the state has banned both adult-use and medical cannabis. Maps of both states will show huge swaths of land that are off-limits to cannabis operators.

Once an appropriate locality has been found, zoning presents an additional hurdle. Localities vary in how they address cannabis zoning issues, but it is common to see licensed businesses restricted to zones approximating their intended use (e.g., an infused products facility may be restricted to light manufacturing zones). On top of these typical restrictions, there may be additional zoning requirements for cannabis operations that are typically more rigorous than regulations for analogous "conventional" businesses. For example, cannabis retail is often barred from opening in commercial core areas, impacting foot traffic and overall viability.

Selective Use Setbacks

Mandated setbacks from so-called "sensitive" land uses present an especially difficult issue for siting a cannabis facility. States and localities vary in defining such "sensitive" uses, but common red flags for cannabis operators include schools, parks, and youth centers. As an additional restriction, local governments often impose minimum setbacks between cannabis facilities, particularly for cannabis retail, as a means of controlling the overall number of stores open in a city or neighborhood.

As an illustrative example, under California state law, the default standard is that a cannabis licensed premises must be located at least 600 feet from any K-12 schools, day care centers, and youth centers in existence at the time the license is issued. The state does acknowledge that zoning is predominantly a local control issue by permitting localities to expressly waive or modify the default setback. However, nothing restricts localities from creating even more stringent setbacks than the state standard, as is frequently the case. The City of Los Angeles, for example, exceeds the state regulations by requiring cannabis retailers to remain at least 700 feet from K-12 schools, public parks, libraries, treatment facilities, day care centers, and permanent supportive housing. The City, as is common, also imposes a minimum distance between cannabis retail locations of 700 feet. Conversely, the requirements for siting a *manufacturing* facility in Los Angeles are less burdensome; the City requires only a 600-foot setback from schools for these facilities.

Existing Facilities

As a final note of caution, a prospective investor or tenant cannot assume that a business is compliantly located and operating simply because it has been operational for a period of time. There are numerous instances where regulators have noticed an ongoing compliance issue long after it should have been caught. Real estate due diligence must include a review of applicable application materials in addition to review of any ongoing operations. If a mistake was made in an application (e.g., the presence of a school was missed), the license or location in question could be at risk despite current operation.

Landlord Risks and Opportunities

Opportunities

- Realize increased revenue with above-market rental fees
- Give aging and underutilized (Class C) industrial space – both individual buildings and entire areas – new life
- Ability to capitalize on upside – equity or profit share (depending on relevant cannabis regulations)
- Tenant improvements – occupants will typically be required to bring building to current code, install security equipment and other features

Risks

- Federally illegal
- Conventional lending does not tolerate federally illegal activities
- High operational and tax cost threatens long-term tenant stability
- Threatens access to bankruptcy protection
- Insurance premiums and carve outs
- For cultivation activity, risk of mold and odor issues
- If cash-based business, potential to be target for theft

(Continued)

- Creditor rights and security challenges – assets may be difficult to collateralize
- Entitlements/zoning more difficult to navigate and time-intensive for tenants to operate
- Landlord's access to the premises in ordinance course is likely restricted by state law

Practice Pointers: Tips for Tenants

- Ask for assignment to an affiliated entity without additional landlord approval
- Emphasize upside to landlord and have "KYT" materials ready
- Consider necessary local and state license disclosures and co-operation needed from landlord, depending on deal structure, in advance
- Anticipate personal guaranty requirement
- Ask about commercial loans and refinancing period
- Carve out commercial cannabis activity from federal law compliance clauses

Notes

1 Medicinal and Adult-Use Cannabis Regulation and Safety Act (MAUCRSA), S.B. 94, ch. 27, § 26032 (2017).
2 "Class C buildings are the oldest, usually over 20 years of age, located in less attractive areas, and need for maintenance." James Chen, "Commercial Real Estate - CRE," *Investopedia*, June 7, 2019, https://www.investopedia.com/terms/c/commercialrealestate.asp.
3 Controlled Substances Act, 21 U.S.C. § 856(a) (2018).

11 Introduction to Cannabis, Securities Law, and Private Placements

Charles S. Alovisetti, Ilya Ross, and Sahar Ayinehsazian

Offer of Sale of Securities Must Be Registered or Exempt from Registration

Section 5 of the Securities Act of 1933 (Securities Act) requires that any offer or sale of securities in the United States either needs to be registered with the U.S. Securities and Exchange Commission (SEC) or sold pursuant to an exemption from registration.[1] An example of a federally registered offering of securities is an Initial Public Offering (IPO). In an IPO or other registered offering, the company files forms with the SEC that provide key facts about itself. The SEC then reviews and comments on these registration forms to ensure adequate disclosure is made (the SEC does not opine on the merits of an offering). In an exempt offering, often referred to as a private placement or unregistered offering, the SEC does not evaluate any registration statement to determine if disclosure requirements are met. Investors must generally make their own determination as to the adequacy of the information.

What Is a Security?

The first question a company raising capital should ask, before delving into any other analysis, is whether it is selling a security. Securities regulations apply only to securities, and not to other assets (e.g., a pound of trim is unlikely to be considered a security). However, in the world of financings, it would be unusual for securities regulations not to come into play. Section 2(a)(1) of the 1933 Securities Act, defines a security as:

> any note, stock, treasury stock, security future, security-based swap, bond, debenture, evidence of indebtedness, certificate of interest or participation in any profit-sharing agreement, collateral-trust certificate, preorganization certificate or subscription, transferable share, investment contract, voting-trust certificate, certificate of deposit for a security, fractional undivided interest in oil, gas, or other mineral rights, any put, call, straddle, option, or privilege on any security, certificate of deposit, or group or index of securities (including any interest therein or based on the value thereof), or any put, call, straddle, option,

or privilege entered into on a national securities exchange relating to foreign currency, or, in general, any interest or instrument commonly known as a "security," or any certificate of interest or participation in, temporary or interim certificate for, receipt for, guarantee of, or warrant or right to subscribe to or purchase, any of the foregoing.[2]

This covers almost all financing structures that a cannabis company might use (typically debt, equity, or convertible debt financings). The Supreme Court has further analyzed this definition and the principal case cited, though dated, is *SEC v. W.J. Howey Co.* Relying on cases decided under state blue-sky laws, this case sets forth the *Howey* test, under which an "investment contract" is "a contract, transaction or scheme whereby a person invests his money in a common enterprise and is led to expect profits solely from the efforts of the promoter or a third party."[3] Transactions which qualify as "investment contracts" are considered securities. Again, for almost all cannabis financings there is not really a question of whether the transactions would qualify as "investment contracts" and the nuance of the case law isn't applicable.

However, in some limited circumstances, particularly when dealing with notes, some forms of debt may not actually be considered securities. In *Reves v. Ernst & Young*, the Supreme Court analyzed and consolidated several lower court decisions regarding certain notes that had not been found to meet the definition of a "security." The Court adopted the "family resemblance" test to determine whether a note is a security. Under this test, a note is presumed to be a security, but this presumption is rebutted if the note resembles one of a judicially developed list of exceptions.[4]

Exemptions

As discussed above, any sale of securities in the United States needs to be registered with the SEC or sold pursuant to an exemption from registration. The below exemptions are the most commonly used in the private financings of cannabis companies.

4(a)(2)

This first exemption is the most ubiquitous and ambiguous. Under Section 4(a)(2) of the Securities Act, registration requirements do not apply to "transactions by an issuer not involving a public offering."[5] The idea is to allow companies to raise money in small private placement transactions for a limited number of offerees who do not require the same protections as rank-and-file investors, who would otherwise need extensive financial, business, and other disclosures set forth in an SEC registration statement. Put simply, when an entity issues stock outside of a public offering, the 4(a)(2) exemption applies and the rules for registration are inapplicable. As most sales of securities are not public offerings, 4(a)(2) is the most widely used exemption.

While there is not a set of objective factors that define the scope of a "public offering," a few guiding principles have developed in practice and evolved through case law. The most significant factor in determining whether an offering of securities complies with 4(a)(2) relates to the number of offerees and whether they have any preexisting relationships with the issuer. Generally, the greater number of offerees, and the more tenuous the relationships between the offerees and the issuer, the harder it is to claim the exemption. Another important factor in determining 4(a)(2) compliance is the sophistication and experience of the offerees. Generally, an offeree who has business knowledge and experience, stemming from relevant education or occupation, would sustain challenges to her sophistication for 4(a)(2) purposes.

In a section 4(a)(2) offering, the issuer must also provide adequate disclosure about the basic information regarding the issuer's financial condition, business, and management to allow any investors to make an educated and informed decision about their investment. The issuer should also take reasonable steps to contain the size of the offering, as larger offerings are more likely to fall outside of the 4(a)(2) protections. Overall, however, the key guiding factors in complying with 4(a)(2) relate to the number of offerees, their sophistication, and whether such offerees had a preexisting relationship with the issuer.

Regulation D

Under the rubric of section 4(a)(2), the SEC has promulgated a safe harbor exemption from registration known as Regulation D (Reg D).[6] While 4(a)(2) does not provide objective factors that determine whether a specific offering is compliant, Reg D assures that if an offering meets certain criteria, it is objectively exempt from registration. For this reason, most private placement offerings rely on Reg D as the appropriate exemption to registration.

There are three exemptions under Reg D (note the descriptions below address only the accreditation and disclosure issues discussed in this chapter and ignore issues related to general solicitation and restricted securities).

i   **Rule 504**: Allows for an exemption for the offer and sale of up to $5,000,000 of securities in a single 12-month period.[7] Unlike some other exemptions, Rule 504 allows for a private sale without any specific disclosure requirements (note that anti-fraud provisions of federal securities laws still apply). Sales can generally be made to an unlimited number of accredited or unaccredited investors.

ii **Rule 506(b)**: In a 506(b) offering it is possible to sell to up to 35 non-accredited investors, who must be sophisticated (i.e., "must have sufficient knowledge and experience in financial and business matters to make them capable of evaluating the merits and risks of the prospective investment"). However, any non-accredited investors must receive specific disclosure documents, unlike accredited investors, where the disclosure requirements are not spelled out.[8] As a result of the Rule 506(d) bad actor disqualification, an offering may not rely on Rule 506(b) if the company raising money, or certain executives or major shareholders thereof, have relevant criminal convictions making them a so-called "bad actor."[9] There are no size limits on funds raised under this exemption.

iii **Rule 506(c)**: Unlike a 506(b) offering, certain active steps must be taken in a 506(c) offering to confirm the accredited status of investors. Unlike Rule 504 or 506(b), a 506(c) offering permits general solicitation and advertising.[10] Like Rule 506(b), this exemption may not be available if a "bad actor" is involved, and there are no size limits on funds raised under this exemption.

Accredited Investor Definition and Considerations

The definition of an accredited investor is determined by the SEC. An accredited investor can be an individual or an entity. Currently, an individual can be considered accredited if he or she meets one of the following criteria: net worth of at least $1,000,000 dollars (excluding the value of his or her primary residence) or income of at least $200,000 each year for the last two years (or $300,000 combined income if married), with the expectation to make the same amount for the current year. For an entity, different criteria can apply depending on its form, but generally speaking, an entity will be considered accredited if all of its equity holders are accredited or if it has more than $5,000,000 in assets. Persons or entities not meeting such standards are referred to as unaccredited or non-accredited investors. While this is not an insignificant amount of money, the threshold is not very high – especially when the person in question is considering a substantial monetary investment in an uncertain venture that, even in the best of circumstances, may not make any money for years to come.

In December 2019, the SEC issued a proposed amendment to the definition of accredited investors. Among other things, it would allow more investors to participate in private offerings by adding new categories of natural persons that may qualify as accredited investors based on their professional knowledge, experience, or certifications. The proposal would also expand the list of entities that may qualify as accredited investors. This included allowing any entity that meets an investments test to qualify, including a "catch-all" category for any entity owning in excess of $5,000,000 in investments.[11]

Beyond restrictions on the number of investors discussed above, there are other reasons not to include unaccredited investors in an offering. For one, it is not unusual to give investors the right to invest in future financing rounds – often referred to as a preemptive right. This is fine, provided no investors are unaccredited, but would be an issue for a company that has existing unaccredited investors with the right to invest in future rounds. Suddenly, a future financing round may inadvertently involve unaccredited investors, requiring a company to spend time and money developing fulsome disclosure documents or risk violating securities law. Another concern, while not immediate, is that if the company wants to go public, the SEC may evaluate all prior issuances of stock by the company and require that it take remedial actions to cure any past violations of securities laws, which might delay or imperil the IPO.

While any emerging company would be wise to restrict its offerings to accredited investors, cannabis companies should be especially vigilant. Securities regulators, both on the federal and state levels, have made it clear that they consider the cannabis industry to be an area of special concern, not because of the federal illegality of cannabis, but because of the increased risk of fraud in such a new and dynamic business. The last thing any cannabis company should want to do is take any action that could expose them to the ire of regulators.

It is also worth mentioning that the underlying policy arguments for restricting offerings (in the absence of fulsome disclosures) to accredited investors become even stronger in the cannabis industry. The risk of failure, and the total loss of investment, is undoubtedly present in an industry that remains federally illegal and operates based on guidelines that could change at any moment. Investing in a cannabis company requires an even higher level of sophistication than a typical deal because of the challenges involved. A company should not accept money from investors who cannot handle the risk of losing their entire investment. Admittedly, this is unfair to the prospective investor, and burned investors placed in a financially precarious situation increase the risk of damaging litigation.

State Law Considerations

Securities laws exist federally, and at the level of each state and territory. These laws are often referred to as "blue sky" laws. The term "blue sky" allegedly comes from the words of Kansas Bank Commissioner J.N. Dolley in 1920, who sought to protect the public from schemes without any more basis than "so many feet of blue sky." While memorable, this quote may be fictional.[12]

State securities laws often predate their federal analogues, which emerged to combat serious abuses in the securities markets. Blue-sky laws vary by state, and compliance can be challenging due to the patchwork nature of the requirements. The varied nature of the state laws can create issues and raise the costs of regulatory compliance associated with raising capital. The National Securities Markets Improvement Act of 1996 (NSMIA) attempted to address the challenges of complying with blue-sky laws by amending Section 18 of the Securities Act to create a category of securities known as "covered securities," which are exempt from state registration and qualification requirements. However, states are still permitted to require a general notice filing and a fee. In most cases, this consists of a copy of the Form D filed with the SEC (discussed below) and a form U-2 (a consent to service of process). State securities regulators also maintain their authority to investigate suspected fraud and unlawful conduct.

The definition of a covered security includes securities issued pursuant to several registration exemptions, including Rule 506(b) and (c), which are the most common exemptions for large private financings. The following chart, derived from the SEC website, shows which exemptions discussed in this chapter qualify for covered security status.

Securities Act Exemption[13]	Is the offering potentially subject to blue-sky laws?
Section 4(a)(2)	Yes
Rule 506(b) [Reg D exemption]	No
Rule 506(c) [Reg D exemption]	No
Rule 504 [Reg D exemption]	Yes

While the Reg D associated state notice and filing fees are generally straightforward, there are some states that have complexities worth mentioning. New York has a difficult system to follow, requiring pre-filing (per Form 99) to comply with Article 23-A of the General Business Law, known as the Martin Act. Many authorities, including the New York State Bar Association (NYSBA), believe the Martin Act is preempted by NSMIA, as it goes beyond a mere notice filing and fee. The NYSBA has been vocal about this point of view and has published a position paper setting forth its arguments.[14] This position, however, has never been tested in court and the New York Attorney General's office declined to amend its filing requirements in response to the position paper. And, under the Martin Act, while there is no private right of action, New York's Attorney General does have wide authority to conduct investigations and even to criminally indict persons for securities violations. Nevertheless, many issuers partially rely on the NYSBA position paper and file the

Form 99 on the federal 15-day post-sale filing schedule, or even omit the Form 99 filing entirely.

Form D Filings

Since the most frequently used exemptions are subject to the requirements of Reg D, it is important to understand what filings are associated with a Reg D offering. Rule 503(a) of Reg D requires an issuer to file a Form D notice with the SEC within 15 days of the first sale of securities. Under federal law, the Form D filing is not a condition to the availability of Rule 504 or 506 for an offering, though the SEC could prohibit issuers from relying on Reg D in the future for past failures to file a Form D.[15] However, it is effectively impossible to comply with the state notice filing requirements if an issuer fails to make a Form D filing, as many states require a copy of Form D to be filed with the state. As a result, some state regulators may view the failure to file a Form D as a nullification of the "covered security" status under NSMIA for which state registration and qualification requirements are preempted. This means that the securities issued pursuant to the offering may be viewed as having ignored blue-sky laws and could create rights of rescission and expose the issuer to sanction.

While it may seem unlikely that a regulator with limited resources and time would become aware of a private financing that is not publicly disclosed, many offerings that turn into regulatory issues come to light because an upset investor reports the issuer to a state securities regulator. The issuer is then put in the difficult position of explaining its noncompliance to the authorities.

A Form D filing can result in unwelcome scrutiny, being a public document that releases sensitive information, which journalists can track and report on. Form D requires the disclosure of the names of its directors and executive officers, the total amount being raised, and the amount sold as of the date of filing (which can be especially sensitive if the raise is off to a slow start). For this reason, some issuers consider relying on 4(a)(2), which is the broad exemption based on the absence of a public offering that lacks the certainty of a specific safe harbor like Reg D. However, this exemption would not provide the "covered security" status of the NSMIA and means that blue-sky laws would have to be analyzed in all applicable states.

Risks of Non-compliance

Cannabis Specific Risks

The sale of securities associated with a cannabis company is subject to the same legal requirements as those of a company in any other industry.

As is the case with many aspects of the cannabis industry, compliance with these rules may be more important due to heightened regulatory scrutiny. For example, the SEC has a message on its website warning investors of fraud risks in the cannabis industry.[16] The Colorado Division of Securities has also issued a very similar warning.[17] Regulators in several different states, including Hawaii and Massachusetts, have followed up on cannabis financings and, in some cases, have issued subpoenas to gather additional information. Cannabis companies should certainly be on the alert for additional regulatory scrutiny and should make sure their offerings are as compliant as possible.

General Risks

Federal Law

Violations of federal securities law can be prosecuted criminally by the SEC. The SEC is also empowered under the Securities Act and Exchange Act to issue orders to cease and desist, bar individuals from the securities industry, and seek civil penalties (though not on behalf of individual investors). Individuals may also bring civil actions under several provisions of the Securities Act, summarized below:

- **Section 11 of the Securities Act** creates a civil claim for investors against issuers, their affiliates, underwriters and officers for misstatements and omissions in an issuer's registration statements, and can be used as recourse for civil liability in primary and secondary offerings.[18]
- **Section 12(a)(1) of the Securities Act** creates a civil cause of action for purchasers of securities against issuers in violation of Section 5 and its requirements that all non-exempt sales of securities be registered with the SEC.[19]
- **Section 12(a)(2) of the Securities Act** creates a cause of action similar to that of **Section 11** against issuers for material misstatements or omissions, but expands the reach of such liability beyond the registration statement filed with the SEC and includes any prospectus or other communication made as part of the sale of securities to the respective purchaser.[20]
- **Section 15 of the Securities Act** makes "control persons" – generally speaking, large shareholders, officers, directors, or others with the right to control the decision making of the issuer – jointly and severally liable with the issuer under Section 11 or 12 liability claims.[21]
- **Section 10(b) of the Exchange Act and Rule 10b-5:** which prohibit making untrue statements or omissions of material facts in connection with the purchase or sale of any security.[22]

- **Section 18 of the Exchange Act** sets forth the primary cause of action arising out of fraud in securities offerings and stretches out to any "instrumentality of interstate commerce" and covers the prohibition on any deceptive or fraudulent practices, including material misstatements or omissions.[23]
- **Section 20 of the Exchange Act** extends to "control persons" joint and several liability with direct violators and abettors of Exchange Act provisions, including, without limitation, Section 10(b)(5).[24]

Finally, in addition to the risks of criminal charges and civil litigation, there are also issues related to IPOs and exits. If a company engages in an IPO, it needs to file a Form S-1 with the SEC. The S-1 requires disclosure of all securities sold in the preceding three years and details about the exemption(s) relied upon by the issuer. Since S-1s may be closely scrutinized by the SEC and the investing public, securities law violations may get unwelcome attention. And in an acquisition scenario, a purchaser may also be interested in past securities violations – either due to near-term plans to go public or fear of inheriting securities-related liabilities. Securities issuance liabilities regulatory issues can arise long after the initial sale.

State Law

In addition to federal law causes of action, investors may also have causes of action against issuers under state law. These state law claims tend to mirror the exposure under federal law. First, as mentioned above, failure to follow blue-sky laws may mean securities were issued without registration and not pursuant to an exemption. This could expose issuers to liabilities under applicable state-level securities laws. Second, civil liability may also exist at the state level if untrue statements of material fact or omissions have occurred. For example, the relevant law in Massachusetts extends civil liability to "[a]ny person who ... offers or sells a security by means of any untrue statement of a material fact or any omission to state a material fact necessary in order to make the statements made, in light of the circumstances under which they are made, not misleading."[25] Finally, for serious violations, state regulators may have the ability to bring criminal charges.

Disclosures and Cannabis

The other area where cannabis-specific concerns come into play is disclosures made in connection with the sale of a security. As discussed above, in a private offering, the SEC or any other regulatory agency does not review disclosure documents in advance. The concern for issuers, however, is that, if disclosures are inadequate, wrong, or misleading, investors could bring suit based on the material misstatement or omission of a material fact. That's why a thorough description of the applicable federal, state, and local laws and regulations can be so important in a cannabis private placement.

Even a potentially minor state or local regulation could derail a cannabis business, which would then rise to a level of materiality. Because of this, investors need to be aware of the regulatory environment to protect an issuer from litigation. The misstatement by a cannabis issuer in an offering document or an investor deck as to when a certain license could be obtained would be fodder for significant shareholder action if the license could not be obtained by such date (assuming the investor can make a strong case that such an expectation was part of the investor's decision, and if the investment subsequently resulted in a loss of value for the investor).

Notes

1 Securities Act of 1933 § 5, 15 U.S.C. § 77e (2018).
2 *Id.* § 77b(a)(1).
3 *SEC v. W. J. Howey Co.*, 328 U.S. 293, 298–99 (1946).
4 *Reves v. Ernst & Young*, 494 U.S. 56, 63–67 (1990).
5 Securities Act of 1933 § 4(a)(2), 15 U.S.C. § 77d(a)(2) (2018).
6 Regulation D – Rules Governing the Limited Offer and Sale of Securities Without Registration Under the Securities Act of 1933, 17 C.F.R. § 230.500 (2019).
7 *Id.* § 230.504. (Prior to adoption of new rules on October 26, 2016, the aggregate amount of securities that could be sold pursuant to Rule 504 was $1,000,000. The same rules change also eliminated Rule 505.)
8 "Investor Bulletin: Private Placements under Regulation D," U.S. Sec. & Exch. Comm'n, Sept. 24, 2014, https://www.sec.gov/oiea/investor-alerts-bulletins/ib_privateplacements.html.
9 Securities Act, § 230.506(d); "Disqualification of Felons and Other "Bad Actors" from Rule 506 Offerings and Related Disclosure Requirements," U.S. Sec. & Exch. Comm'n, Sept. 19, 2013, https://www.sec.gov/info/smallbus/secg/bad-actor-small-entity-compliance-guide.htm
10 "Investor Alert: Advertising for Unregistered Securities Offerings," U.S. Sec. & Exch. Comm'n, Sept. 23, 2013, https://www.investor.gov/introduction-investing/general-resources/news-alerts/alerts-bulletins/investor-alerts/investor-50.
11 Amending the "Accredited Investor" Definition, 85 Fed. Reg. 2574 (Jan. 15, 2020) (to be codified at 17 CFR 230, 240).
12 Jonathan R. Macey and Geoffrey P. Miller, "Origin of the Blue Sky Laws," 70 *Tex. L. Rev.* 347, 359–60 at n. 59 (1991); Lawrence R. Gelber, "The Gelber Law Glossary," Gelber Law, http://www.gelberlaw.net/Glossary.html#B.
13 Chart derived from data at the SEC webpage, "Frequently Asked Questions about Exempt Offerings," U.S. Sec. & Exch. Comm'n, https://www.sec.gov/smallbusiness/exemptofferings/faq.
14 Committee on Securities Regulation of the New York State Bar Association, "Private Offering Exemptions and Exclusions under the New York State Martin Act and Section 18 of the Securities Act of 1933," 6-2 *N.Y. Bus. L. J.* 10 (2002).

15 "Securities Act Rules," U.S. Sec. & Exch. Comm'n, Nov. 6, 2017, https://www.sec.gov/divisions/corpfin/guidance/securitiesactrules-interps.htm (explaining SEC Compliance and Disclosure Interpretations (C&DI) of sections 257.07 and 257.08).
16 "Investor Alert: Marijuana-Related Investments," U.S. Sec. & Exch. Comm'n, May 16, 2014, https://www.sec.gov/oiea/investor-alerts-bulletins/ia_marijuana.html.
17 "Marijuana-Related Investments: Greener Pastures or Just another Scam?," Colorado Dep't of Reg. Agencies, Oct., 2018, https://drive.google.com/file/d/1YG351VvPETpM_O5mHT6vSPEhw9XCShE5/view.
18 Securities Act of 1933 § 11, 15 U.S.C. § 77k (2018).
19 *Id.* § 77l(a)(1).
20 *Id.* § 77l(a)(2).
21 *Id.* § 77o.
22 *Id.* § 78j.
23 Securities Exchange Act of 1934 § 18, 15 U.S.C. § 78r.
24 *Id.* § 78t.
25 Massachusetts Uniform Securities Act, Mass. Gen. Laws Tit. XV, ch. 110A, § 410(a)(2) (2019).

12 Introduction to Cannabis and Banking

Sahar Ayinehsazian and Charles S. Alovisetti

Introduction

Duffle bags of pungent smelling cash and tellers armed with copious amounts of Febreze – this is the quintessential image of the early days of cannabis banking following the release of the FinCEN guidance by the FinCEN on February 14, 2014. While nearly seven years later, the FinCEN guidance's seven short pages remain the cornerstone of cannabis banking, which, for the purposes of this chapter refers to a cannabis-related business's ability to transparently access depository services, financial institutions' treatment of cannabis money has greatly evolved. This evolution is apparent in both the sophistication of various bank and credit unions' cannabis "Know Your Customer" due diligence programs and the steadily growing number of financial institutions that are safely and successfully servicing state-legal cannabis businesses, as reported by FinCEN.[1] Nonetheless, despite sweeping national support for federal legalization, and continued state-by-state legalization of the cannabis industry, regular access to banking services remains an obstacle for state-legal cannabis-related businesses, largely because of cannabis' federal status as a Schedule I substance under the CSA.

Federal Policy

The FinCEN Guidance and the Sessions Memo

On February 14, 2014, Deputy Attorney General James M. Cole released what is known as the 2014 Cole Memo. This memo, which coincided with the release of the FinCEN guidance, extended the discretionary protections and enforcement priorities in the earlier Cole memos to financial institutions servicing the cannabis industry.

The 2014 Cole Memo is one of the memos rescinded by Attorney General Jefferson Sessions in his January 4, 2018 letter.[2] To date, Attorney General Sessions' rescission of the Cole Memo has not affected the status of the FinCEN guidance, and the Department of the Treasury has given no indication that it intends to rescind the FinCEN guidance. Though it was originally intended that the Cole Memo and the FinCEN guidance would work in tandem, the FinCEN guidance is a stand-alone document which explicitly lists the eight enforcement priorities cited in the Cole Memo. Consequently, any authority the FinCEN guidance has remains intact.

The FinCEN guidance details the due diligence procedures financial institutions should undertake in onboarding and maintaining cannabis-related clients to ensure that those businesses are compliant with applicable state law. Since the release of the FinCEN guidance, various states like California, New York, and Washington have created their own guidelines for cannabis-related banking services.[3] Likewise, numerous state governors and regulators continue to call on the federal government to facilitate the cannabis industry's access to banking services.[4]

While the rescission of the Cole Memo had an initial chilling effect on cannabis banking, it is unlikely that access to banking will cease altogether, as this is neither in the interest of financial institutions servicing the industry nor FinCEN. In order to best position themselves to obtain or maintain bank accounts, cannabis-related businesses should focus heavily on transparency and compliance. Specifically, cannabis-related businesses should ensure they properly maintain all required licenses and only deposit money into their business banks' accounts that can be traced back to either (1) a legitimate investment in the business or (2) the state-legal sale of cannabis. Finally, cannabis businesses should ensure that they can prove that they are fully complying with all applicable state and local laws.

The SAFE Act

On September 25, 2019, the House of Representatives passed H.R. 1595, known as the SAFE Banking Act ("SAFE Act"). The SAFE Act, which had been proposed unsuccessfully in numerous prior sessions of Congress, seeks to create protections for depository institutions that provide financial services to state-legal cannabis-related businesses.

The SAFE Act generally prohibits a federal banking regulator from penalizing a depository institution for providing banking services to a legitimate cannabis-related business. Specifically, the bill prohibits a federal banking regulator from (1) terminating or limiting the deposit insurance or share insurance of a depository institution solely because the institution provides financial services to a legitimate cannabis-related business; (2) prohibiting or otherwise discouraging a depository institution from offering financial services to such a business; (3) recommending, incentivizing, or encouraging a depository institution not to offer financial services to an account holder solely because the account holder is affiliated with such a business; (4) taking any adverse or corrective supervisory action on a loan made to a person solely because the person either owns such a business or owns real estate or equipment leased or sold to such a business; or (5) penalizing a depository institution for engaging in a financial service for such a business.

As specified by the SAFE Act, a depository institution or a Federal Reserve bank shall not, under federal law, be liable or subject to forfeiture for providing a loan or other financial services to a legitimate cannabis-related business.[5]

Although the SAFE Act made history by passing the House of Representatives, its fate in the Senate remains to be seen as this book goes to press. This uncertain fate became even more precarious on December 18, 2019, when Senate Banking Committee Chairman Mike Crapo outlined his concerns regarding the SAFE Act and suggested provisions that would make the legislation unworkable.[6]

Nonetheless, the unprecedented bipartisan support for the SAFE Act is a testament to the growing support for cannabis banking at the federal level, which signals a green light to financial institutions considering serving the cannabis industry.

As of May 12, 2020, the SAFE Act language was included in the House version of an additional Coronavirus relief package called the "Health and Economic Recovery Omnibus Emergency Solutions Act" ("HEROES Act").[7] As it currently stands, the SAFE Act language in the HEROES Act is largely, if not entirely, the same as the version that passed the House on September 25, 2019. The ultimate fate of the SAFE Act is uncertain. Once the full House passes this bill, it will be up to the Senate to acquiesce to the language — and there are questions about how much of an appetite the Senate has for passing the entire bill, putting aside the cannabis portion.[8]

Challenges and Solutions

The cannabis industry's limited access to banking services is largely the result of financial institutions' fears of the loss of their insurance or account with the Federal Reserve, increased due diligence costs, and reputational risks. However, as discussed below, these concerns have not created issues for the banks and credit unions that have chosen to provide services to state-legal cannabis businesses.

Insurance

The Federal Deposit Insurance Corporation ("FDIC") and the National Credit Union Association ("NCUA") have not been as vocal about cannabis banking as FinCEN. Nonetheless, both have long been aware of the FinCEN guidance and have shared the guidelines with their examiners and instructed them on how to determine whether financial institutions servicing cannabis businesses are complying with the FinCEN guidance, as evinced by the 2014 letters from the FDIC and NCUA to the Washington State Department of Financial Services.[9]

It should further be noted that no financial institution has ever lost its FDIC or NCUA insurance as a result of providing banking services to state-legal cannabis-related businesses in accordance with the FinCEN guidance.

Federal Reserve Account

Another cause for hesitation by financial institutions considering offering services to cannabis-related businesses is their concern regarding losing their account with the Federal Reserve. Like the FDIC and NCUA, the Federal Reserve has not provided much public comment on the issue. However, the Federal Reserve has previously communicated that it too has incorporated the FinCEN guidance into its examination materials.[10] To date, no financial institution has lost its account with the Federal Reserve as a result of providing banking services to state-legal cannabis-related businesses in accordance with the FinCEN guidance.

Increased Diligence Requirements

Financial institutions must perform due diligence on cannabis-related businesses both while onboarding the business and for the duration of the time such a business remains a client. While the details of onboarding and ongoing due diligence depend on each individual financial institution, all such diligence must adhere closely to the FinCEN guidance. As such, onboarding due diligence may be as simple as reviewing a cannabis business's licenses and corporate documents, or as intensive as going through such a business's license applications and enforcement violations in detail.

Financial institutions are required by the BSA to file a SAR for any business they believe willfully disguises activities or violates federal law. Since the cultivation, processing, and sale of cannabis for any reason remain illegal under federal law, banks must continue to file SARs when working with cannabis-related businesses, despite the fact that state laws regulate such activity.

The FinCEN Memo breaks SAR reporting for cannabis-related businesses into three groups based on risk level. The first type of SAR, called "MARIJUANA LIMITED," is to be filed for businesses a financial institution believes do not violate any of the federal government's eight priorities. In this case the SAR will be limited to identity and address information about the business. The filing institution is obligated to file the SAR solely because the subject is engaged in a cannabis-related business (and because no additional suspicious activity has been identified).

The second type of SAR, called "MARIJUANA PRIORITY," is to be filed for cannabis-related businesses a financial institution believes may be violating one or more of the federal enforcement priorities. In this case, the SAR must include, along with identifying and address information, comprehensive details on the enforcement priorities the financial institution believes have been violated and the dates, amounts, and any other details relevant to the suspicious activity.

The final type of SAR, known as "MARIJUANA TERMINATION," is to be filed for cannabis- related businesses with which a financial institution terminates their relationship due to continued violations of federal enforcement priorities, or other issues preventing the financial institution from maintaining an effective anti-money laundering compliance program. When this occurs, FinCEN urges the financial institution to share information about the business with other banks. These reports need not be filed if a financial institution terminates the relationship for unrelated reasons.

Additionally, the FinCEN guidance requires financial institutions to continuously monitor their cannabis-related clients for any of the "red flags" listed in the guidance. Unsurprisingly, such heightened due diligence can increase a bank's internal costs. To combat this issue, several third parties have developed compliance software or other products for financial institutions that service the state-legal cannabis industry. These products help financial institutions to navigate the regulatory compliance demands of servicing the cannabis industry and provide tools and resources for due diligence.

Reputational Risks

Because of the stigma previously attached to cannabis, many financial institutions have been wary of working with cannabis businesses for fear of driving away their non-cannabis clients. However, as cannabis legalization gains greater national support, the reputational risks of banking for the cannabis industry continue to diminish. According to a recent study, financial institutions will likely strengthen their reputation and attract new customers by servicing cannabis businesses.[11] In fact, the majority of those surveyed indicated servicing big box stores like Walmart, the adult entertainment industry, and pharmaceutical, oil, and tobacco companies would reflect far more poorly on a financial institution than servicing state-legal cannabis businesses. And, as discussed in Chapter 1, in addition to the practical risks listed above, financial institutions that work with the cannabis industry are theoretically at risk for criminal or civil sanction as a result of the broad scope of drug laws in the United States.

Merchant Processing

While an entire chapter could be dedicated to merchant processing or lack thereof in the cannabis industry, any discussion of cannabis banking would be incomplete without at least a mention of the topic. Although cannabis banking continues to progress, merchant processing, or, simply put, the ability to pay for cannabis products with credit or debit card, remains largely impossible for cannabis businesses. This is due first and foremost to the fact that there is no Merchant Category Code ("MCC") for cannabis goods or services. An MCC is used to classify a business by the types of goods or services it provides – without an MCC, a business cannot process credit or debit card payments. Additionally, the major credit card networks continue to insist that cannabis-related transactions may not take place on their networks. Finally, financial institutions in the United States have almost unanimously refused to serve as the processing bank or the acquiring bank for merchants processing cannabis-related transactions.

While many companies have attempted to enable cannabis-related merchant processing, these attempts have been short lived, at best, and resulted in massive losses for users, at worst.[12]

Hemp Banking

Guidance released on December 3, 2019 by a range of U.S. regulatory bodies specified that

> [b]ecause hemp is no longer a Schedule I controlled substance under the Controlled Substances Act, [financial institutions] are not required to file a [SAR] on customers solely because they are engaged in the growth or cultivation of hemp, in accordance with applicable laws and regulations. For hemp-related customers, banks are expected to follow standard SAR Procedures and file a SAR if indicia of suspicious activity warrants.[13]

Financial institutions serving hemp-operators, therefore, will no longer have to comply with FinCEN's cannabis-specific SAR filing requirements, thereby saving the institutions a great deal of time and effort.

Although the guidance eased the SAR requirements applicable to hemp operators, it did stipulate that banks serving the hemp industry "must have a [Bank Secrecy Act/Anti Money Laundering] compliance program commensurate with the level of complexity involved."[14] Additionally,

> [w]hen deciding to serve hemp-related businesses, banks must comply with applicable regulatory requirements for customer identification, suspicious activity reporting, currency transaction reporting and risk-based customer due diligence, including the collection of beneficial ownership information for legal entity customers.[15]

Conclusion

Although cannabis-related businesses still face challenges in accessing banking services, their ability to bank continues to improve. As more financial institutions shed their fears in light of the realization that federal banking regulators do not condemn cannabis banking, cannabis-related businesses are increasingly able to operate much like other "normal" businesses.

Notes

1 According to FinCEN's 2Q2019 Marijuana Banking Update there were 713 depository institutions actively banking cannabis businesses throughout the U.S. as of June 30, 2019. https://www.fincen.gov/sites/default/files/shared/291404_1st_Q_FY2020_Marijuana_Banking_Update_Public.pdf.
2 "Marijuana Enforcement," U.S. Dep't. of Justice, Office of the Attorney General, Jan. 4, 2018, https://www.justice.gov/opa/press-release/file/1022196/download.
3 "Cannabis Banking Guidance," Cal. Dep't. of Business Oversight, Oct. 2, 2019, https://dbo.ca.gov/wp-content/uploads/sites/296/2019/10/FINAL-DBO-Cannabis-Banking-Guidance-Memo.pdf; "Guidance on Provision of Financial Services to Medical Marijuana & Industrial Hemp-Related Businesses in New York State," N.Y. Dep't of Financial Services, July 3, 2018, https://www.dfs.ny.gov/system/files/documents/2020/03/il180703.pdf; "Marijuana in Washington State - Financial Services Issues," Wash. Dep't of Financial Inst., https://dfi.wa.gov/banks/marijuana; "Examination Procedures for Credit Unions with Member Accounts in the I502 Marijuana Business (LCB-licensed marijuana businesses) 2016 Update: Medical Marijuana Endorsements," DFI, May 20, 2016, https://dfi.wa.gov/documents/credit-unions/marijuana-exam-procedures.pdf.
4 "Letter to Congressional Leaders," DFI, June 13, 2019, https://dfi.wa.gov/sites/default/files/06-13-19-letter.pdf; "Marijuana and Banking Resources," Penn. Dep't of Banking Securities, https://www.dobs.pa.gov/Businesses/Pages/Marijuana-and-Banking-Resources.aspx (last visited May 14, 2020).
5 H.R.1595 –Secure And Fair Enforcement Banking Act of 2019, Congress.gov, https://www.congress.gov/bill/116th-congress/house-bill/1595?q=%7B%22search%22%3A%5B%22SAFE+Banking+Act%22%5D%7D (last visited May 14, 2020).
6 "Chairman Crapo Outlines Concerns with Cannabis Banking Legislation," U.S. Senate Committee on Banking, Housing, and Urban Affairs, Dec. 19, 2018, https://www.banking.senate.gov/newsroom/majority/chairman-crapo-outlines-concerns-with-cannabis-banking-legislation.
7 "Health and Economic Recovery Omnibus Emergency Solutions Act," U.S. House of Representatives, May 12, 2020, https://docs.house.gov/billsthisweek/20200511/BILLS-116hr6800ih.pdf.
8 Kyle Jaeger, "Marijuana Banking Access Included in House Leadership's Coronavirus Relief Bill," *Marijuana Moment*, May 12, 2020, https://www.marijuanamoment.net/marijuana-banking-access-included-in-house-leaderships-coronavirus-relief-bill/.
9 "Letter to Mr. Scott Jarvis," Nat. Credit Union Admin., July 18, 2014, https://dfi.wa.gov/documents/banks/ncua-marijuana-letter.pdf; "Letter to Mr. Scott Jarvis," Fed. Deposit Insurance Corp., June 27, 2014, https://dfi.wa.gov/documents/banks/fdic-bsa-letter.pdf.
10 "Letter to Governor Jay Inslee," Board of Governors of the Federal Reserve System, Aug. 13, 2014, https://dfi.wa.gov/documents/banks/gov-inslee-interagency-response.pdf.

11 http://dhmresearch.com/wp-content/uploads/2016/12/DHM-Research-LTPR-Marijuana-Banking-White-Paper-December-2016.pdf.

12 Complaint, First Data Merchant Services LLC v. MM Development Co., No. 1:19-cv-10964-PKC (S.D.N.Y 2019); In the Matter of Linx Card, Inc., No. MT-18-0050 (Or. Dep't of Consumer Affairs and Business Serv., Div. Financial Reg. May 7, 2019).

13 "Agencies Clarify Requirements for Providing Financial Services to Hemp-Related Businesses," Board of Governors of the Federal Reserve System, Federal Deposit Insurance Corporation, Financial Crimes Enforcement Network, Office of the Comptroller of the Currency, and Conference of State Bank Supervisors, Dec. 2, 2019, https://www.federalreserve.gov/newsevents/pressreleases/bcreg20191203a.htm.

14 *Id.*

15 *Id.*

13 Introduction to Cannabis and Insurance

Charles S. Alovisetti

Introduction

Insurance, at its core, is a contractual transfer of risk. Individuals or companies who can't afford to take certain risks (e.g., they would be financially ruined by their house burning down) effectively pool these risks with other people by obtaining an insurance policy. An insurance underwriter will value the risk by using actuarial history and charge a price based on its estimation of the risk. By underwriting many policies, and taking on multiple risks, an insurer is able to leverage statistics to make sure that, overall, it will come out ahead, even if some of the risks come to pass. As discussed below, the absence of this history poses a challenge for insuring the cannabis industry.

Risks Faced by Cannabis Companies

Cannabis companies face many of the same risks faced by businesses in other industries, in addition to risks unique to the industry. Like other industries, cannabis businesses need to deal with a wide array of risks: product liability claims, theft, fire, natural disasters, economic downturns, changes in regulations, employment-related litigation claims, loss of product, shareholder claims against directors and officers, malpractice suits, and many other hazards. In addition to these risks, cannabis companies face unique threats: federal enforcement, product liability issues in a new industry (the vaping crisis for example), high risk of employee theft (some experts claim around 90% of financial and product loss is due to employee theft), hostile regulators, rapidly changing regulations, difficultly accessing banking services, difficulty accessing lines of credit, and others.[1] To add to the challenges of cannabis companies, one of the critical methods businesses have used for risk management – insurance – is expensive, difficult to obtain and, in many cases, simply unavailable.

Regulation of Insurance

Regulation of Insurance

The insurance industry is generally regulated at the state level, and pursuant to federal law, the McCarran-Ferguson Act, the insurance industry is largely exempt from federal regulation.[2] State-level regulation divides insurers into two main buckets:

- **Admitted Insurer or Licensed Insurer**: An insurance carrier that is regulated by a state Department of Insurance (or similar regulatory body). The regulator will monitor the financial condition and conduct of the insurers and will also regulate the insurer's policy forms (i.e., the content of their policies) or rates, or both. These insurers contribute to a state fund, called a guaranty fund, that can pay claims if the licensed insurers fail.
- **Surplus Line Insurers or Non-Admitted Insurers**: These are insurance carriers who are subject to different regulations from those that cover admitted or standard carriers and are often free from the form or rate regulations imposed on admitted insurers. Since they are not strictly regulated by the state where the insurance is, surplus line insurers are required to obtain a special surplus line license and are regulated in the state or country where they are domiciled. If a surplus line insurer were to fail, there is no guaranty fund to protect the insured.

State Cannabis Regulations and Insurance

When evaluating insurance policies, it's important to consult the cannabis and hemp regulations in each jurisdiction of operation. Despite the challenges of obtaining insurance, some state regulatory regimes mandate obtaining certain policies. For example, in Colorado, a cannabis product manufacturer must obtain products liability insurance prior to selling certain high-risk products such as nasal sprays or rectally administrated products. A certificate of product liability insurance needs to be provided to the regulators. Thankfully for producers, there are no requirements as to policy limits. In California, regulators had proposed a requirement in draft regulations that cannabis businesses carry insurance provided by a carrier "authorized to do business in California by the Secretary of State."[3] Commentators at the time noted that this requirement would have been challenging to comply with as admitted carriers were not providing insurance policies for cannabis companies in California at the time, and this draft regulation did not make it into the final rules.

Contract Law and Public Policy

Since insurance is contractual, most disputes boil down to a court's interpretation of a contract. However, insurance law is not purely a matter of contractual interpretation, and public policy considerations do arise. One of the central principals in insurance law is that ambiguity in an insurance policy must be construed in favor the policyholder (since the insurer will have been the drafter and ambiguity is typically construed against the drafter). A corollary to this is the principal that the insuring provisions of a policy are construed liberally and the exclusions narrowly.

These principals arise in the cannabis context when there is a dispute as to whether the exclusions (e.g., contraband) preclude recovery for a company. Finally, courts have developed a tort of "bad faith" in response to insurers denying coverage and taking advantage of policyholders in the event of a loss or claim.[4]

There have been a number of cases that have tested the question of whether cannabis operations were uninsurable because of public policy against insuring illegal actions and whether an insurance company, having written a policy for a company they knew was in the cannabis industry, could then deny coverage based on federal illegality. In *Tracy v. USAA Casualty Insurance*, a case from 2012, an individual cannabis grower made a claim under her homeowners' policy when her plants were stolen. The policy covered loss caused by theft of "trees, shrubs, plants or lawns, on the residence premises."[5] She was denied coverage and sued. The court, applying Hawaiian substantive law, held that requiring the insurer to provide coverage would be contrary to federal law (as reflected in the CSA and *Gonzales v. Raich*) and public policy.[6] For the non-lawyers, and the lawyers who haven't thought about civil procedure since law school, note that this case was in federal court due to diversity (i.e., the amount in dispute was over $75,000 and the parties were from different states) and, therefore, the court applied the substantive law of Hawai'i and federal procedural law.[7] This matters because a number of key cannabis states, including California, Oregon, Nevada, Massachusetts, and Colorado, have statutes that explicitly make cannabis contracts enforceable. That doesn't completely resolve the issue, however. First, each of these statutes only makes contracts related to cannabis operations authorized by the state in question enforceable (as covered in Chapter 17). If an insurance claim involved operations across several jurisdictions, an argument could be made that the statute did not apply, since it would only cover activity authorized by the state in question. Second, it may still be a federal court ruling on a contract regarding a federally illegal activity, so some degree of uncertainty is still present.

A subsequent case in Colorado, also in federal court, came to a very different conclusion in 2016. In *Green Earth v. Atain*, a business operating a retain and grow facility sustained a loss due to smoke and ash from a nearby wildfire entering its grow facility and damaging plants. Green Earth made a claim under its policy for damage to its cannabis plants.[8] Atain, the insurance company, denied the claim on several grounds. Green Earth then sued alleging breach of contract, bad faith breach of insurance contract, and unreasonable delay. The insurer rejected the allegations, claiming the living plants were not covered as they fell within the "growing crops" exclusion of the policy. Atain also argued that harvested cannabis was within the "contraband" exclusion and that the policy was void on public policy grounds since cannabis is federally illegal. The court found for Atain on the "growing crops" exclusion issue, but rejected the "contraband" exclusion argument and the argument that the policy itself was unenforceable due to public policy concerns. On the contraband argument, the court looked not just at the federal black letter law, but also the federal policy of non-enforcement. The court noted there had been an "erosion of any clear and consistent federal public policy in this area." This policy of non-enforcement, combined with the fact the insurer was clearly aware of the nature of Green Earth's business at the time the policy was written, lead to the court to award damages to Green Earth for the value of the harvested cannabis.

Types of Insurance

There are a wide number of specialized insurance coverages available and parties typically purchase several policies to protect themselves from losses. These policies are generally divided into two forms: third-party insurance, which provides liability coverage when the insured injures another person (e.g., the portion of auto insurance that covers another person's expenses in an accident), and first-party insurance, which provides coverage to an insured who suffers injury (e.g., the portion of auto insurance that covers damage to an insured's car).

Below are some types of policies applicable to cannabis businesses:

- **Commercial General Liability (CGL) Insurance**: A broad type of insurance policy that provides liability insurance for general business risks.
- **Cyber Insurance**: Covers internet-based risks, such as data breaches, that are often excluded from commercial general liability insurance.
- **Directors and Officers Liability ("D&O") Insurance**: Insurance payable to the directors and officers of a company, or to the organization(s) itself, for losses or advancement of defense costs in the event an insured suffers such a loss as a result of a legal action brought for alleged wrongful acts in their capacity as directors and officers. D&O insurance can be prohibitively expensive for public cannabis companies.
- **Employment Practices Liability Insurance (EPLI)**: Liability insurance covering wrongful acts arising from the employment process. Example claims include: wrongful termination, discrimination, sexual harassment, and retaliation. As a general rule, such insurance covers only negligence, not intentional acts.

(Continued)

- **Errors and Omissions Insurance (E&O)**: A type of professional liability insurance that protects companies, their workers, and other professionals against claims of poor work or negligent actions.
- **Excess and Umbrella Insurance**: Both are designed to be additional layers of coverage above primary insurance policies. They are similar but not the same. Umbrella policies not only offer high liability limits, but can also broaden coverage for things not covered by the underlying policy. Excess liability policies provide coverage above the limits of the underlying coverage and do not offer broader protection than the underlying policy (and can sometimes be more restrictive).
- **Federal Crop Insurance**: The federal crop insurance program provides subsidized crop insurance policies for farmers. These policies are generally either yield-based (i.e., if there is a smaller harvest than normal) or revenue-based (protection against crop revenue loss from declines in yield, price, or both).[9] Premiums are paid in part (63% on average in 2017) by the Federal Crop Insurance Corporation as part of the federal government's support for the agricultural industry.[10]
- **Products Liability Insurance**: A form of general liability insurance covering damages arising from the use of a company's goods or products to property or people.
- **Property & Casualty (Home, Auto, Renter's) (P&C) Insurance**: An umbrella term including many forms of insurance, including auto insurance and homeowner's insurance. Typically covers belongings and another person's expenses in the aftermath of an accident.
- **Reinsurance**: Can also be called insurance for insurers or stop-loss insurance. Reinsurance is where an issuer spreads the risk of its portfolio to other parties to reduce the odds of paying a large obligation. The entity that accepts a portion of the potential obligation is known as the reinsurer. It has proved difficult obtaining reinsurance in the cannabis industry, which has impacted the availability of insurance.
- **Representations and Warranties Insurance**: An insurance policy used in mergers and acquisitions to protect against losses arising due to the seller's breach of certain of its representations in the acquisition agreement. Limited availability in the U.S. cannabis market and often at a price point that does not make commercial sense. More realistic to obtain this type of policy for a hemp or CBD transaction.

Within these categories there are two different types of policies:

- **Claims-Made Policy**: A policy providing coverage triggered when a claim is made against the insured during the policy period, regardless of when the act that gave rise to the claim took place (though in some cases the act must have taken place on or after a retroactive date). This is one of two main types of insurance policies, the other being occurrence-based policies.
- **Occurrence-Based Policy**: Policy that covers losses that happened during the period of coverage, regardless of when a claim is filed. The advantage of this type of policy is that even if a policy is cancelled at a future date, or there is a lapse, coverage for events that occurred when the policy was in effect would still exist. These policies are very difficult for cannabis companies to obtain.

Insurance Terminology

Insurance is an industry with a unique terminology that is hard to grasp for outsiders, meaning that any explanation of insurance can easily devolve into a vocabulary lesson.

Understanding the following terms will help explain the basics of insurance and understand the unique issues impacting cannabis companies:

- **Agents/Brokers (in the insurance context)**: Act as middlemen between someone needing insurance and the insurer and are typically subject to licensure and regulation by the state.
- **Additional Insured Endorsement**: Coverage for someone who is not actually paying the premium, but who the policy holder has agreed to cover under the policy.
- **Captive Insurance**: A formal method of self-insurance that involves setting up a subsidiary company that receives and holds premiums paid by the parent company. There can be tax benefits to using captive insurance and it has been used for tax abuse in some cases.
- **Contribution**: Rule that specifies what happens when a person buys insurance from two or more companies and an insurable event occurs. Under this principle, if a policyholder files a

(Continued)

claim with one carrier, that insurer can collect a proportional amount from the other involved insurance companies.

- **Deductible (sometimes called Retention)**: The amount of money you pay in an insurance claim before the insurance coverage begins and the insurer starts paying you. Some insurance policies in the cannabis industry will have higher than normal deductibles.
- **Exclusion**: A policy provision that excludes coverage for a type of risk and narrows the scope of coverage provided by the insurer. In the cannabis context, watch out for insurance policies that carve out violations of the CSA.
- **Insurance Carrier or Insurer**: This is the insurance company that writes an insurance policy and accepts the risks. Insurance carriers are divided into admitted insurers and non-admitted insurers (also called surplus line insurers).
- **Policy Limit**: The maximum dollar amount that an insurance company will pay out in relation to a specific insurance policy claim. This is often broken into an individual limit (most payable for a single claim) and an aggregate limit (most payable for all claims in a single year). Insurance premiums are often quoted as a percentage of the policy limit (e.g., cannabis D&O has been quoted to the authors as 25% of each million dollars of policy limit). Cannabis companies often find it difficult to obtain insurance policies with policy limits equivalent to those available to non-cannabis companies.
- **Reservation of Rights Letter**: A letter insurers will send to prevent them from being bound to provide coverage since duty to defend is broader than duty to indemnify and insurers may need to defend suits before coverage can be determined. Cannabis companies should be aware that just because an insurer has elected to defend a suit, this does not mean the insurer will pay a claim.
- **Self-Insurance**: This is when a business does not obtain third-party insurance, but instead sets aside a pool of money to be used if needed. Captive insurance can be a more formal way of self-insuring.
- **Specialty Lines Insurance**: The segment of the insurance industry where the more difficult and unusual risks are written. Theoretically can insure essentially anything (e.g., Mick Jagger's voice).
- **Sublimit**: A limitation in an insurance policy that provides a cap on coverage for a certain type of loss (e.g., in the cannabis industry, insurers can apply a low sublimit to coverage for

> assault & battery, which presents a problem for operations located in high crime areas). It is a part of, as opposed to an addition to, the limit that would otherwise apply to the loss.
> - **Subrogation**: A term meaning the legal right of an insurer to stand in for an insured and pursue a third party that caused an insurance loss to the insured.

Insurers and Difficulties of Insuring the Cannabis Industry

Lack of Underwriters

Insurers have been reluctant to cover the cannabis industry for several reasons. First, there is concern that working with the cannabis industry could expose them to criminal or civil liability. While this may be a conservative approach given the absence of federal enforcement (as described in Chapter 1), this is a real concern given the expansive nature of federal drug laws. Second, as mentioned above, the industry needs actuarial data to price risk. If they are wrong on the assessment of the likelihood of risk, they will lose money. While insurers can look at analogous industries (though there are not perfect analogs available given the unique legal situation of cannabis) to help understand risk, the state legal cannabis industry is very new and does not have the historical data that is available for other industries. And worse, much of the existing data is based on errant self-reporting by cannabis industry participants.[11] As a result of these two facts, insurance companies are in a challenging position when it comes to the ability to determine risk.

In addition to the challenges faced in the insurance marketplace, a major player, Lloyd's of London, stopped insuring cannabis companies in the United States due to federal illegality in 2015.[12] Lloyd's of London is a unique specialty lines insurance provider.[13] It is not an individual insurance company, but a brokered market in which approximately 100 underwriting syndicates both compete and co-operate to provide specialty insurance. This combination enables Lloyd's to offer a wealth of choice, knowledge, experience and expertise under one roof. As a major, albeit declining in relative importance, specialty lines insurer and reinsurer, Lloyd's withdrawal from the U.S. cannabis market significantly reduced the availability of insurance.[14]

To date the market for cannabis insurance has largely been met by surplus line insurers (albeit to a limited extent). However, states are slowly permitting admitted carriers to sell insurance to cannabis companies. California, under former California Insurance Commissioner Dave

Jones, has been a leader in this field, with an admitted cannabis insurance product debuting in 2017 with other products following.[15] Currently there are multiple admitted insurance policy products available in California.

Finally, due to federal illegality, there is currently no true crop insurance available for cannabis companies. However, the 2018 Farm Bill allows the U.S. Department of Agriculture (USDA) to provide hemp producers with crop insurance programs. In January 2020 it was determined that the USDA's pilot insurance program will provide certain coverage for eligible producers in select counties in 21 states. The policies insure producers against yield losses due to natural causes, like weather and crop disease, but not against crop losses resulting from hot hemp (Chapter 2 explains the significance of this term).[16]

Prohibitive Costs

It can be difficult for cannabis-related businesses to obtain adequate insurance policies. It is certainly possible to obtain insurance for cannabis companies, though not in the forms and at the policy limits they would like, but it can be prohibitively expensive. For example, D&O insurance for public cannabis companies can require premiums equal to, or even greater than, 25% of the policy limits. Meaning a company would need to spend $250,000 each year to have a million-dollar policy limit. At that price, it may not be economical to obtain coverage. We have also learned that many reputable carriers will not issue rep & warranty insurance for cannabis companies in the U.S. other than hemp or CBD companies. Other reports have indicated it is possible to obtain such coverage, but at a cost that does not make commercial sense.[17]

Practical Steps

Self-Insurance Options

The reality is that many cannabis businesses are opting for self-insurance as a default solution because they either cannot obtain the insurance coverage they want or they cannot afford the requested premiums. However, they may not be setting aside enough capital to address the risks they are taking. This is less self-insurance than simple risk taking. Some in the captive insurance industry have suggested the cannabis industry is a major opportunity, but it does not appear as though anyone has successfully introduced the concept to the cannabis space (although some companies have set up small captives).[18] This is likely because, once you've taken into account the size of the risks and the capital expenditure needed to drive growth, most cannabis companies do not have the capital or cash flow necessary to make a captive insurance policy work. In other words, captive insurance also suffers from prohibitive costs.

Dealing with Insurance Policies

First, when evaluating insurance options, operators need to carefully read any policies before signing. Do not take brokers at their word – what matters is what is written into a policy. We have seen instances of a broker assuring a company that a policy is cannabis friendly, only to discover that the policy excluded violations of the controlled substances act. It may be wise to consult an insurance coverage attorney during this process. Second, if a company is working with an unknown or less than reputable carrier (due to the paucity of choices for cannabis companies), or if it is obtaining a specialty insurance product, please consider whether any claims have been paid by the carrier, or pursuant to the specialty insurance. If there is not a history of claim payment, this is significant a risk to consider, as the coverage may prove illusory. If working with a non-admitted carrier, the financial stability of the insurer should also be considered. Third, think ahead regarding what policies are needed – many cannabis companies have large coverage gaps and should consider comprehensive policy reviews to evaluate their exposure.[19] For example, analysts have been predicting a wave of product liability lawsuits in the cannabis industry for a period of time now. These lawsuits could be related to product contamination or recall, pesticides, vaping illness, or improper labeling that fails to include proper warnings, and could impact many different segments of the cannabis industry, including retailers, distributors, producers, and growers. If possible, it would be better to obtain coverage in advance of the coming wave of product liability claims. Finally, regardless of what insurance policies are obtained, it is always good policy for a company to improve its internal controls and risk management procedures.

Notes

1 John Schroyer, "For Marijuana Companies, Biggest Security Concern Comes from the Inside," *Marijuana Business Daily*, May 26, 2015, https://mjbiz-daily.com/for-marijuana-companies-biggest-security-concern-comes-from-the-inside/.
2 McCarran-Ferguson Act 15 U.S.C. §§ 1011-1015 (2018).
3 Francis Joseph Mootz and Jason Horst, "Cannabis and Insurance," 23, 3 *Lewis & Clark L. Rev.*, June 30, 2019, https://papers.ssrn.com/sol3/papers.cfm?abstract_id=3412595.
4 *Id.*
5 *Tracy v. USAA Cas. Ins. Co.*, CIVIL NO. 11-00487 LEK-KSC (D. Haw., Mar. 16, 2012) (order granting defendant's motion for summary judgment), https://casetext.com/case/tracy-v-usaa-cas-ins-co.
6 *Id.*
7 *Id.*
8 *Green Earth Wellness Center, LLC v. Atain Specialty Insurance Company*, No. 1:2013cv03452 - Document 105 (D. Colo. 2016) (Opinion and Order granting in part and denying in part Motion for Summary Judgment), https://law.justia.com/cases/federal/district-courts/colorado/codce/1:2013cv03452/145181/105/.

9 Isabel Rosa and Renée Johnson, "Federal Crop Insurance: Specialty Crops," Congressional Research Service, No. R45459, Jan. 14, 2019, https://fas.org/sgp/crs/misc/R45459.pdf.

10 *Id.*

11 "Interviews conducted by the authors with numerous insurance brokers, who requested anonymity in order to be able to speak freely," Month, Year to Month, Year. [See CMoS, 17th ed., Rules 14.211–14.214].

12 Amy O'Connor, "Lloyd's Stops Insuring Marijuana Firms Due to U.S. Law Conflicts," *Insurance Journal*, June 24, 2015, https://www.insurancejournal.com/news/national/2015/06/24/372808.htm.

13 "About Lloyd's," Lloyds.com, https://www.lloyds.com/about-lloyds.

14 Carolyn Cohn, "London Losing Ground in Global Reinsurance Market: Report," *Reuters*, May 9, 2017, https://www.reuters.com/article/us-reinsurance-london/london-losing-ground-in-global-reinsurance-market-report-idUSKBN1851IA.

15 Mootz and Horst, "Cannabis and Insurance."

16 United States Department of Agriculture, "USDA Announces Pilot Insurance Coverage for Hemp Growers," Dec. 23, 2019, https://www.rma.usda.gov/News-Room/Press/National-News-Archive/2019-News/2019-News/USDA-Announces-Pilot-Insurance-Coverage-for-Hemp-Growers.

17 "Interviews with insurance brokers."

18 "The Cannabis Industry: An Opportunity for Growth," *Captive Insurance Times*, Apr. 18, 2018, http://www.captiveinsurancetimes.com/specialistfeatures/specialistfeature.php?specialist_id=223; "Interviews with insurance brokers."

19 "Interviews with insurance brokers."

14 Introduction to Cannabis and Licensing

Charles S. Alovisetti, Jessica Scardina, and Emily Hackman

Introduction

Operating a direct cannabis business (i.e., a company that takes title to cannabis and may grow, process, distribute, and sell cannabis under the applicable state laws) requires the company to obtain and maintain appropriate state and local licensure. Accordingly, applying for and obtaining a cannabis license is often the first step taken by a cannabis business. Retaining the required licenses and approvals is critical to the success of cannabis businesses. The type of licenses held will dictate the scope and activities of permitted cannabis operations.

Obtaining a License

There are typically two ways in which states and localities distribute cannabis licenses: a merit-based process (sometimes called a competitive process) and a ministerial or non-competitive process:

Merit-Based Licensure Process

In a merit-based application process, the issuing authority (whether the state or locality) often limits the number of licenses to be issued, establishes a short application window with a hard deadline for submission of applications, scores applications based on pre-determined evaluation criteria, and awards licenses to applicants with the highest ranked applications. Merit-based licensing processes are typically only used at the state level for medical cannabis applications. There are currently no adult-use licensing systems that have a statewide competitive licensing process, but some localities in adult-use states do have merit-based application processes, particularly common for retail licenses. In local merit-based application processes, applicants may even be required to participate in an interview or give a presentation on the proposed business.

Merit-based licensing schemes vary considerably between states. For example, Pennsylvania granted a total of 13 grower/processor licenses for the entire state in its second licensing round (bringing the state license total to 25, including the 12 from the initial round of applications).[1] In New York State, 43 applicants applied for licensure but only 5 applicants were successful. New York State's licenses allow the holder to grow, process, and sell their own products.[2] Subsequently, New York State expanded its program to issue an additional five licenses. With significantly more applicants than licenses offered, merit-based processes require states to score and rank applicants based on pre-determined criteria, granting licenses only to a small group of select winners. With so much money at stake, it is not surprising that merit-based licensing has led to complaints of favoritism, bribery, and official corruption, with the FBI and local law enforcement actively investigating potential cases.[3] As a result, applicants for pot licenses should be aware of red flags that could signal the presence of public corruption in the licensing process.[4]

In addition to the specific criteria related to an applicant's ability to produce quality medical cannabis in a safe and hygienic environment, states often ask about amorphous criteria such as commitment to public welfare or diversity. For example, New York State has a criterion that stated, "that it is in the public interest that such registration be granted to the applicant."[5] Other factors may include, but are not limited to: local support for the applicant from governmental authorities or community organizations and members, strong financial stability, a demonstration of sufficient and transparent cash flow, the strength and experience of the team, proposed quality assurance protocols, facility capabilities, design and location, and community engagement and community benefit plans.

Ministerial Licensure Process

In a ministerial licensure process, any applicant who can demonstrate that they sufficiently satisfy the statutory, zoning, and other legal requirements is granted a license to operate. There is no need to obtain a higher score than other applicants. There is typically no imposed cap on the number of licenses to be issued, though there may be natural soft caps in place based on the availability of eligible properties that meet both proper zoning and setbacks. The application process is typically done on a rolling basis. This means you can apply for a license at any time, not just at the beginning of an authority's licensing process, or at specific intervals. This is not to suggest that acquiring a ministerial license is an easy or inexpensive process. There are many obstacles to overcome, including obtaining local approvals, demonstrating financial stability, passing extensive background checks, and finding appropriately zoned property. In our experience, finding eligible property can be the biggest obstacle to obtaining a non-competitive license.

Local Licensing

Adding an additional layer of complexity to the cannabis business license application process in some states is the existence of two different application processes: the state process and the local process, which may happen concurrently or one after the other. In these jurisdictions, a state may have a non-competitive licensing process in place, while cities and towns within the state – as permitted by state statute – administer their own, merit-based licensing processes. California is the most prominent example of this kind of dual licensing structure. At the state level, all three agencies charged with oversight of the licensing process for cannabis businesses in California – the Bureau of Cannabis Control along with the state Departments of Food and Agriculture and Public Health – accept applications for commercial cannabis licenses on a rolling basis, and there is no state-imposed cap on the number of licensed California cannabis businesses. However, local California governments such as the City of West Hollywood have promulgated their own rules and regulations governing commercial cannabis activity, including competitive application processes that limit the number of cannabis business licenses available in those municipalities.

The existence of both a non-competitive state license application and competitive or capped local applications can create tensions and confusion for both prospective cannabis operators and regulators, while intensifying an already competitive process in municipalities with attractive markets. The City of West Hollywood, for instance, received over 300 applications from 120 different applicants for a total of 40 available local licenses (5 license types for which the City identified the top 8 winners). The City of Pasadena received 122 applications for the retail license category and selected the top 6. Even jurisdictions, such as the City of Los Angeles, that capped the number of licenses available, but so far has chosen to use a first-come, first serve ministerial process, still leave the majority of applicants dissatisfied and without a license. These competing licensing processes at the state and local levels exacerbate the issue of license scarcity in the face of a high volume of applications. Cannabis businesses in these states can face a high level of uncertainty in areas where various municipalities have either banned or approved commercial cannabis activity. California provides a case study in the dissonance created in states with such dual licensing structures: as of 2019, about 2/3 of California municipalities had passed local measures prohibiting some form of commercial cannabis operation.[6] Such local ordinances are often pointed to as a contributing factor in the disappointing rate of growth of California's recreational cannabis market since the state legalized adult-use cannabis in 2016 (note, however, that state licensing was first available on January 1, 2018).

These competitive local licensing processes bring their own requirements of diversity and commitment to causes such as social equity, and
in many cases can require applicants to meet specific stringent local requirements to create successful applications, or risk exclusion from the
process. Additionally, local governments can exploit state licensing structures that allow for localities to enter into additional contracts with prospective cannabis businesses before they can begin operation. Although
such contracts are not technically a separate local licensing structure,
they can have a significant impact on an applicant's chances for licensure
or future profits. In Massachusetts, for example, cannabis businesses
must enter into a "Host Community Agreement" with the municipality
in which they intend to operate, and ambiguous language in the relevant
statute provides cities and towns wide latitude in charging businesses to
operate within their boundaries. Statutorily imposed contracts between
localities and applicants for licensure present many of the same challenges as dual state and local licensing processes. Prospective cannabis
businesses that intend to operate in states that allow such agreements
should be mindful of their consequences on licensure and potential future profits.

Different License Types

States that permit the commercial sale and distribution of cannabis have
implemented a variety of different approaches to licensing these businesses. These states tend to differ on the types of licenses offered, the
number of licenses available, and the processes for awarding them. While
some states require only a single license for the cultivation, processing,
and dispensing of cannabis, other states offer a variety of license types,
each of which specifically permits the licensee to engage in a different
step of cannabis production. In the latter model, businesses may acquire
multiple licenses, including at the same facility, to integrate their operations. For example, Colorado currently licenses 11 types of activities
for cannabis businesses and offers permits for other ancillary business
activities, such as delivery and off-premises storage. In contrast, North
Dakota's medical model offers a single "Compassionate Care Center" license, and California's collapsed adult-use and medical model offers nine
different categories of licenses with 29 different license types available,
including a temporary cannabis event license. In addition to the types
of license offered, the number of licenses granted and the processes for
awarding them vary significantly from state to state. The below describes
the different cannabis license types found in the US:

Medical v. Adult-Use[7]

Cannabis licenses are generally either medical or adult-use (called recreational or retail in some states). A medical license will only authorize

medical cannabis operations and an adult-use license only permits adult-use cannabis operations. There are typically regulations governing how these systems can interact (e.g., whether medical cannabis can be transferred to an adult-use retailer) and if licensees can be co-located (e.g., whether a store with both medical and adult-use licenses can engage in both types of sales). In many states a cannabis company will hold two sets of parallel licenses – one for adult-use cannabis activity and one for medical cannabis activity. Due to different regulatory regimes and tax rates, the cost and type of cannabis products often differ between the adult-use and medical sides, so a distinct medical cannabis market remains even in states that have legalized cannabis for adult-use. However, there have been significant decreases in medical cannabis patient numbers once a state adopts broader legalization measures.[8]

Vertically Integrated Licenses

In some medical cannabis programs, there is only one type of license that permits a wide range of commercial cannabis activity. Examples of this kind of program include those in effect in limited medical cannabis states like New Jersey, New York, and Florida (although Florida now also separately licenses testing facilities). States that do not issue vertically integrated licenses will instead issue different licenses for specific activities, as demonstrated by the array of available licenses, listed in more detail below. And some states have a hybrid approach, such as Massachusetts, which offers a vertically integrated license for its medical program, but separate licenses for its adult-use program.

Cultivation

States vary in the types of cultivation licenses they issue, but many share the goal of restricting the amount of cannabis grown under a specific license. Some states will restrict total canopy (i.e., an area to be calculated in square feet and measured using clearly identifiable boundaries of all areas(s) that will contain mature plants at any point in time) permitted to a license or a licensed business or both. Massachusetts, for example, does both by issuing tiered licenses that limit the total canopy available under a specific license and by limiting any licensed business to a maximum of 100,000 square feet of canopy.[9] Other states, such as Colorado, cap the total number of plants a licensee is permitted to grow at any one time; this number includes all vegetative and flowering plants but not immature plants (also known as clones). If a licensee is utilizing only a small percentage of its authorized plant count, the regulatory body can reduce the licensee's authorized plant count. Licensees must demonstrate need, through submission of sales and cultivation records, in order to increase their authorized plant count. Cultivation licenses can be for indoor, outdoor (sun-grown), or mixed-light (a combination of artificial and natural light) operations, depending on the state and locality license offerings.

Manufacturing (Other Name: Processing, Extraction)

Most states have a license type for extraction and infusion operations called a manufacturing, processing, or extraction license. For companies seeking to focus on branded infused products and extracts, this is typically the only license they need to hold. Because it remains illegal to ship cannabis across state lines, some infused product brands have sought out manufacturing licenses in new markets to enable them to make and sell products in these jurisdictions. The simpler path to expansion for most brands has been to enter into white labeling agreements, in which one company produces goods for sale by another company under its own brand, with businesses that already hold manufacturing licenses in other markets.

Dispensary (Other Names: Retail)

A dispensary license permits the holder to operate a cannabis retail store. Depending on the state, a dispensary license may permit the operation of multiple stores. In Pennsylvania, dispensary licenses permit the holder to own and operate three stores.

Testing

Some states have separate licenses for testing facilities. Other licensed businesses are required to obtain testing services from these labs before selling products. It is common for states to prohibit a company or individual from owning a testing license and holding any equity interest in another type of cannabis license to avoid conflicts of interest.

Transportation and Distribution

Some states require third party businesses that transport cannabis or cannabis-derived cash, or both, between licensed businesses to hold a separate transportation license. Transporter license holders are also generally permitted to engage in some form of limited cannabis storage ancillary to their shipment duties.

Delivery

Delivery of cannabis from store to purchaser's home address does not exist in many jurisdictions. Some states do not permit deliveries at all and others, including California, require certain licensees to conduct cannabis deliveries. In a jurisdiction with delivery licenses, companies may need to obtain a separate license or approval to conduct deliveries. These are a newer license type and have not been widely issued. For example, Massachusetts, which has a separate delivery license type, has yet to issue one of these licenses, as the application form was not released until May 28, 2020.[10] For the first two years, Massachusetts will restrict these delivery licenses to "businesses controlled by, and with majority ownership comprised of, Economic Empowerment Applicants or Social Equity Participants."[11] Colorado currently only permits delivery of medical cannabis.

Micro Licenses (Other Names: Accelerator, Microbusiness)

Many states have created smaller scale and less capital-intensive license types meant to accommodate smaller businesses that cannot afford the facilities or requirements of multiple licenses. For example, California has a microbusiness license that allows a licensee to cultivate cannabis in a limited size area and to act as distributor, manufacturer, and retailer. Another license with a similar goal is the Accelerator license in Colorado.

Social Consumption (Other Names: Hospitality or Cannabis Consumption)

Social consumption licenses permit businesses to allow onsite consumption (e.g., a cannabis café). Some states offer a temporary form of this license for special events. Public consumption licenses, like delivery licenses, are newer license types. Most states either do not issue public consumption licenses or have issued them in limited numbers.

Miscellaneous Cannabis License Types

In addition to the more common license types, there are also license types that are found in a limited number of states: business operators, distributors, and research and development. A business operator licensee is permitted to operate another licensee's facility for a percentage of the revenue or profit generated by the license. A distributor license, which notably exists in California, is typically broader than a transporter license and includes responsibilities to collect state cannabis taxes, arrange for testing of cannabis goods, and conduct quality assurance review of cannabis products to ensure they comply with packaging and labeling requirements. In California, cannabis goods can only be transported to a dispensary by a distributor and not a transporter (except clones for retail sale). Research and development licenses are meant to legalize possession of cannabis in order to conduct research activities.

Non-Cannabis Licensing for Cannabis Companies

In addition to the required cannabis licenses, cannabis companies typically must obtain various other state and local licenses, permits, and approvals to properly conduct their businesses. These requirements can lead to significant delays and operational expenses. These can include state and local tax licenses, conditional use permits, fire, building, and security permits, health department approvals, and more. For example, Denver, Colorado, requires Denver-based manufacturing companies conducting volatile extractions to maintain Class 1, Division 1, explosion-proof facilities, which are costly to construct and permit.

Licensing Actions

Change of Ownership

From a corporate transaction perspective, effecting a change or transfer of ownership of a license can be the most meaningful licensing action beyond winning a license in a competitive application. There is a great deal of variation in how different states treat changes of ownership. Some states, like California, will treat an asset sale or transfer of a license between entities very differently from a deal where the equity of a license holding company changes hands. If the entity listed as the owner of a license is going to change, California will require an entirely new state application and processing this can take months. In places like Colorado, however, a transfer of a license between entities is treated in the same manner as a change of equity ownership and will, absent other differences, take the same amount of time for approval.

In addition to state-level license change issues, local jurisdictions may also require some kind of licensing action at the local level in the event of a change of ownership. In other states, however, localities will not be involved at all in changes of ownership or will defer the majority of the regulatory authority to the state agency. Even within states there can be a great deal of variety as to the level of involvement of a locality.

Change of Location

In many states, licenses are tied to a specific location. This is more often the case in states with a non-vertically integrated licensing model. For these regimes, regulatory approval is needed to move a licensed premise to a different location. Depending on the state in question, it may not be possible to pursue both a change of location and a change of ownership at the same time. This means a company would need to resolve any changes of location either prior to, or immediately after, consummating a transaction that requires a change of ownership.

Renewals

Licenses, once issued, must be renewed in certain regular intervals (the length of which can vary widely between states, though annual renewals are the most common). It is common for a licensing fee to be due at renewal. Renewals are generally routine actions; however, there can be a great deal of variation between states in terms of what kinds of disclosures are required at renewal (e.g., renewal forms may explicitly require disclosure of all company financing). The degree of required disclosures can impact the timing of corporate transactions, as the obligation to disclose certain agreements can result in further regulatory inquiries.

Penalties

Regulatory penalties vary widely between states and range in severity. The most common regulatory penalty is a verbal or written notice of the alleged violation and a requirement to fix the violation in a timely manner. Other regulatory penalties include fines and the suspension and revocation of licenses. Bad actors can also find themselves banned from participating, even passively, in the cannabis industry. Penalties can have wide ranging impacts on multi-state operations, as states generally require disclosure of regulatory sanctions in other jurisdictions. A history of regulatory penalties can also make it difficult to win competitive licensing processes, where the requirement to disclose past regulatory violations is common.

Hemp Licensing

Hemp licensing is generally far less competitive than cannabis licensing. Because of this, issues around winning and maintaining licenses through licensing actions are less important in the hemp industry than in the cannabis industry. It is often possible to simply obtain a new hemp license instead of worrying about transfer issues. The different types of hemp licenses are discussed in Chapter 2.

Notes

1 "PA Unveils 13 Medical Marijuana Grower/Processor Licenses; Flower Sales Set," *Marijuana Business Daily*, July 31, 2018, https://mjbizdaily.com/pennsylvania-unveils-13-new-medical-marijuana-grower-processor-licenses/.
2 Matthew Hamilton, "New York Licenses Five New Medical Marijuana Companies," *Albany Times Union*, July 28, 2017, https://www.timesunion.com/7day-state/article/New-York-licenses-five-new-medical-marijuana-11652954.php.
3 Tom Angell, "FBI Seeks Tips on Marijuana Industry Corruption," *Forbes*, Aug. 16, 2019, https://www.forbes.com/sites/tomangell/2019/08/16/fbi-seeks-tips-on-marijuana-industry-corruption/#6425a3484ca7;"FBIProbingPotential

Public Corruption in California Capital's Marijuana Industry," *Marijuana Business Daily*, Oct. 14, 2019, https://mjbizdaily.com/fbi-probing-potential-public-corruption-in-sacramento-marijuana-industry/; Sushree Mohanty, "Cannabis Corruption in the US: Trouble before Elections?," *Market Realist*, Oct. 15, 2019, https://marketrealist.com/2019/10/cannabis-corruption-us-trouble-before-elections/; "Corruption in the Cannabis Industry," *Cannabexchange*, Apr. 11, 2020, https://cannabexchange.com/corruption-in-the-cannabis-industry/.

4 Tom Firestone and Tanya Hoke, "Cannabis-Related Due Diligence: What Are the Red Flags for Corruption?," *The FCPA Blog*, Oct. 29, 2019, https://fcpablog.com/2019/10/29/cannabis-related-due-diligence-what-are-the-red-flags-for-corruption/.

5 N.Y. Comp. Codes R. & Regs. Tit. 10, § 1004.6(b)(7) (2017).

6 John Schroyer and Eli McVey, "Chart: Most California Municipalities Ban Commercial Cannabis Activity," *Marijuana Business Daily*, Feb. 18, 2019, https://mjbizdaily.com/chart-most-of-california-municipalities-ban-commercial-cannabis-activity/.

7 The only exception is a 2019 Oregon law that's not really an exception since it doesn't go into effect until permitted by federal law: Kristian Foden-Vencil, "Oregon House Passes Bill to Transport Cannabis across State Lines," *Oregon Public Broadcasting*, June 11, 2019, https://www.opb.org/news/article/oregon-house-bill-cannabis-state-lines/.

8 Gillian Flaccus and Angeliki Kastanis, "As States like Colorado Legalize Recreational Marijuana, Medical Cannabis Patients Drop Dramatically," *Colorado Sun*, June 12, 2019, https://coloradosun.com/2019/06/12/colorado-medical-marijuana-recreational-marijuana-stats/.

9 Massachusetts Cannabis Control Commission, "Guidance on Types of Marijuana Establishment Licenses," n.d., https://mass-cannabis-control.com/wp-content/uploads/2018/04/Guidance-License-Types.pdf.

10 Melissa Hanson, "Massachusetts Marijuana Delivery License Applications on Track to Launch in May, Reserved for Economic Empowerment and Social Equity Applicants," *MassLive*, May 07, 2020, https://www.masslive.com/marijuana/2020/05/massachusetts-marijuana-delivery-license-applications-on-track-to-launch-in-may-reserved-for-economic-empowerment-and-social-equity-applicants.html; Massachusetts Cannabis Control Commission, "Frequently Asked Questions (FAQs) about Delivery," May 28, 2020, https://mass-cannabis-control.com/wp-content/uploads/2020/05/052720-Delivery-FAQs.pdf.

11 *Id.*

15 Introduction to Cannabis and Social Equity

Cassia Furman and Kelsey Middleton

Introduction

For many, cannabis legalization is a social justice issue. While the cannabis industry has taken massive strides toward eradicating nation-wide cannabis prohibition – shifting federal legalization from aspirational to probable, and normalizing the public perception of cannabis and its consumers – the question of how to properly acknowledge the legacy of the United States' war on drugs remains at issue. As states and localities across the country develop cannabis licensing programs, efforts to meaningfully account for the legacy of discriminatory policing and mass incarceration of minority groups are gaining traction at local, state, and federal levels of government. This chapter explores the legacy of the "war on drugs" in brief as well as the role and impact of "social equity" cannabis programs that seek to redress the disproportionate impact of the war on drugs on communities of color.

The Legacy of the War on Drugs

The criminalization of psychoactive substances in the United States began with San Francisco's 1875 ordinance that banned opium dens and made it a misdemeanor to keep or visit any establishment where opium was used. A San Francisco Chronicle report would later reveal that the San Francisco Board of Supervisors took such action as a response to learning about "'opium-smoking establishments kept by Chinese, for the exclusive use of white men and women'—and of 'young men and women of respectable parentage' going there."[1] In 1909, Congress made opium smoking a federal offense with the Anti-Opium Act; legislation later criticized for exempting the consumption and injection of certain opiates commonly used among whites.

The criminalization of opium marked only the beginning of the fraught relationship between race, politics, and drug regulation in America, most notably impacting the nation's Black and Brown communities. Building off the legacy of the Anti-Opium Act, Henry Anslinger, the first commissioner of the Federal Bureau of Narcotics (a precursor to the modern Drug Enforcement Administration) and an influential figure in the passage of the 1937 Marihuana Tax Act, stated, "Marijuana is the most violence-causing drug in the history of mankind. ... Most marijuana smokers are Negroes, Hispanics, Filipinos and entertainers. Their satanic music, jazz and swing, result from marijuana usage."[2] Given these statements and the historical context, the racist, xenophobic policies underlying drug prohibition, including cannabis prohibition, are easily observed. Misinformation concerning drug use was frequently invoked to distinguish "the other" – frequently people of color – from the white American majority and to foster fear and apprehension of the "other" groups to consolidate political support.

In a June 17, 1971, press conference, President Nixon famously declared drug abuse to be America's "public enemy number one," commencing the modern war on drugs. While the war on drugs may have been racially and politically neutral on its face, the enforcement of drug war offenses was far from evenhanded. John Ehrlichman, former policy advisor to President Nixon, openly admitted this approach when he stated:

> The Nixon campaign in 1968, and the Nixon White House after that, had two enemies: the antiwar left and [B]lack people. You understand what I'm saying? We knew we couldn't make it illegal to be either against the war or [B]lack, but by getting the public to associate the hippies with marijuana and [B]lacks with heroin, and then criminalizing both heavily, we could disrupt those communities. We could arrest their leaders, raid their homes, break up their meetings, and vilify them night after night on the evening news. Did we know we were lying about the drugs? Of course we did.[3]

As America's federal drug policies were implemented and institutionalized, Black and Brown people were arrested and incarcerated at disproportionate rates. Sentences doled out to Black and Brown people remain harsher than those given to white offenders for similar crimes.[4] In 2015, Black people made up about 32% of the United States population but comprised 56% of all incarcerated people.[5] And while Black people represent 12.5% of illicit drugs users, they comprised 29% of those arrested for drug offenses and 33% of those incarcerated in state facilities for drug offenses.[6] As Michelle Alexander observed in *The New Jim Crow*, "Nothing has contributed more to the systematic mass incarceration of people of color in the United States than the War on Drugs."

Despite increasing awareness of the flawed, if not amoral, motivations spurring the war on drugs, and the growing of list of states opting to decriminalize or regulate cannabis, vestiges of the drug war linger in the

21st century. An ACLU study conducted in April 2020 showed that despite a decrease of cannabis arrests at a national level since 2010, the rate of decline has stagnated and, in some instances, even reversed upward despite the popularity of cannabis policy reform movements.[7] The study further revealed that war on drugs policies continue to disproportionately target people of color, particularly Black people. In 2020, Black people are 3.6 times more likely than white people to be arrested for cannabis possession, despite similar usage rates.[8]

Development and Impact of Social Equity Programs

Introduction

While decriminalization and legalization of medical and adult use cannabis at the state level, as well as increasing pressure to legalize at the federal level, may herald an end to the country's most egregious discriminatory drug law policies and enforcement tactics, it does not adequately recompense or represent the interests of persons and communities most impacted by the war on drugs. As the first waves of cannabis businesses open, racial minorities – particularly Blacks and Hispanics – have yet to enjoy the promise of the burgeoning legal cannabis industry to the same degree or at the same rate as their majority counterparts. Barriers to entry are particularly high in the cannabis industry due to the limited licenses available in most state legal marketplaces, which artificially constricts the market and inflates cost. At the same time, the American media reports daily on worsening income inequality in the country. Given the obstacles, it is not surprising that recent data reveals 81% of cannabis executives are white.[9] Within this challenging landscape, community leaders and local government officials struggle to develop and implement meaningful social equity programs.

Demographics and Eligibility

Ideally, a social equity program would ensure that the demographics eligible for the program are adequately represented and prepared to compete with competitors who are likely better resourced. Defining eligible demographics, however, has proven challenging for governments due to political conflicts and legal constraints. Politically, defining the eligible demographic is difficult because there is not a consensus as to who should comprise the group of persons eligible for the benefits and privileges provided by the social equity program. From a race-neutral perspective, cannabis users are the population that has been most harmed by cannabis prohibition. From a race-conscious perspective, however, persons that have suffered consequences of committing a drug war crime – predominantly Blacks and Hispanics – have been most harmed by cannabis prohibition. To complicate matters further, there are other gradations within this spectrum worthy of meaningful consideration. Governments have acknowledged that women, veterans, and persons facing housing insecurity have experienced certain hardships due to cannabis prohibition and the war on drugs. These characteristics often intersect with race, socioeconomic status, and other characteristics that can render a group more vulnerable.

Constitutional Considerations

Although many factors may explain the disparity of ownership and representation in the cannabis industry, it is plausible that the criteria by which applicants are assessed does not successfully provide for an adequate representation of racial and ethnic minorities. Presumably out of a well-founded concern that a race-conscious licensing scheme would run afoul of the Equal Protection Clause and any applicable state laws, cannabis agencies have been reticent to explicitly consider race in the provision of cannabis business licenses. Instead, lawmakers rely on so-called proxies for race, such as geography and income, to attain the desired level of racial and ethnic minority participation. Although "proxy" programs are easier for governments to implement, they are not a substitute for affirmative action parameters, which by their nature more directly prioritize people of color. And while affirmative action programs remain on somewhat precarious constitutional grounds, the Supreme Court has not held that institutions are prohibited from considering race or ethnicity entirely, leaving the door open for further consideration of race-conscious social equity programming.

The Equal Protection Clause of the 14th Amendment provides, "No state shall deny to any person within its jurisdiction the equal protection of the laws." Whenever the government makes a law that classifies persons according to a protected characteristic, such as race, the law is subject to strict scrutiny. Under strict scrutiny, the government must demonstrate a compelling interest motivating the law, and the means toward securing that interest must be necessary or narrowly tailored.[10] Though the adage "strict in theory, but fatal in fact" has long been associated with this stringent level of review, affirmative action programs have managed to narrowly withstand constitutional inquiry.[11] *Fisher v. University of Texas at Austin*, (2016) (commonly referred to as *Fisher II*) is the Supreme Court's most recent iteration of the Equal Protection doctrine as it pertains to affirmative action programs.[12] *Fisher II* involved a challenge to the University of Texas at Austin's undergraduate admissions policy alleging that the university's consideration of race as part of its holistic review process disadvantaged the plaintiff, Ms. Fisher, and other white applicants in violation of the Equal Protection Clause. The Court held that the university's admissions policy did not violate the Constitution because the use of race in the overall admissions scheme was deemed narrowly tailored to the university's interest of maintaining the benefits that flow from a diverse student body. But the Court also required the university to

> continue to use data to scrutinize the fairness of its admissions program; to assess whether changing demographics have undermined the need for a race-conscious policy and to identify the effects, both positive and negative, of the affirmative action measures it deems necessary.[13]

Fisher II introduced three parameters that are helpful to examine the constitutionality of race-conscious cannabis equity programs:

1 Race-based programs must meet strict scrutiny.
2 Race-conscious programs may not operate as quotas, but some deference is afforded to institutions in defining their "critical mass."
3 No deference is granted to institutions / government in the determination of whether the use of race is narrowly tailored. The institution bears the burden of proving a non-racial approach would not promote the interests of diversity.

Satisfying Strict Scrutiny

To pass constitutional muster, a race-conscious program must be necessary or narrowly tailored to a compelling government interest. *Fisher II* clarified that both the goal and implementation of the race-conscious remedy or program must meet strict scrutiny. The hallmarks of a narrowly tailored program include individualized consideration of each applicant in which race is but "a factor of a factor" in a holistic review process together with the absence of quotas, separate admission tracks, or other mechanisms that insulate applicants who belong to certain racial or ethnic groups from competition. Following these parameters, cannabis licensing agencies that use a merit licensing scheme – one that involves a comprehensive overview of the applicant's business, credentials of high-level officers, narratives demonstrating compliance with applicable laws, and criminal background checks – are better poised to include race among the many factors they consider when reviewing applicants. Any consideration of race must be flexible and non-mechanical, however. A review that doles out any number of points solely because of one's race is not likely to pass constitutional muster.

Although the Supreme Court has ruled quotas are unconstitutional, it has also held that metrics may play a limited role in defining a "critical mass" of minority engagement.[14] It follows that cannabis agencies would be afforded some latitude to define their "critical mass" or optimal degree of minority engagement; preferably, a degree of engagement that reflects the demographics and needs of the communities they serve. As courts are permitted to examine numerical evidence when evaluating whether plans are narrowly tailored, a plan that seems to prioritize or license a disproportionate number of minority applicants in relation to the demographics of the respective jurisdiction may raise red flags. This creates a predicament for the proponents of race-conscious programs. The goal cannot be the attainment of a certain number or proportion of minorities, but it also cannot be so immeasurable that it does not permit judicial scrutiny of the efficacy of the policies adopted to reach the goal.

Proponents of race-conscious licensing schemes must also demonstrate a compelling interest for which the race-based classification is drawn. The Court has accepted various interests as compelling. While none are directly applicable to the cannabis industry, many of the interests are analogous to those espoused by social equity program stakeholders, including: obtaining the benefits that flow from diversity such as cross-racial understanding; breaking down stereotypes; cultivating leaders with legitimacy in the eyes of the citizenry; acquiring the competencies required of future leaders; and remedying past discrimination.

Compiling Evidence to Demonstrate Necessity

Given the nascency of the cannabis industry, little existing data is available to show disparities unique to the business of cannabis or indeed, to adequately document industry demographics as a threshold measure. The lack of data complicates development of social equity programs because, per the Supreme Court tests, prior to resorting to race-conscious means, institutions are required to show that race-neutral means were first attempted to secure a critical mass of minority engagement. How exactly to apply this test to the emerging cannabis industry remains largely unknown. However, when the State of Maryland explored a race-conscious cannabis equity program in 2017, the state was directed to conduct a study to display a significant statistical disparity between the availability of minority workers and the use of minority workers by the government entity.[15] The study confirmed that minorities and women were not adequately represented in the industry, and provided the evidence necessary to support the use of race-based and gender-based measures by the state to remediate past discrimination.[16] Existing studies ordered by local governments to analyze disparities in general business opportunities among racial minorities could also be extrapolated to support race-conscious cannabis licensing criteria specifically.

While local governments face a high bar and uncertainty in choosing to select race-conscious cannabis social equity criteria, the opportunity is clear for those willing to take on this challenge. Agencies should keep thorough records of their race-neutral outreach and engagement efforts and measure their effectiveness at increasing the participation of target populations since courts will evaluate these records to determine whether the use of a race-conscious scheme is appropriate. There must also be a strong evidence of past discrimination at the time a race-conscious program is established. It remains unclear whether police beat records or similar statistics evidencing the widespread discriminatory policing of Black and Brown people for cannabis-based offenses may be used to show discrimination in the cannabis industry, as the nexus is somewhat tangential, but this is at least a logical starting point.[17]

Characteristics of Existing Social Equity Programs

Introduction

Within the constitutional restraints discussed above, states like Illinois and Michigan, and California cities including Oakland, San Francisco, and Los Angeles, are leading the country in the development and implementation of cannabis social equity programs. As a whole, the programs are intended to promote equity in the cannabis industry and create business opportunities for persons who have been disadvantaged by the war on drugs, cannabis prohibition, and other factors such as, race, gender, poverty, and housing insecurity. None of these programs have been in existence for more than a few years, and many have not yet been fully implemented as of May 2020. Common program components include not only direct licensing support, fee reductions and deferrals, and cannabis business education and training, but also ancillary services such as expungement clinics and business start-up loan programs.

Program Components and Qualifications

Common among the nascent social equity programs is the use of a multi-factored system to assess one's eligibility for the program. Almost all existing equity programs consider the following factors: low-income relative to the jurisdiction's average median income, residency in a "disproportionately impacted area," and prior cannabis crime arrests or convictions. Some jurisdictions have also opted to tailor their eligibility criteria to better reflect their population and the needs of their communities. For example, Humboldt County, California's Local Equity Program, Project Trellis, considers a wide variety of community-focused factors in assessing eligibility including, homelessness; experiencing sexual assault, exploitation, domestic violence, or human trafficking while participating in the cannabis industry; gender, race, and sexual orientation of an individual working in the Humboldt County cannabis industry; and, whether the applicant seeks a cannabis permit to operate in a location with a poverty rate of 17% or above.

Lessons Learned

Despite considerable progress, the cannabis industry has yet to design or implement a licensing scheme that can produce an adequate representation of racial and ethnic minorities in cannabis business licensing and ownership. The capacity of "race neutral" programs to resolve disproportionate impact is limited. In addition to constitutional issues, program implementation is challenged by funding availability. Ironically, a common social equity program qualifier is low income, but cannabis businesses are notoriously expensive to get off the ground. Technical support is largely provided by local government staff with limited resources and business experience. To navigate complex application and operational requirements, well-intentioned government officials frequently advise social equity applicants to consult with a lawyer or other consultant, which is not the most helpful suggestion to a low-income applicant. The reality for social equity applicants is that outside investment is typically needed to open the doors, but the program parameters sometimes have a chilling effect because investors are faced with non-market terms for participation.

The difficulties in establishing program eligibility and then selecting among a pool of hopefuls competing for a limited number of licenses compounds issues for local government officials and applicants alike. Administrative defects and charges of perceived corruption and fraud are frequently associated with the programs in these early days. This is perhaps a byproduct of the inherent difficulties of merging the (relative) cultural elite and low-income communities in a capitalist setting without navigable guideposts. The tension between the race-conscious program intent, but race-neutral implementation, coupled with the high stakes easily leads to presumptions of corruption or predatory practices, even if all parties (government administration, social equity partners, and capital investors) are well meaning.

Looking Forward

Although early cannabis social equity programs have been imperfect, the potential remains to establish better tools for communication among stakeholders, increase trust, and to realize positive outcomes. In addition to considering race-conscious program elements, incorporating more holistic measures such as community reinvestment funds (to be funded from existing cannabis taxes, rather than placing additional burdens on operators) and corporate social responsibility as program requirements has the potential to positively benefit a greater number of individuals, most particularly disproportionately impacted communities of color. Earmarking lower cost licenses for social equity priority such as delivery, packaging, and distribution/transportation also has the potential to spread program reach and impact. The development and large-scale implementation of a model social equity ordinance, in line with the efforts undertaken by the Minority Cannabis Bar Association and other affinity groups, can provide state and local governments with much-needed resources and help create a framework for communication among stakeholders that fosters trust and alignment, rather than fear and doubt. Expungement, sentence reform, and early parole should remain priorities and program components; it is only too clear in 2020 that the United States has not successfully mitigated the legacy of the drug war nor moved to a 'post-racial' society. The cannabis industry is uniquely positioned to both recognize the responsibility and realize the promise of its social justice origins. The next several years will be critical in determining the ongoing viability of social equity programs and businesses, and our ongoing focus and commitment as an industry is essential.

Notes

1 Nikolay Anguelov, *From Criminalizing to Decriminalizing Marijuana: The Politics of Social Control* (New York: Lexington Books, 2018) at 4.
2 Laura Smith, "How a Racist Hate-Monger Masterminded America's War on Drugs: Harry Anslinger Conflated Drug Use, Race, and Music to Criminalize Non-Whiteness and Create a Prison-Industrial Complex," *Timeline*, Feb. 27, 2018, https://timeline.com/harry-anslinger-racist-war-on-drugs-prison-industrial-complex-fb5cbc281189.
3 Erik Sherman, "Nixon's Drug War, an Excuse to Lock up Blacks and Protestors, Continues," *Forbes*, May 23, 2016, https://www.forbes.com/sites/eriksherman/2016/03/23/nixons-drug-war-an-excuse-to-lock-up-blacks-and-protesters-continues/#1a3cee6942c8.
4 Marc Mauer and Ryan S. King, "A 25-Year Quagmire: The War on Drugs and Its Impact on American Society," *The Sentencing Project*, Sept. 2007, https://www.sentencingproject.org/wp-content/uploads/2016/01/A-25-Year-Quagmire-The-War-On-Drugs-and-Its-Impact-on-American-Society.pdf.
5 "Criminal Justice Fact Sheet: Drug Sentencing Disparities," *NAACP*, https://www.naacp.org/criminal-justice-fact-sheet/.
6 *Id.*
7 Ezekiel Edwards and Brooke Madubuonwu, "A Tale of Two Countries: Racially Targeted Arrests in the Era of Marijuana Reform," *ACLU*, Apr. 17, 2020, https://www.aclu.org/news/criminal-law-reform/a-tale-of-two-countries-racially-targeted-arrests-in-the-era-of-marijuana-reform/?initms_aff=nat&initms_chan=web&utm_medium=web&initms=200420_420_marijuanareport_vanity&utm_source=earned&utm_campaign=420&utm_content=200420_criminallaw_marijuanareport_vanity&ms_aff=nat&ms_chan=web&ms=200420_420_marijuanareport_vanity&redirect=marijuana.
8 *Id.*

9 Eli McVey, "Chart: Percentage of Cannabis Business Owners and Founders by Race," *Marijuana Business Daily*, Sept. 11, 2017, https://mjbizdaily.com/chart-19-cannabis-businesses-owned-founded-racial-minorities/.

10 *United States v. Carolene Products Co.*, 304 U.S. 144 (1938) n. 4; *Korematsu v. United States*, 323 U.S. 214 (1944).

11 *Adarand v. Pena*, 515 U.S. 200, 202 (1995)

> It is not true that strict scrutiny is strict in theory, but fatal in fact. Government is not disqualified from acting in response to the unhappy persistence of both the practice and lingering effects of racial discrimination against minority groups in this country.

12 *Fisher v. University of Texas*, 579 U.S., 133 S. Ct. 2411 (2013).

13 *Id.*, 133 S. Ct. at 2419 (2016).

14 *Grutter v. Bollinger*, 539 U.S. 306, 336 (2003) ("'[S]ome attention to numbers,' without more, does not transform a flexible admissions system into a rigid quota.")

15 Brentin Mock, "Race and Weed in Maryland," *CityLab*, May 4, 2017, https://www.citylab.com/equity/2017/05/racial-equity-in-the-cannabis-trade-spreads-to-maryland/524838/.

16 Doug Donovan, "Maryland's Plan to Diversify Medical Cannabis Market Attracts 160 Applicants for 14 New Licenses Despite Snags," *Baltimore Sun*, May 29, 2019, https://www.baltimoresun.com/business/bs-md-cannabis-licenses-20190528-story.html.

17 *Richmond v. Croson*, 488 U.S. 469 (1989), seems to suggest that the statistics must come from within a particular industry.

16 Introduction to Cannabis and Advertising

Cassia Furman, Andrea Golan, and Charles S. Alovisetti

Introduction

Cannabis marketing and advertising is a broad topic, encompassing a diverse range of sub-topics, such as health care law and FDA regulation, digital privacy laws, and aiding and abetting violations of the CSA. Moreover, the advertising of cannabis and hemp are regulated differently. The FDA now oversees hemp advertising in the context of health-related claims, while the cannabis industry remains federally illegal and thus is not overseen by federal regulators. Advertising can be a particularly challenging area for cannabis operators given that "compliance" with local or state advertising regulations has a subjective element and enforcement is inconsistent. Even operators making conscientious advertising decisions (for example, eschewing the use of cartoons or similar images appealing to children) can face sanctions from officials reaching the opposite conclusion. Subjective enforcement is also evident across social media platforms, where one company's cannabis content can inspire thousands of "likes" and "followers," while another company sees its account terminated for nearly identical images and messaging.

Difficulties for operators are exacerbated by the lack of uniform consensus around appropriate advertising, even within a given state or municipality. The lack of certainty often compels operators seeking to maintain a competitive advantage over "disruptor" competitors to push the envelope on ad content in an effort to drive sales. The margin of error is compounded in the digital age by the ease of searching a company's marketing and advertising history online. Companies have faced regulatory issues related to an ad or label previously removed from its active content, but still prone to resurfacing on a regulator's browser search months or even years later.

Finally, the landscape is further complicated by the fragmented nature of state laws governing cannabis markets. Each state, and many local governments, has unique laws, creating complications in the digital age for both cannabis operators and prospective advertisers, who must already contend with the potential federal illegality of an advertiser's activity, as well as possible federal sanction. Federal law prevents cannabis products from traveling across state lines. Cannabis licenses are often highly controlled and limited in number, resulting in scarcity. Some states impose residency requirements to own or operate a cannabis business, further complicating multi-state operations. To deal with such constraints, some companies license their intellectual property to cannabis businesses in each state, but are then operating at a distance, possibly without a strong understanding of state-specific advertising and packaging requirements.

Despite the challenges, and in some cases inspired by them, cannabis companies continue to develop innovative advertising and marketing campaigns. These campaigns are critical to differentiating brands in a segmented market where there are still few dominant trade names and marks. This chapter offers a broad survey of topics relevant to cannabis operators and prospective advertisers.

The Controlled Substances Act

The Controlled Substance Act prohibits:

- Unauthorized use of the Internet to "deliver, distribute, or dispense a controlled substance," such as cannabis, as well as aiding and abetting the unauthorized use of the Internet to do so.[1]
- Knowing or intentional use of a "communication facility" to commit, cause, or facilitate the commission of a felony violation of the CSA, which includes manufacturing, distributing, or dispensing a controlled substance.[2]
- Placing in "any newspaper, magazine, handbill, or other publications, any written advertisement knowing that it has the purpose of seeking or offering illegally to receive, buy, or distribute" a controlled substance.[3]
- "Knowingly or intentionally us[ing] the Internet, or caus[ing] the Internet to be used, to advertise the sale of, or to offer to sell, distribute, or dispense" controlled substances.[4]

Traditionally an advertiser's assessment of whether to run cannabis content is determined by the CSA, which classifies cannabis as a Schedule I substance. The CSA's ban on *any person* advertising illegal drugs, however, includes exemptions for advertising "which merely advocates the use of a similar material, which advocates a position or practice, and *does not attempt to propose or facilitate an actual transaction in a Schedule I controlled substance*"[5] (Emphasis added). This exemption is unlikely to apply to cannabis operators and ancillary businesses, given that providing a platform for the purchase and sale of illegal narcotics goes beyond mere advocacy.

The CSA further provides that it is unlawful for *any person* to

> knowingly or intentionally use the Internet, or cause the Internet to be used, to advertise the sale of, or to offer to sell, distribute, or dispense, a controlled substance where such sale, distribution, or dispensing is not authorized by [the CSA] or by the Controlled Substances Import and Export Act.[6]

As related to ancillary businesses that use the Internet to advertise cannabis products and operators or facilitate cannabis sales, the CSA prohibits the use of the Internet to "deliver, distribute, or dispense a controlled substance," such as cannabis, as well as aiding and abetting the unauthorized use of the Internet to do so.[7] Similarly, the CSA prohibits the knowing or intentional use of a "communication facility" to commit, cause, or facilitate the commission of a felony violation of the Act, which includes manufacturing, distributing, or dispensing a controlled substance.[8]

Although the CSA restrictions appear daunting, certain mitigating factors have led some advertisers – largely outside the premium publishing markets – to be more comfortable with cannabis advertising. First, various court decisions, mostly involving drug deals outside of the cannabis realm, have limited the scope of liability associated with communication facilities. In *Abuelhawa v. United States*, 556 U.S. 816, 823–24 (2009), the federal government recorded six calls between a suspected dealer and the defendant. The defendant was charged with six felonies on the theory that each of the phone calls was made in violation of 21 U.S.C.S. § 843(b), despite the fact that the defendant ultimately purchased only a misdemeanor quantity of cocaine. Noting that Congress meant to treat purchasing drugs for personal use more leniently than felony distribution, the unanimous Court held that using a telephone to make a misdemeanor drug purchase does not facilitate felony drug distribution in violation of § 843(b). The Court's conclusion that the CSA's communication facility provisions are aimed at those who "coordinat[e] illegal drug operations," reasonably distinguishes publishers printing ads for a third party from criminal activity, although reported court decisions to date do not firmly establish this point.

Likewise, aiding and abetting liability requires the intent to facilitate the entire underlying crime. Intending to profit from publishing ads for a cannabis business is not the same as intending to facilitate the cannabis business' sale of cannabis. The government "must prove the commission of the predicate drug offense beyond a reasonable doubt in order to sustain a conviction under section 843(b)." *United States v. Dotson*, 871 F.2d 1318, 1322 (6th Cir. 1989). In *Dotson*, the defendant appealed a conviction for using a communication device, specifically a telephone, to facilitate the distribution of, and possession with intent to distribute, a controlled substance (cocaine) in violation of 21 U.S.C. § 843(b). In order to sustain a conviction under section 843(b), the court held that the government must prove three formal elements: (1) a knowing or intentional (2) use of a communication facility (3) to facilitate the commission of a drug offense (*Dotson*, 871 F.2d at 1321, citing *United States v. McGhee*, 854 F.2d 905, 908 (6th Cir. 1988)). The third element contains the further requirement that the "government prove the commission of the underlying substantive drug offense beyond a reasonable doubt." Based on this reasoning and the fact that the jury instruction did not adequately communicate the government's burden to establish the underlying drug offense, the Sixth Circuit Court of Appeals vacated the district court judgment against the defendant.

Key Advertising Mediums

Radio and Television

The cannabis industry, in its current phase, began to emerge in roughly 2012, when cannabis was legalized for adult use in Colorado and Washington. Consequently, state-legal cannabis businesses have largely relied on more recent media, like the Internet and cannabis-focused print media, rather than radio and television, to advertise. While the Federal Communications Commission (FCC) has not explicitly banned cannabis-related television and radio advertisements, other governmental agencies may view running cannabis advertisements as prosecutable, thereby endangering an entity's FCC license. Additionally, most states' cannabis advertising regulations require some form of confirmation that the recipients, or the majority thereof, of cannabis-related advertising are registered patients or caregivers or at least 21 years old. Age verification can be especially challenging with television and radio advertisements, making it a less favorable advertising medium for cannabis-related companies.

Print Media

Cannabis has had a long history of industry-dedicated magazines, in large part due to its inability to access general print media, such as newspapers. Although some non-cannabis–specific print publications are relaxing restrictions on cannabis-related advertising, much of the print advertising for cannabis-related businesses still tends to appear largely in cannabis-specific print publications. Advertising in print publications tends to make it easier for operators to vet recipients and comply with state-specific age verification requirements.

Out of Home Advertising

Out of home advertising largely consists of billboards. This advertising medium is increasingly popular amongst cannabis-related operators, especially non-plant–touching ancillary businesses. While most states with robust cannabis regulatory frameworks address out of home advertising, such restrictions are generally applicable to licensed plant-touching operators, rather than ancillary businesses. Nonetheless, where such advertising is permitted, it is generally best practice to avoid siting a cannabis-related billboard within close proximity to a school or interstate highway.

Social Media

Perhaps one of the most popular advertising mediums for cannabis-related businesses, social media generally offers cannabis-related businesses greater advertising freedom. This is largely because social media outlets, such as Instagram, TikTok, and Facebook, tend to be monitored irregularly. Additionally, social media makes it easier for cannabis-related businesses to perform age verification. Nonetheless, numerous plant-touching and ancillary businesses have had their social media accounts deleted, in some cases multiple times. This is because major social media outlets like Instagram and Facebook prohibit or heavily restrict cannabis advertising on their platforms.[9] Search engines like Google have followed suit, explicitly prohibiting cannabis advertisements.[10] TikTok, the social media platform which revolves around sharing 15-second video clips, does not directly address cannabis content, but nonetheless specifically prohibits content that displays or encourages drugs or drug consumption and content that depicts minors consuming or possessing drugs, alcohol, or tobacco.[11] Section "Other Marketing Issues" examines issues with social media "influencers" in greater detail.

Other Marketing Issues

Influencer Marketing

Cannabis companies are increasingly turning to influencer marketing as an appealing and often less expensive alternative to conventional advertising. In spite of the growing number of states where cannabis is legal, it remains difficult to find advertisers, particularly premium publishers, willing to violate the federal prohibition on advertising a Schedule I controlled substance. The use of influencers both presents a creative solution to this issue and mirrors larger advertising and marketing trends. Influencer campaigns allow cannabis companies to leverage the reach of an influencer's social media following to promote their brands, products, or services across state lines.

Even so, cannabis influencer marketing comes with its own unique set of challenges. Companies must comply with FTC endorsement guidelines, as well as state laws governing cannabis marketing and advertising.

The cannabis advertising policies of social media platforms can be just as tricky. Contracts with influencers are also a key consideration. The rules can be complicated, and in the event an influencer breaks those rules, both the influencer and the brand will be held responsible.

FTC Endorsement Guides

The FTC Endorsement Guides, formally known as the Guides Concerning the Use of Endorsements and Testimonials in Advertising, were first enacted in 1980 and amended in 2009. The over-arching premise of these non-binding guides is that consumers have a right to know whether an opinion is independent or incentivized. In the words of FTC Commissioner, Rohit Chopra, "When companies launder advertising by paying an influencer to pretend that their endorsement or review is untainted by a financial relationship, this is illegal payola."[12]

The FTC Endorsement Guides require a clear and conspicuous disclosure of material connections between endorsers and advertisers. It is important to consider what the FTC deems to be an "endorsement," a "material connection," or a "clear disclosure." Simply showing the product or tagging the brand in a post can be deemed an endorsement. Paying someone to endorse a brand is a material connection, but the FTC says it can be less than that. A free or discounted product, a perk, or a chance to win a free product, are all deemed to be material connections. Employment, personal, and family relationships are also considered material connections requiring disclosure. A clear disclosure is one that plainly lets the public know the connection between the influencer and the brand. The disclosure must be conveyed at the beginning of a post. Readers should not have to click for an expanded explanation in order to see the disclosure. Cannabis influencers also must be careful not to make claims that a product can treat a health condition or cure disease unless it can be backed up by competent and reliable scientific evidence. The FTC requirements for substantiation of claims discussed earlier in the chapter also extend to influencer endorsements.

These standards are evolving. In early 2020, the FTC announced its intent to update the voluntary guidance as well as its enforcement approach by requiring social media platforms to implement policies for disclosure. Additionally, it will be mandating influencer contracts to specify the disclosure rules to which influencers and companies must adhere.[13] The FTC also plans to codify elements of the existing non-binding guides into formal rules so that violators can be liable for civil penalties and damages.[14]

State Advertising and Marketing Regulations

In addition to FTC guidelines, cannabis companies face a conflicting patchwork of state advertising laws. For example, in California any advertising "calculated to induce the sale of cannabis" can only be displayed after the advertiser has confirmed, using reliable up-to-date audience composition data, that at least 71.6% of the audience viewing the advertising is reasonably expected to be 21 years of age or older.[15] Other states, such as Washington, require certain language to be included in every cannabis advertisement warning of the product's intoxicating effects and health risks. As advertisers must comply with these rules, so must influencers advertising on their behalf. In most states with a regulated cannabis market, the acts of an agent of a cannabis licensee (i.e., the influencer) are imputed to the licensee.

Social Media Platform Policies

Cannabis companies must also be mindful of social media platform policies prohibiting the advertising or sale of cannabis. Even companies with a longstanding presence on a particular social media platform may see their content suddenly removed, without prior notice or ability to remove offensive content. In many cases competitors play the role of "watchdog," reporting user violations to the platform and triggering complaint-based enforcement activity. Historically, brands and their influencers were compelled to tread carefully by avoiding images of cannabis or cannabis paraphernalia on social media platforms, lest risking account closures for violation. While this appears to be happening less often, with anecdotal reports of some platforms even welcoming cannabis content (particularly if content involves an influencer with a large platform following), the risk of account closure, and the loss of organically grown followers, is real. To lower the risk of account closure, one should avoid posts that depict consumption, show images of minors, seem to appeal to youth, or appear to promote teen vaping.

Influencer Contracts

Influencers new to the cannabis space are likely unaware of all the applicable legal requirements that come into play when making a seemingly simple endorsement for a cannabis company. Cannabis companies should have detailed contracts in place that explain, in plain English, content posting guidelines. A separate signed acknowledgment that the influencer has read the guidelines is advisable. Examples of adequate disclosures should be spelled out. "Thanks, Brand" is not a sufficient disclosure, while "Thanks Brand for the free [product]" meets the FTC clear disclosure requirement. Agreements should be tailored to the type of campaign and address items such as how many posts will be made, how often, and in what time frame. Other items to consider are whether to require pre-approval of posts, requirements to use specific hashtags, and who owns the content created by the influencer. This list is by no means exhaustive. Consult with legal counsel to create a robust contract that clearly sets forth each party's obligations.

Mobile Applications

Mobile applications not only enable companies to advertise their products and services, but also enhance user interactivity. An illustration of the complex interplay between federal cannabis prohibition and e-commerce is the use of mobile applications to control devices such as vaporizers, which came to an unanticipated head in 2019 when an outbreak of electronic cigarette ("e-cigarette") and vaping-related lung injuries and deaths, now known as "EVALI," emerged without warning.[16] The rise in use of e-cigarettes and vaporization devices, which started gaining popularity in 2007, largely coincided with the legalization of medical and recreational cannabis. The proliferation of e-cigarette and nicotine vaping devices went largely unregulated until the 2019 outbreak of lung injuries associated with use of e-cigarettes and vaporizer products. From June 2019 to January 2020, over 2500 cases of e-cigarette or vaping-associated lung injury were reported to the Centers for Disease Control and Prevention (CDC).[17]

In addition to e-cigarette and nicotine vaping devices, vaporizer products containing THC were also identified as a culprit in the spate of lung injuries and deaths. Lawmakers responding to the public health crisis caused by the EVALI outbreak often failed to distinguish between cannabis vaping products sold through the regulated market and contaminated cannabis products sold through the black market. Some policymakers also used the crisis as an opportunity to vilify cannabis use in general by lumping it with the rising rates of teen addiction to legal e-cigarettes, which had already been declared an epidemic by the U.S. Surgeon General. Some states and municipalities called for bans on all flavored products. Others called for temporary bans on all vaping products, including both cannabis and tobacco, while others tried (and are trying) to pass laws prohibiting sale of all e-cigarettes. President Trump called on the FDA to ban flavored e-cigarettes entirely, while Congress considered a ban on cannabis products already illegal under federal law.

In the midst of these public health concerns, Apple announced a sweeping ban on all apps in its iOS App Store that encourage or facilitate the consumption of vape products. Citing the spread of vaping devices as a public health crises and a youth epidemic, Apple removed 181 apps representing a mix of store apps, games, and hardware companion apps.[18] Apps that facilitate the sale of cannabis, tobacco, or controlled substances were already prohibited.[19]

Google Play, the other major platform for mobile apps, also made a significant policy change in 2019. The pivot was made on the heels of an FTC lawsuit alleging that Google was not adequately vetting apps for age-appropriate content for placement in the children and family section of the Play Store.[20] In addition to prohibiting apps that facilitate the sale of tobacco, including e-cigarettes, Google Play does not allow apps that "facilitate the sale of marijuana or marijuana products, regardless of legality."[21] Google Play's policies outline some examples of common violations, including: allowing users to order cannabis through an in-app shopping cart feature; assisting users in arranging delivery or pick-up of cannabis; and facilitating the sale of products containing THC.[22]

Apple's App Store and Google's Play Store have adopted policies which tie back to the language in the CSA discussed earlier in this chapter. The CSA makes it a felony, punishable up to four years in prison, to place an advertisement knowing it has the purpose of offering to illegally receive, buy, or distribute a Schedule 1 controlled substance.[23] The CSA also prohibits using the Internet to advertise the sale of, or to offer to sell, distribute, or dispense an unauthorized controlled substance.[24] Therefore, Apple and Google Play will not allow a cannabis-related mobile app to allow an in-app purchase or arrange delivery. Such functionality would be considered facilitating a sale.

However, a mobile app may direct users to the nearest store or delivery service outside of the mobile application, provided the user's geographic location is verified by the app to confirm residence in a state where cannabis is legal. If the app user were located in a state where cannabis had not been legalized, directing the user to such information would also be a direct violation of the CSA. For example, while Eaze, a popular cannabis delivery service, currently has an active app on the Apple App Store and Google Play store, the app itself does not facilitate cannabis sales and delivery, but instead leads users to Eaze's website for such services. Like the CSA, Apple and Google Play policies carve out an exception for advertising material which "merely advocates the use" of a controlled substance or "advocates a position or practice" without facilitating an actual transaction.[25] In practice, this means cannabis-related mobile apps may promote the use of cannabis through educational, health, lifestyle, or scientific information.

Setting aside the CSA's limitations on advertising cannabis, cannabis-vaping apps are confronting an additional hurdle to admission into Apple's App Store and Google's Play Store. Integrated vaping apps made an appearance in 2019, offering innovative features such as allowing users to identify the measure of cannabinoids while taking a draw, setting limits on the "dose" of each inhalation, or allowing users to lock their devices via the app. When Apple announced its ban on vaping apps in late 2019, it permitted Apple device users who already downloaded the apps to continue using them. Otherwise, any app that Apple deems to encourage the use of vape products is not permitted in the Apple Store.

For the moment, Google Play maintains a more liberal policy for admitting vaping apps. Like Apple, Google Play does not allow apps that facilitate the sale of e-cigarettes.[26] However, Google Play does not similarly prohibit apps that encourage consumption of vape products. Rather,

Google Play does not allow apps that encourage irresponsible use or depict or encourage the use of tobacco (including e-cigarettes) to minors. Consequently, vaping apps (cannabis or otherwise) are generally permitted in the Google Play Store, provided they do not display imagery, text, or characters that promote irresponsible use or consumption by minors. Until there is a shift in federal policy and cannabis is removed from the CSA, Apple and Google are unlikely to make any policy changes in this area. For vaping-related apps, that shift is more likely to move in the other direction as various regulatory and legislative bodies move to ban or severely restrict the sale, advertising, and marketing of e-cigarette and vaping products.

Best Practices

While cannabis-related companies cannot altogether avoid the risks and headaches affiliated with cannabis-related advertisements, incorporating the best practices listed below may mitigate the risk of enforcement:

- All cannabis-related companies, even ancillary companies who do not hold a state commercial cannabis license, should strictly comply with all applicable state and local cannabis advertising regulations.
- Avoid advertising to the general public and, where possible, ensure that all recipients of advertisements are registered patients and caregivers or at least 21 years old.
- Avoid the encouragement of state-illicit cannabis use. This includes, but is not limited to, refraining from advertising adult-use cannabis use in medical-only states.
- Use a method of age verification when advertising involves direct, individualized communication, such as text messages.
- Ensure all advertising is truthful and appropriately substantiated and does not create a misleading impression.
- Ensure that advertising is not made attractive to children – an area of frequent enforcement. This includes, but is not limited to, avoiding the following in advertisements: (1) cartoons; (2) likenesses to images, characters, or phrases popularly used to advertise to children; and (3) imitations of candy packaging or the use of phrases associated with children's candy products.
- Use models who are, and appear to be, at least 21 years old.
- Where applicable, include cannabis license numbers.
- Avoid advertising cannabis and alcohol together.
- Limit advertisements to state-licensed cannabis operators.

Notes

1 Controlled Substances Act, 21 U.S.C. § 801, at § 841(h)(1)(A) (2018).
2 21 U.S.C. § 843(b) (2018).
3 21 U.S.C. § 843(c)(1) (2018).
4 21 U.S.C. § 843(c)(2)(A) (2018).
5 21 U.S.C. § 843(c)(1) (2018).
6 21 U.S.C. § 843(c)(2) (2018).
7 21 U.S.C. § 841(h)(1)(A) (2018).
8 21 U.S.C. § 843(b) (2018).
9 "Terms of Use," *Instagram*, Apr. 19, 2018, https://help.instagram.com/581066165581870 ("You can't do anything unlawful, misleading, or fraudulent or for an illegal or unauthorized purpose."); "What Is Instagram's Policy on the Sale of Marijuana?," *Instagram*, https://help.instagram.com/789164081427334?helprep=related

> Instagram doesn't allow people or organizations to use the platform to advertise or sell marijuana, regardless of the Seller's state or county. Our policy prohibits any marijuana seller, including dispensaries, from promoting their business by providing contact information like phone numbers, email addresses, street addresses, or by using the 'contact us' tab in Instagram Business Accounts. **However, we do allow people to include a website link on their bio information**.
>
> (Emphasis added)

"Advertising Policies, Prohibited Content," *Facebook*, https://facebook.com/policies/ads ("Ads must not constitute, facilitate, or promote illegal products, services or activities"); "Advertising Policies, Drugs & Drug-Related Products," *Facebook*, https://www.facebook.com/policies/ads/prohibited_content/drugs ("Ads must not promote the sale or use of illegal, prescription or recreational drugs [...] Avoid using images of smoking-related accessories (like bongs and rolling papers) [...] Avoid using images of either recreational or medical marijuana").

10 "Advertising Policies, Dangerous Products or Services," *Google*, https://support.google.com/adspolicy/answer/6014299?hl=en

> The following is not allowed: [a]ds for substances that alter mental state for the purpose of recreation or otherwise [to] induce "highs" [such as] cocaine, crystal meth, heroin and other illegal opioids, [and] marijuana; [a]ds for products or services marketed as facilitating recreational drug use [such as] pipes, bongs, [and] cannabis coffee shops.

11 "Community Guidelines," *TikTok*, Jan. 2020, https://www.tiktok.com/community-guidelines?lang=en.
12 Rohit Chopra, "Regarding the Endorsement Guides Review," Commission File No. P204500, *Federal Trade Commission*, Feb. 12, 2020, https://www.ftc.gov/system/files/documents/public_statements/1566445/p204500_-_endorsement_guides_reg_review_-_chopra_stmt.pdf.
13 *Id.*
14 *Id.*
15 *Id.*
16 The term "EVALI," coined by the CDC, is an acronym that stands for 'e-cigarette, or vaping, product use-associated lung injury.' "Outbreak of Lung Injury Associated with E-Cigarette Use, or Vaping," *Center for Disease Control and Prevention*, Mar. 17, 2020, https://www.cdc.gov/tobacco/basic_information/e-cigarettes/severe-lung-disease/healthcare-providers/index.html.

17 Coady Wing, Ashley C. Bradford, Aaron E. Carroll, et al., "Association of State Marijuana Legalization Policies for Medical and Recreational Use with Vaping-Associated Lung Disease," *JAMA Network*, Apr. 6, 2020, https://jamanetwork.com/journals/jamanetworkopen/fullarticle/2763966.

18 Ina Fried and Mike Allen, "Exclusive: Apple to Remove Vaping Apps from Store," *Axios*, Nov. 15, 2019, https://www.axios.com/exclusive-apple-to-remove-vaping-apps-from-store-8669fd94-e92a-4ce4-a9e2-ce5afa598b67.html.

19 "App Store Review Guidelines," *Apple*, https://developer.apple.com/app-store/review/guidelines/#safety.

> Apps that encourage consumption of tobacco and vape products, illegal drugs, or excessive amounts of alcohol are not permitted on the App Store. Apps that encourage minors to consume any of these substances will be rejected. Facilitating the sale of marijuana, tobacco, or controlled substances (except for licensed pharmacies) isn't allowed.

20 A coalition of 22 consumer and public health advocacy groups filed a complaint with FTC, requesting it to investigate Google's unfair and deceptive practices in marketing apps to Children. "Apps Which Google Rates as Safe for Kids Violate Their Privacy and Expose Them to Other Harms," *Campaign for a Commercial Free Childhood*, Dec. 19, 2018, https://commercialfreechildhood.org/apps-which-google-rates-safe-kids-violate-their-privacy-and-expose-them-other-harms/.

21 "Restricted Content," *Google Play*, https://play.google.com/about/restricted-content/inappropriate-content/#!?zippy_activeEL=tobacco-alcohol#tobacco-alcohol.

22 *Id.*

23 21 U.S.C. § 843(c) (2018).

24 21 U.S.C. § 843(c)(2)(A) (2018).

25 21 U.S.C. § 843(c)(1) (2018).

26 "Restricted Content," *Google Play*, https://play.google.com/about/restricted-content/inappropriate-content/#!?zippy_activeEL=tobacco-alcohol#tobacco-alcohol.

Part III

Getting in the Game

Doing Deals in the
Cannabis Industry

17 Introduction to Cannabis and Business Formation

Charles S. Alovisetti, Elliot Y. Choi, and Catie Wightman

Introduction

Setting up a cannabis company correctly from the start is critical, especially if the goal is to take on outside capital, exit through a sale, take a company public, or acquire other companies with stock. Investors, buyers, and capital markets each have certain expectations regarding entity structures and corporate governance, and they often require entity restructuring (including conversion into another entity form) or adjustments to economics if a company's corporate governance is not up to par.

There are additional complexities and unique considerations for any entity in the cannabis industry, whether a license-holding company or an ancillary business (commonly referred to as "non-plant touching"). Not all cannabis companies are the same; for example, a family-owned farm has different considerations than does a business looking to go public. These considerations make it crucial for a cannabis company to take the time at the outset to set itself up correctly. Fixing mistakes later is time-consuming and costly.

First Decision: Entity Choice

An initial critical issue when starting a new business is which entity type to use. There are numerous entity types available, but most startups are set up as corporations or limited liability companies (LLCs). The advantages and disadvantages of these two entity types are discussed below.

Taxation

LLCs and corporations are taxed in fundamentally different ways. A corporation is a separate tax-paying entity, meaning that a corporation pays an income tax (currently 21% at the federal level). If dividends are issued to shareholders of a corporation, those shareholders must pay an additional tax on these dividends. That taxation structure is commonly called "double taxation." An LLC, on the other hand, is a pass-through entity for tax purposes, and any taxable gains are directly allocated to the members of an LLC who pay taxes on those gains based on each member's individual income tax bracket (up to 37% at the federal level).[1]

Moreover, if a corporation loses money, the losses are only available to reduce the taxes on the corporation itself and cannot be passed through to the shareholders. However, with an LLC, losses, deductions, and other tax benefits generally pass through to the members and can be used to offset other income on their individual tax returns (though this offset is subject to some key limitations).

While double taxation of a corporation can result in earnings being subject to a higher effective tax rate before making it into the shareholders' hands and may initially seem like a material downside to organizing as a corporation, there are some advantages to the corporate form. A corporation can help shield shareholders from personal tax liability under Section 280E of the Internal Revenue Code, which disallows ordinary business deductions if a business is engaged in trafficking a substance on schedule I or II of the Controlled Substances Act. The impact of Section 280E is critical for a cannabis corporation as "marihuana" remains on schedule I, although recently hemp has been removed through the enactment of the 2018 Farm Bill. Since the average cannabis company's tax rate is usually significantly higher than that of a business not subject to Section 280E, members of LLCs are often allocated phantom income, meaning these members owe more taxes than the cash distributions they received according to their ownership stake. This is not an issue in a corporation, since initial tax liability falls on the corporation. The corporate form also protects the shareholders, who generally only need to pay taxes when they receive a dividend.

The pass-through taxation of an LLC can create issues when the company takes on debt. The cancellation of debt, which may occur in certain circumstances such as a convertible note financing or bankruptcy, could create taxable income for an LLC resulting in recognition of ordinary income to the members in an amount equal to the canceled debt. Members may have losses previously allocated to them to offset this gain, but this is not always the case. Pass through taxation can also complicate convertible note financing transactions, a popular capital-raising structure for early stage companies.

It is no surprise that cannabis companies are at a far higher risk of an IRS audit. There are several high-profile cases where the IRS audited a cannabis company and determined that the company took deductions that were disallowed under Section 280E. Normal business deductions are not available to cannabis companies, but many push the envelope to reduce the significant tax burden caused by Section 280E.

Generally, an IRS audit occurs at the corporate or partnership level, and back taxes (and any related penalties) are paid by the corporation or the partnership, not by the shareholders or partners.[2] However, if a cannabis business is taxed as a pass-through entity, the IRS may follow the money in an audit and hold the owners personally liable for the taxes that should have been paid. A corporation can avoid this personal liability to its owners, provided there is no malfeasance on the part of the owners.

Changes implemented after December 31, 2017 under the Bipartisan Budget Act of 2015 (BBA) may make it less likely that owners will be exposed to personal tax liabilities.[3] These changes do not necessarily mean that owners of pass-through entities will avoid any personal liability, so all decisions based on the new rules should be carefully vetted with tax counsel. It is possible for some entities with fewer than 100 partners to opt out of the new audit rules.[4]

Another tax consideration is that most startups reinvest their revenue in operations, so it is rare for a startup to have excess cash that can be distributed to owners outside of an exit event. Compared to an LLC, it may be more tax efficient for a corporation to retain cash to reinvest in operations. A corporation currently pays 21% tax on its earnings, while members of an LLC are taxed on their allocated share of the LLC's income at their personal tax rates (which may be in excess of 21%), regardless of whether any cash is distributed to them. After distributing cash to allow members of an LLC to make their personal tax payments, an LLC may be left with less cash than a similarly situated corporation, leaving less capital available to reinvest in the LLC's operations.

Taxation can also impact administrative functions and create additional costs. Partnership tax accounting is complex and tracking the capital accounts of each member of an LLC can be time intensive. Roughly speaking, a capital account is the tax basis of a member of an LLC based on the running total of the member's contributions, profits and losses, and investment. An LLC must also send out a K-1 form to each of its owners at the end of every tax year. This form states the profit and loss allocated to each owner. Each owner must include this K-1 in their respective filings and pay taxes or take a deduction for any allocation of profit or loss. If a startup has a wide owner base, sending out K-1s can add to its accounting burden. LLC owners also face additional administrative burdens, and each may be required to file a tax return in multiple states.

Foreign Investments and Taxation

Foreign investors may prefer to invest in corporations rather than LLCs, since an investment in a corporation can allow them to avoid the obligation to file U.S. income tax returns. Pass-through taxation of LLCs can result in foreign investors facing unique downsides when investing in an LLC.

First, foreign investors are generally not subject to tax in the U.S., but an investment in an LLC could result in U.S. tax obligations for income effectively connected to U.S. trade or business (called Effectively

Connected Income or ECI). This would obligate foreign investors to make a federal income tax filing in the United States.

Second, countries that treat LLCs as corporations, such as Canada, do not attribute the taxes paid by LLCs to their owners. A Canadian investor may not benefit from foreign tax credits for taxes paid to the IRS and can end up facing double taxation, even with an LLC. This is why Canadian companies making investments in the U.S. often opt for limited partnerships (LPs). However, the LP entity form is generally not appropriate for startup companies. In addition to the burden on the investors themselves, an LLC also has withholding obligations on certain types of income allotted to foreign owners, even in the absence of cash distributions.

The issues related to foreign investors are often resolved by setting up a blocker corporation – a U.S. or foreign entity classified as a corporation for U.S. income tax purposes – between the startup LLC and the foreign investors. This is common practice in the investment fund context, but it adds a layer of complexity and expense that could be a deal-breaker, especially for a small investment in a startup. It is also possible for an LLC to "check the box" and elect to be taxed as a corporation, which would resolve issues related to foreign investors.

Other Tax Issues

In addition to the fundamental differences in how corporations and LLCs are taxed, three other tax features bear consideration. (These are extremely simplified descriptions of tax differences between corporations and LLCs.)

1   A corporation, but not an LLC, can take advantage of the Qualified Small Business Stock (QSBS) benefit set forth in Section 1202 of the Internal Revenue Code. Subject to certain qualifications, if a person holds QSBS for a five-year period, they may be able to exclude up to $10 million of capital gains on an exit.
2   An LLC can distribute appreciated property tax-free to its members, which can enable spin-off transactions. If a corporation distributed property to its shareholders, the property would be a taxable dividend.
3   If the owners of an LLC or corporation are also employees of the startup, entity choice can significantly affect employment taxes. An LLC's members are generally subject to self-employment tax on their share of income, but a corporation's shareholders are not. However, if a corporation is profitable and does not make any dividends while paying above-market salaries to its owner and employees, this can create issues.

Governance

In addition to different administrative costs and taxation, LLCs and corporations are also subject to different rules regarding governance. Unlike an LLC, which has broad authority to set up its governance and economic terms as the owners see fit, a corporation must follow certain clear governance structures established by corporate statutes and case law. These governance structures include the management of the corporation by a board of directors elected by the shareholders, and the appointment by the board of directors of officers to run the day-to-day operations. Shareholders cannot manage day-to-day operations, but an LLC can be structured so that the members can manage day-to-day operations. Only by making shareholder proposals or by electing directors do the shareholders influence the operations of the corporation. Unlike LLCs, a corporation, by law, is required to put certain major decisions to a shareholder vote. For example, under Delaware law, a corporation selling all or substantially all of its assets must approve such decisions by votes of both the board of directors and at least a majority of its shareholders. In addition, there are formalities a corporation should follow. For example, board meetings must be properly noticed and held, and formal written records, called minutes, must be kept for these events.

Unlike corporations, LLCs are typically permitted by state law to set forth the terms of their governance and economic distributions in an operating agreement. An LLC can be run directly by its members, by a manager, or in some other unique fashion determined by its owners. LLCs can also avoid the corporate formalities of corporations and establish their own rules for meetings and decision making. LLCs may prove useful in the case of a startup, where flexibility regarding governance is desirable.

Exits

The tax consequences of selling an LLC and corporation differ and can have a major impact on potential exits. One option available to a corporation, but not an LLC, is the ability to take advantage of a tax-free reorganization. With a Section 368 reorganization, if structured correctly, a buyer can acquire a corporation in exchange for stock of the buyer without creating a taxable transaction, whereas acquiring an LLC in exchange for stock of the buyer may result in a taxable event. Many public companies in the cannabis space like using Section 368 reorganizations since it allows them to use their stock as consideration for acquisitions without creating tax liability, and many of the largest cannabis transactions are stock-only deals.

On the other hand, selling assets is more tax-efficient for an LLC than for a corporation. If an LLC sells its assets, the owners will only pay one level of tax on the gain recognized from the assets sold. A corporation, however, has two levels of tax on an asset sale: the corporation must pay for any gain recognized on the assets, and the shareholders pay taxes on any gain paid out as a dividend. Since many buyers in the cannabis industry are nervous about hidden liabilities, they may want to opt for an asset acquisition over a stock deal or merger, assuming the corresponding regulations allow for asset sales. An asset sale also allows the buyers to get a basis step-up in the acquired assets, which is a significant tax advantage.

A corporation can also be better suited for an IPO, as almost all publicly traded companies are corporations. However, it is possible to structure an IPO with an LLC or convert an LLC to a corporation prior to an IPO, but these options can increase complexity, costs, and time to complete the IPO.

Incentive Equity

The structure of a corporation's incentive equity plan, generally structured as stock options, can also be an advantage since employees are more familiar with stock options. It is possible for an LLC to grant its employees incentive equity called "profit interests" which, while different, approximate stock options in a corporation. However, many employees do not appreciate the value of profit interests in the same way they understand stock options. The greater understanding of the real value of stock options can be useful to a startup when attracting employees.

Legal Costs and Investor Views

Investors, including venture capitalist and angel investors, have traditionally preferred corporations rather than LLCs as investment targets. More sophisticated investors are far more comfortable with LLCs now than in the past, but corporations are still preferred.

The fact that corporations have traditionally been the choice for startup companies means that many of the legal forms used for raising capital are standardized for corporations. Form documents are now available for earlier stage equity financings (often called "seed-stage financing").[5] For example, the National Venture Capital Association (NVCA) has developed a collection of form seed-stage financing documents that are posted on its website for use with corporations, but not for LLCs.[6] The Y Combinator has developed a Simple Agreement for Future Equity form (commonly known as a SAFE) for corporations that is also frequently used for seed-stage financings. These forms were developed to help reduce legal costs and friction associated with negotiating financings. While the time may seem ripe for someone to create equivalent LLC forms, those forms do not currently exist. In addition, partnership tax is far more complicated than C corporation tax, and this complexity can add to the time and expense of preparing documentation for an LLC transaction.

Another common form of seed-stage financings is a convertible note raise. It can be tricky to use convertible notes with LLCs as compared to corporations. With an LLC, convertible notes should be structured carefully to avoid adverse tax consequences (e.g., members having to recognize gain due to forgiveness of indebtedness income) and overly complex calculations.

Other Options

There are several other entity types, including limited partnerships, limited liability partnerships, limited liability limited partnerships, cooperatives, sole proprietorships, and non-profit corporations. These entities have their uses, but they are rarely appropriate for a startup business for a number of reasons. Some require governance structures that are too complex for startups, and others make it too difficult to finance the company.

Final Considerations

Choosing the right entity type is not a decision with a clear-cut right and wrong answer that applies to all scenarios. The choice depends on the individual facts and circumstances, some of which are not known at the time an entity is formed. And while entity selection is rarely an irreversible decision because it is usually possible to convert one entity form into another, conversion down the line can have adverse tax consequences and can result in significant legal costs. It is therefore worthwhile to take the time to make an informed initial decision.

Second Decision: Jurisdiction of Formation

Once an entity form is selected, the next question is where to form the entity. The standard advice for startups is to form the entity (at the least the holding company that will be used to raise capital) in Delaware, regardless of where their physical operations will be located. That is because investors prefer Delaware.

The state of Delaware has developed a series of laws, including the Delaware General Corporation Law (DGCL), as well as a court system and case law familiar with the types of legal issues faced by corporations. Seasoned investors and their counsel thoroughly know and rely on these laws, which is why, absent unique circumstances, startups are generally advised to form in Delaware and qualify as foreign corporations in their other states of operation.

So, what about cannabis startups? Because some courts have decided not to enforce cannabis contracts due to policy concerns regarding the federally illegal status of cannabis, legal practitioners debate whether it is a better idea to use a state like Nevada, California, Colorado, or Massachusetts, where adult-use cannabis is legal at the state level. The logic is that an adult-use cannabis company should take advantage of the corporate law of a state where such activity is expressly permitted.

While Delaware does not have a legal adult-use market for cannabis, companies that choose to incorporate in Delaware likely are not violating Delaware law if they are only serving the adult-use market in states where it is legal. Regulated industries, such as gaming, alcohol, and motor vehicle manufacturing, often deal with conflicting regulations and laws in different states. These companies are not required to follow Delaware laws in all jurisdictions just because they are incorporated in Delaware. However, because cannabis is still federally illegal, there is still a risk that Delaware could treat cannabis companies differently than federally legal businesses.

Side Note: Delaware Repurchase Provisions

In addition to concerns about investor preferences and contract enforceability, another issue for cannabis startups is a potential need to repurchase shares held by investors or employees. If a startup holds or plans to hold a cannabis license or is otherwise closely connected to a licensed entity (a lender, for example), it will likely be subject to background checks and vetting of owners. That means having a bad apple shareholder could put the whole business at risk. In order to mitigate this risk, cannabis startups are advised to consider adding a provision to their governing documents that permit the repurchase of shares from an equity holder who creates a licensing issue.

In Delaware, the right to redeem shares must be included in the certificate of incorporation or corresponding resolutions authorizing the shares[7]; the right of redemption will not be inferred from ambiguous words or phrases. This right is further set forth in Section 151(b)(2) of the DGCL, which authorizes redemption of stock by a corporation that holds a government license or franchise in order to prevent the loss of such license, franchise, or membership, or to reinstate it.[8] The certificate of incorporation or the resolution or resolutions issuing such stock must set out the terms, conditions, and procedures applicable to redemption, including the redemption price, which may consist of "cash, property or rights, including securities of the same or another corporation."[9]

Forming an Entity in Other Jurisdictions: State Cannabis Contract Enforceability

Another factor in selecting a jurisdiction is whether state statutes explicitly make cannabis contracts enforceable. For example, in Colorado, C.R.S. Section 13-22-601 states,

> [i]t is the public policy of the state of Colorado that a contract is not void or voidable as against public policy if it pertains to lawful

activities authorized by section 16 of article XVIII of the state constitution and article 453.4 of title 12, C.R.S.

Note that this Colorado statutory reference explicitly references a constitutional amendment and statutes that permit commercial cannabis activity in Colorado. It does not mention anything regarding activities outside the state of Colorado, which is a critical component for any national cannabis company.

This issue arises in California as well, where the applicable statute Cal. Civ. Code Section 1550.5 reads:

> [n]otwithstanding any law, including, but not limited to, Section 1550, 1667, and 1668 and federal law, commercial activity related to medicinal cannabis or adult-use cannabis conducted in compliance with California law and any applicable local standards, requirements, and regulations shall be deemed to be all of the following: (1) A lawful object of a contract[,] (2) Not contrary to an express provision of law, any policy of express law, or good morals[,] (3) Not against public policy.

Again, the statute only covers the policy issues around enforceability to the extent the cannabis contract deals with licensed activity in the state in question (California). Similar statutes are also on the books in Nevada[10] and Massachusetts.[11]

Given the absence of explicit public policy support for contracts dealing with out of state activities, which would be the case for any national or multi-state cannabis startup, it may not be advantageous to form in an adult-use cannabis state, when compared to the advantages of forming in Delaware.

Notes

1 Corporations meeting certain requirements can make an S corporation election and be taxed as a pass-through entity in the same fashion as an LLC. Most cannabis businesses would not meet these requirements. It is also possible for an LLC to elect to be taxed as a C corporation, which would allow it to avoid the complexities of pass-through taxation discussed below, while still taking advantage of the greater flexibility of the LLC form. However, it is uncommon for LLCs to make this election, since most businesses would instead choose a corporate form more familiar to investors and potential buyers. (Unless otherwise noted, it is assumed that corporations have not made an S corporation election and LLCs have not elected to be taxed as C corporations and are pass-through entities for tax purposes.)
2 Darleen Pulliam and Sharon K. Burnett, "The IRS's New Streamlined Audit Rules for Partnerships," *The CPA Journal*, Nov. 2017, https://www.cpajournal.com/2017/11/01/irss-new-streamlined-audit-rules-partnerships/.

3 "Partnership Audit Rules for Cannabis Companies," Green Growth CPAs, Mar. 6, 2019, https://blog.greengrowthcpas.com/partnership-audit-rules-cannabis-companies.

4 *Id.*

5 *"Version 3.2,"* Series Seed, https://www.seriesseed.com/.

6 "Model Legal Documents," NVCA, https://nvca.org/model-legal-documents/.

7 *SV Investment Partners v. Thoughtworks,* 7 A.3d 973 (Del. Ch. 2010).

8 Del. Code Ann. tit. 8, § 151(b)(2) (2019).

9 *Id.*

10 Nev. Rev. Stat. § 453D.140 (2019).

11 Mass. Gen. Laws ch. 94G, § 10 (2019).

18 Introduction to Cannabis, Due Diligence, and Deal Structuring

Charles S. Alovisetti, Elliot Y. Choi, and Sahar Ayinehsazian

Introduction

Because of the jurisdiction-specific nature of state and local cannabis and hemp laws, it is difficult to provide guidance on due diligence that will be applicable across all jurisdictions. However, there are regulatory commonalities, despite the disparities in these laws. This article focuses on properly identifying these common issues rather than on black letter law.

Deal Structure

Permissibility of Transaction

The cannabis industry is full of companies and promoters seeking to put deals together now and worry about regulatory compliance later. In most cases, the real aim is to push forward profitable activities while maintaining the appearance of compliance. This aggressive approach can pay off, but there are often negative impacts that must be managed. Additionally, transactions can unwind and severe sanctions can potentially be imposed.

Although a significant fine can be devastating for many companies, it may be worth it for a large public company to close a deal quickly. Irrespective of the ability to withstand large fines, all parties should enter a deal fully aware of when they are pushing regulatory limits. Thus, the first step of due diligence is always to look at the transaction from an aerial view, to determine whether it is permissible and what potentially negative regulatory outcomes may arise.

Most importantly, potential buyers should not assume that a license can be sold simply because a broker has advertised it for sale. Likewise, when it comes to regulatory workarounds, it is best to trust, but also to verify. Finally, the buyer should think through any disclosure issues that might arise before beginning work in earnest on a transaction. Depending on the state, there may not be a materiality threshold at which regulators care about ownership. Some regulators expect to know the names of all parties to a transaction, no matter how insignificant or passive. In some cases, local regulators' disclosure requirements differ significantly from state requirements.

Mergers and Acquisitions

The first step in confirming an M&A transaction's deal structure is to ensure that the license in question, or the licensed entity, can be sold. Many states prohibit the transfer of cannabis licenses, making it imperative that the licensed *entity* be sold. Some states, like Maryland, have enacted laws that prohibit the sale of a licensed entity until the business has been operational for a certain period. Other states have residency requirements, limiting the pool of potential buyers. Deal structure analysis may also be necessary at the local level, depending on the state in question. For example, California localities vary greatly in how they handle cannabis license ownership changes, ranging from pre-closing approval requirements to a simple post-closing notification. It is important to understand local requirements early in the process in order to appropriately address any discrepancies with state requirements.

Regulators may also take an inconsistent approach as to what constitutes a sale of a cannabis- or hemp-related license. For example, as stated above, merely changing the ownership of a company that holds a cannabis license may not necessarily constitute a sale, especially if the ownership of that company has not completely changed. Further, the definition of ownership also varies between states as well as localities. In jurisdictions prohibiting the transfer of a cannabis or hemp license from one entity to another, it may be preferable to structure the transaction as a stock deal or merger, rather than an asset sale.

Another very common issue with cannabis deal structures is perceived or actual violations of ownership restrictions. An early form of ownership restriction that is becoming less common is a residency restriction. Some states, such as Washington State, require that all owners (those directly participating in or entitled to the revenue or profit of a business in addition to equity holders) be residents of the state. A restriction becoming more common in states with a limited number of licenses, like Pennsylvania, is a prohibition on owning more than a certain number of licenses. In the same vein, many jurisdictions apply a strict numerical cap on the number of licenses that can be held by one person or entity. Almost all states restrict the ability of an entity with an interest in a cultivation, manufacturing, distribution, transportation, or dispensary/retail license to have an interest in a testing license as well. Sellers often propose alternative deal structures to avoid a clear license cap violation, but regulators have taken mixed approaches to scrutinizing these structures. Having too much control over a license can constitute de facto ownership for license cap purposes.

One common workaround for these issues is to have the licensed entity enter into a management agreement, often containing an option to purchase the licensed entity itself for nominal consideration once transferability is legal. This may or may not resolve an ownership restriction, depending on the state. Increasingly, regulators have required preapproval of management agreements or have banned them entirely.

Debt Financings

There is a theoretical question as to the risk of a cannabis debt agreement being found unenforceable for public policy reasons. (At this point, we have not seen major loans challenged.) As discussed in the preceding chapter, many states have changed their laws to explicitly make cannabis contracts enforceable. These laws are limited to operations pursuant to the laws of the state in question and do not cover multi-state operations (which is often the case for larger loans). Enforceability may also impact closing opinions delivered in a financing.

The collateral package for a cannabis loan raises several regulatory concerns. Whether cannabis, cannabis products, and cannabis licenses can be collateralized varies across states. For example, very few states explicitly prohibit taking a security interest in cannabis or cannabis products, but all states prohibit the ownership of cannabis (personal possession aside) by a non-cannabis licensee. Likewise, there is rarely an explicit prohibition on attaching liens to cannabis licenses themselves. Nonetheless, some regulators take the position that such liens are forbidden, due to the approval process typically necessary to transfer such licenses or license holding entities. The enforceability of such non-explicit restrictions remains to be seen. Pledge agreements, where the underlying equity is in an entity that directly or indirectly holds a cannabis license, also require careful consideration so as not to violate provisions requiring approval of the change of ownership of a cannabis business. As with collateral issues, this often requires multi-state and locality analysis.

In addition to collateral issues, another major regulatory question for debt financings is determining the permissible level of control over a licensed entity. Regulations in this area of law are not very useful; almost no regulations provide practical advice about what kind of affirmative or negative covenants may be acceptable without implicating control. If a lender was seen as controlling a licensed entity, this would be a clear regulatory violation, as only the owners of a licensed entity may exercise control.

Warrant coverage in a debt transaction sometimes has a regulatory impact. Depending on the state, holding a convertible equity position in a licensed business may constitute ownership, requiring disclosure and approval of the lender as an equity holder and the other issues discussed in the section on equity financings below.

Finally, lenders and operators need to consider whether the loan will need to be disclosed or pre-approved by the regulators, and if so, at what point this disclosure must occur. This is an area of state cannabis regulations where there is a somewhat higher degree of regulatory guidance. Parties to a loan must think through any background check issues that may arise from pre-approval or disclosure of a loan.

Equity Financings

In equity financings, new owner approvals present the most common structuring issues. In some jurisdictions like Illinois, any owner, no matter how little or indirect their interest in a licensee may be, must be approved and added to the list of owners of a license. In other states, like Florida, where adding owners is easier, there may be a materiality threshold below which new owners do not need to be disclosed or pre-approved. It is, therefore, essential to understand the authority in question and its interplay with the proposed deal. In a jurisdiction with strict approval processes for new owners like Colorado prior to the implementation of HB 1090, companies often seek to bring owners into intellectual property holding companies or management companies. Similar structures are used in states like Arizona, which prohibit for-profit entities from owning licenses. Investors should understand the structure of their investment to determining what they are truly buying, as some companies are not open about the fact that the investment may not be in the licensed entity.

In some states, ownership caps are tied to materiality thresholds. For example, in Massachusetts, no entity or individual may control or own more than 10% of more than three adult-use licenses of the same type. It is important to ensure that potential investors do not prevent the consummation of an acquisition by violating these restrictions.

Equity investors should understand how any license violations of an issuer will impact their other license holding entities and future licenses. If an investor owns equity in several companies that have licenses in different states, a compliance issue with one of these licenses may trigger an obligation to disclose the violation to the other states. Such disclosure violations are generally more common in the context of competitive licensing processes.

Intellectual Property Licensing Deals

Intellectual property (IP) licensing arrangements are increasingly common in the cannabis space, given the prohibition on interstate transfers of cannabis. As such, a cannabis company with an established presence in one state may ultimately choose to enter an IP licensing deal in another state, instead of obtaining its own license. To maintain consistency, IP licensing agreements often have strict specifications, including strictures on the use of certain non-cannabis terpenes. It is imperative that such agreements do not inadvertently give too much control over the cannabis licensee to the IP holder, thereby triggering regulatory approval requirements.

In analyzing whether an IP licensing deal can be accomplished, the form of payment is also critical. Direct (i.e., percentage-based) participation in the revenue or profit of a licensed business can create ownership issues in many states, such as California. If ownership is implicated, regulatory approval and background checks may be needed. For this reason, many deals are structured as packaging arrangements, whereby the IP holder sells packages to the licensed cannabis business, which in turn uses the packages for the sale of the cannabis product.

Regardless of the form of payment, control of the licensed business operations and premises must remain entirely with the license holder. It may be permissible for employees of the IP holder to come onto the premises to assist with production, but they must remain subject to the control and direction of the licensee. Companies have gotten into trouble for turning over their facilities, without supervision, to an IP holder that wants to take direct control of the production process.

In addition, some states like Nevada and New York require pre-approval of new products, product logos, or product names sold by a licensed business. All states have requirements such as dosing guidelines, as well as packaging and labeling rules, regarding products sold by licensing businesses. These rules must be reviewed in advance of closing the transaction to ensure the new products will not create any violations.

Ancillary Transactions

Many investors prefer to invest in ancillary or non-plant touching companies because of a perceived lower risk as compared to plant touching cannabis companies. Investors might also assume that equity holders of ancillary companies are not subject to regulatory scrutiny or background checks, but this is not necessarily the case. It is better to confirm up front whether the proposed deal is contingent on investors avoiding background checks. The exact nature of an ancillary company and the jurisdictions in which it operates should be scrutinized in order to determine whether a background check will be necessary. It is also important to remember that even if no background check or regulatory disclosure is required as a matter of course, regulators often maintain broad authority to investigate further, including obtaining investor information.

Status of Licenses

Licenses

The most obvious diligence step with respect to a cannabis company target is to ensure that all its licenses are in good standing and that regulators recognize the individuals and entities that claim to hold them as the proper owners. Some states make this easy by providing online directories of licenses, though it is unusual for local jurisdictions to publicly report this information. In cases of non-public data, target companies will need to provide up-to-date copies of licenses and, where necessary, license applications. Regulators in some jurisdictions may release information to individuals with the written consent of licensees.

Not all licenses are equal. Typically, a state regulator will initially award a provisional license that becomes final once the company has passed inspections and is ready to operate. A provisional license can be subject to additional ownership change restrictions. There is usually a deadline by which a provisional license must become operational or risk relinquishment. Thinly capitalized companies have frequently faced challenges after winning licenses, scrambling to raise capital to fund build-outs within regulatory timing constraints. Notably, however, many states are lenient on these timelines, and there have been numerous cases where companies were given additional time to get up and running. It is still important to be aware of all timing constraints. Even in states where cannabis operations have been active for a long period of time, it is still important to confirm whether licenses are active. Failure to use a license, without mitigating circumstances, could result in an administrative action.

In some cases, it is necessary to carefully review the application materials in order to fully confirm a license. In other cases, such as when a license can be confirmed online for a business that has been operational for a long period of time, reviewing an application may not be as important. In certain jurisdictions, like Ohio, regulators expect any entity awarded a license to fulfill any plans set forth in a license application. If a company says on an application that it will hire workers in a certain community, some regulators will hold a company to that promise, which creates licensing risks if these plans are not brought to fruition. There also may be errors in an application that only come to light later during build-out.[1] Errors in an application could have adverse consequences, including the right of the regulators to rescind or cause forfeiture of the license.

Background Checks

In addition to the typical value of running background checks on key members of the management team, collecting biographical information about the executives and founders of a company can also help shed light on licensing risks. Most licensing regimes have strict requirements about the backgrounds and criminal statuses of cannabis company owners and employees. If an owner or executive has past issues that were not disclosed to the regulators or that indicate a risk to future licensure, such issues must be addressed in negotiations. Otherwise, they can have a ripple effect of negative outcomes for investors. For example, a founder with a drinking problem could be convicted a felony DUI, causing that founder to be removed from the ownership of a company as well as her management role because of the strict requirements most licensing regimes have about the backgrounds and criminal statuses of cannabis company owners and employees.

Legacy Regulatory Violations

It is particularly important to check a business's past regulatory issues, because regulators often view a violation as attached to an individual license, so that the violation will travel with the license through any transfer of ownership. Consequently, regulators may be less lenient in the future regarding compliance issues, due to a perceived history of bad acts. In addition, if there is a current administrative action against a licensed business, this may delay or prevent regulatory approval for a transaction such as a change of ownership.

Compliance

Enforcement Overview

It is hard to predict when and how cannabis regulations will be enforced. Long periods of lax enforcement can be followed by quick decisive action, compounded by the fact that regulators in new jurisdictions are often overwhelmed with the process of setting up a new framework and lack the resources to uncover licensing issues. Enforcement is often political and varies dramatically across jurisdictions and over time. For example, in Massachusetts, where there are caps on how many licenses a single company can own, several publicly traded companies had commercial arrangements with more licenses than the state limitations allowed. After the *Boston Globe* came out with a series of articles exposing these arrangements, regulators quickly began investigations that negatively impacted these companies' share prices.[2] Such a risk would have been difficult to determine during a diligence process.

Adding to the difficulty of sniffing out past and potential regulatory violations is the fact that not all states provide public information about licensing violations. Localities are also less likely to provide public information about licensing violations. For states and localities that do not publish violations, investors and acquirors will need to rely on disclosures from the companies themselves.

Due to the multiple challenges surrounding the identification of compliance issues, compliance diligence is often focused on the culture of compliance at a company. Almost all cannabis companies at this stage claim to take compliance seriously; however, this is often purely a marketing line. Cannabis compliance is exceptionally challenging due to the ever-shifting regulatory environment, the number of unique jurisdictions that any large company must consider, and the dynamic nature of the industry itself.

> Companies that take compliance seriously typically have some combination of the following: an internal compliance team with a direct line to senior management, dedicated regulatory counsel covering all relevant jurisdictions, internal or external compliance audits, lobbyists on retainer, an understanding of the common compliance issues that cannabis companies face, and a willingness to forego business opportunities in order to follow the law.

Ancillary Companies

Simply because a company does not hold a cannabis license does not mean it is free from worrying about compliance with state cannabis rules and regulations. If an ancillary company works with or provides services to licensed businesses, it must avoid regulatory issues to prevent causing trouble for its licensed counterparties. Compliance is increasingly important for ancillary businesses, as cannabis regulators expand their enforcement powers onto ancillary companies as well as licensees.

Products Liability and Vaping

As the cannabis industry expands, so too will litigation from consumers alleging injury from the use of cannabis products. The recent vaping crisis can provide insight into potential product liability risks. A company that appropriately handles the vaping challenges is likely to be at lower risk of product liability claims in the future, though all cannabis and hemp companies face some risks. Under general principles of product liability law, if a product causes personal injury or harm to a person, anyone in the chain of distribution, including a seller, can be held liable for placing that product into the stream of commerce.

With reference to the recent vaping illness crisis, the following steps may be helpful in evaluating a target company's risk of liability:

1   Consider whether any injuries or deaths have been linked to a company's products. Most of the vaping fatalities are linked to products distributed by unlicensed illegal producers. It would be a very bad sign for a licensed company to be directly implicated in a vaping illness.

2   Consider whether the company has complied with the rapidly evolving state laws regarding vaporized products.
3   Review any company statements released in connection with the vaping crisis.
4   Consider whether the company has mechanisms in place to deal with a recall. A well-run company should have structures in place to respond to consumer complaints and potential product recalls.
5   Finally, consider whether a company has adequate insurance coverage in the event of product liability claims.

Other Significant Issues

As discussed elsewhere in this book, the following are areas of concern for cannabis companies and should be reviewed carefully during a due diligence process: insurance, real estate, banking and payment processing, and Section 280E exposure. For hemp and CBD companies, these are common trouble areas: intermingling of hemp and cannabis operations, product marketing, FDA compliance, state compliance issues (see Chapter 4), and the source of any CBD used.

Notes

1   An example here that the authors saw in action is a license winner that had one of its planned locations in an area that did not permit cannabis operations due to setbacks. When state regulators discovered this issue, which only happened after the award of a provisional state license, it created several problems for the company.
2   Todd Wallack, "Beyond Massachusetts, States Struggle to Limit Marijuana Behemoths," *Boston Globe*, Mar. 21, 2019.

Index

Note: Page numbers followed by "n" refers to endnotes.

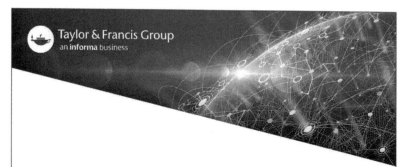